Philosophy of Religion

Philosophy of Religion

LOUIS P. POJMAN

WAVELAND
PRESS, INC.
Long Grove, Illinois

For information about this book, contact:
Waveland Press, Inc.
4180 IL Route 83, Suite 101
Long Grove, IL 60047-9580
(847) 634-0081
info@waveland.com
www.waveland.com

10-digit ISBN 1-57766-611-9
13-digit ISBN 978-1-57766-611-0

Printed in the United States of America

7 6 5 4 3 2

FOR JONATHAN HARRISON

PREFACE

M Y GOAL IN WRITING THIS BOOK in philosophy of religion is to produce a text which is analytically rigorous, accessible to students, and
balanced in presentation and which covers the major issues, ranging from
the traditional arguments for and against the existence of God through
personal identity and immortality to the questions of the relationship
between faith and reason and the relationship between morality and religion. I have endeavored to discuss these issues succinctly and lucidly,
avoiding unnecessary jargon, and have striven to present in an impartial
(though not neutral) and sympathetic manner the main theories and
arguments on each topic discussed in this work. Although the presenta-
tions in the various cases tend toward different conclusions, I have sought
to provide enough material for students and teachers to develop strands of
arguments in ways that differ from my own tendencies. This becomes high-
lighted in the Conclusion, in which I discuss the *person-relativity* of evidence
and the possibility of a cumulative case for theism.

It seems that I have been writing this book all of my life. I grew up in a
household divided on religion. My mother and most of my relatives were
devout Roman Catholics, whereas my father was a convinced, rationalistic
atheist. From an early age the metaphysical tension of my home life in-
duced wonderment about God, the problem of evil, immortality, and the
relation between ethics and religion. The struggle between faith and
doubt has accompanied me throughout my life. Indeed, I went into philosophy in order to understand the arguments and evidence for and
against the existence of God and related metaphysical issues, and I am still
filled with wonder at the subject, struggling to find the truth on these issues. Is there any question more important than whether a benevolent

God, to whom we are accountable, exists? To quote the Oxford philosopher Anthony Kenny:

> If there is no God, then God is incalculably the greatest single creation of the human imagination. No other creation of the imagination has been so fertile of ideas, so great an inspiration to philosophy, to literature, to painting, sculpture, architecture, and drama. Set beside the idea of God, the most original inventions of mathematicians and the most unforgetable characters in drama are minor products of the imagination: Hamlet and the square root of minus one pale into insignificance by comparison.

I am more convinced of the merit of the subject than of the various answers to the central metaphysical questions, and I hope that the importance of the issues discussed in this work is adequately communicated to the students who will be using it. My underlying goal is to promote deeper and clearer understanding and reflection, not any specific set of definite answers.

In addition to the standard arguments for and against the existence of God, I address the challenge of evolutionary theory to religious explanations (especially Chapters 3 and 6), the possibility that hope is an adequate substitute for belief (Chapter 10), and the prospects of building a cumulative case for the existence of God. My book deals with the matter of the ethics of belief (i.e., do we have a moral duty to believe according to the available evidence?). There are original discussions of religious experience and the relationship between ethics and religion. I also discuss contemporary work in philosophy of religion (e.g., the works of J. L. Mackie, Alvin Plantinga, and William Lane Craig).

There are a number of useful texts in this field, and I have used and profited from many of them. My book is different in that, whereas most of these take a distinctly evangelical Christian perspective, I have endeavored to write from an impartial perspective, seeing various options and points of view on the various issues while helping to guide students in their own search for truth over these emotion-laden, crucial issues.

A number of people have influenced my thinking about this subject. I was fortunate to study with great philosophers on both sides of the faith divide: Alvin Plantinga, J. L. Mackie, John Macquarrie, Basil Mitchell, and Anthony Kenny. While a student at Oxford University, I had the privilege of hearing Richard Swinburne's illustrious "Wilde Lectures on the Existence of God." Wallace Matson's work caught my attention after graduate school, as has of late the work of Jonathan Harrison, especially his magnificent *God, Freedom and Immortality* (Avebury 1999). No philosopher has impressed me more than he, for his penetrating insights, cogency of arguments, and clarity of vision on this and other philosophical issues. To Jonathan Harrison this book is dedicated with profound gratitude.

I owe a debt of gratitude to Ken King, philosophy editor at Mayfield. Ken signed me for and published my first anthology textbook, which was in the philosophy of religion. It is only fitting that I should culminate a relationship over 14 years with this single authored work in that same subject. I am also grateful for the reviewers who provided trenchant criticisms on an earlier draft of this work, resulting in a better book: Tiina Allik, Loyola University in New Orleans; Paul Bloomfield, University of Arizona; J. William Forgie, University of California, Santa Barbara; Theodore Guleserian, Arizona State University; Joseph J. Lynch, California Polytechnic State University, San Luis Obispo; G. Randolph Mayes, California State University, Sacramento; Jon S. Moran, Southwest Missouri State University; Dr. David A. Spiecer, University of South Florida; and Gail Stenstad, East Tennessee State University. Most of all, I am indebted to my wife, lover, and best friend, Trudy, who read every page and made significant suggestions for improving the work.

Louis P. Pojman

CONTENTS

1

INTRODUCTION

Reason must be our last judge in everything. I do not mean that we must consult reason and examine whether a proposition revealed from God can be made out by natural principles, and if not, that then we must reject it; but consult it we must, and by it examine whether it be a revelation from God or no; and if reason finds it to be revealed from God, reason then declares for it as much as for any other truth, and makes it one of her dictates.

—JOHN LOCKE

THE ROLE OF RELIGION IN HUMAN HISTORY

No OTHER SUBJECT HAS EXERCISED as profound a role in human history as religion.* Offering a comprehensive explanation of the universe and our place in it, religion offers us a compass on a cosmic map of reality. Through its sacred books, lessons in cosmic map reading enable us to find our way through what might otherwise be a labyrinth of chaos and confusion. Religion tells us where we came from, where we are in the cosmic scheme of things, and where we are going, as well as where we ought to be going and how to get there. It provides both an explanatory system and justification for morality. It legitimizes social mores, morality itself, as well as rituals for the dedication of children, rites of passage, marriage, and the passage from death to the beyond.

Moreover, religion is value laden. It typically gives us a sense of dignity and self-worth. "We hold these truths to be self-evident," wrote Thomas

---

*Religion: from the Middle English *religioun* and Latin *religio:* having to do with the supernatural, the transcendent reality.

Jefferson in the Declaration of Independence, "that all men are created equal, that they are endowed by their Creator with certain unalienable rights, that among these are life, liberty and the pursuit of happiness." This could only be said within a religious or deeply metaphysical framework. Certainly, a purely naturalistic and evolutionary account of humanity does not justify a doctrine of equal and *positive* human value and equal positive rights. Evolution tells us that there is no more objective value in a human being than in a cockroach or kidney bean. But the major world religions, especially the Jewish–Christian–Muslim varieties, hold that we are made in the image and likeness of Almighty God. We have an impressive pedigree. Whoever helps or harms a human, says **theism,** helps or harms one of God's children. Similarly, a naturalistic account of human nature, seeing human behavior as much subject to physical laws as physical bodies are, has difficulty explaining, let alone justifying, belief in human free will. But religion, while not pretending to give an exact description of how it works, takes free will for granted, as a mysterious gift of God, hence providing a richer and more compelling intuitive basis of moral responsibility and moral desert than does secularism.

Religion offers comfort in sorrow, hope in despair and death, courage in danger, and joy in the midst of all life brings. It tells us that the world is not a mere impersonal materialistic conundrum but a friendly home provided for us by our heavenly Father. As William James says, "if religion is true, the universe is no longer a mere it to us, but a Thou, and any relation that may be possible from person to person might be possible here."

The sacred tomes of the world—the Vedas, the Bhagavad Gita, the Bible, the Koran, the Dhahammapada—are literary classics in their own right. In the Western tradition, who has not marveled at the elegance of the Creation story in Genesis 1 ("In the beginning God created the heavens and the earth"), at Joseph's triumph in spite of his brothers selling him into slavery in Egypt, at Moses' leading the children of Israel out of bondage in Egypt, at David's courageous challenge of the Philistine giant Goliath or his tragic and amorous affair with Bathsheba, at the mighty works of Joshua, Samson, Elijah, and Daniel, at the birth of Jesus, his Sermon on the Mount, the Golden Rule, Paul's hymn of love (1 Corinthians 13), or the parables of the Prodigal Son and the Good Samaritan. If a picture is worth a thousand words, a good parable is worth a thousand pages of moral discourse.

Religion has inspired millions—from the pyramids in Egypt to the Pantheon in Athens, from the Hindu Juggernaut and temples along the sacred Ganges River in Benares to the Gothic cathedrals of Cologne, Chartres, Westminster Abbey, and Notre Dame—these tributes rise as a triumph of the human hope for a transcendent reality; its art—from the Muslim mosaics in Grenada and the Dome of the Rock in Jerusalem to Michelangelo's Sistine Chapel—is without peer; its music—from Hindu and Buddhist chants (the "Om" mantra) through Bach's cantatas, Mozart's masses, and Handel's *Messiah* to thousands of hymns and spirituals—has lit the hearts in weal and woe of people in all times and places. In fact, I know atheists who stand in reverential awe when Handel's "Alleluia Chorus" is performed and secularists who weep when John Newton's "Amazing Grace" is sung. What would a secular *St. Matthew's Passion* be like? A cacophony? Even many of our scientists saw themselves as carrying out a divine mission; Isaac Newton believed his work was religious worship, uncovering God's laws. Indeed, so pervasive and ubiquitous is our religious heritage that few notice that every time we date a letter or check or contract, we pay homage to the founder of Christianity, dividing our calendar into B.C. and A.D. (*anno Domini,* the year of our Lord). We have just entered the third millennium since what?

Religion holds power over humanity like nothing else. The leaders of the city of Ephesus said of their encounter with Christian missionaries in the first century A.D., "These who have turned the world upside down have come hither also." Saints and martyrs have been created in its crucible, reformations and revolutions ignited by its flame, outcasts and criminals catapulted to a higher level of existence by its power. Auschwitz survivor Olga Lengyel writes that almost the only people to keep their dignity in that Nazi concentration camp were people animated by faith—"priests and nuns in the camp [who] proved that they had real strength of character." When I worked with the poor in Bedford-Stuyvesant, Brooklyn, in the 1960s, the work of the Pentecostal Christian minister David Wilkerson astounded the civil authorities, for drug addicts who were considered incorrigible suddenly would "kick the habit cold-turkey" on being converted. Such is the power of religion.

Nonetheless, in spite of its enormous dynamics, its power and influence are no guarantees of truth. It could be that the impact of religion in human affairs only shows that humans are myth-making and myth-craving animals. We need a comprehensive explanatory theory, if only a Big Myth, to help us make it through the darkness of existence, whether it be a religion, Nazism, Marxism, environmentalism, or astrology. Indeed, at a recent meeting of the American Academy for the Advancement of Science, its president, Loyal Rue, fearing that the loss of traditional religious belief had created a meaning vacuum in our culture, advocated before that distinguished body of scientists that we deceive ourselves by means of a "Noble Lie" into believing that we and the universe have objective value.[1]

On the other hand, some, such as Friedrich Nietzsche, have urged us to get used to the idea of God's death:

> "Where is God gone?" the madman cried out. "I will tell you! We have killed him—you and I. We're all his murderers! But how have we done it? How were we able to drink up the sea? Who gave us the sponge to wipe away the whole horizon? What did we do when we loosened this earth from its sun? Whither does it now move? Whither do we move? Away from all suns? Do we not dash on unceasingly? Backwards, sidewards, forwards, in all directions? Is there still an above and below? Do we not stray, as through infinite nothingness? Has it not become colder? Does not night come on continually, darker and darker? Shall we have to light lanterns in the morning? God is dead! God remains dead! And we have killed him! How shall we console ourselves, the most murderous of all murderers? The holiest and the mightiest that the world has hitherto possessed, has been led to death under our knife—who will wipe the blood from us? With what water could we clean ourselves? (*Joyful Wisdom*)

If God is dead or, more precisely, never existed, then we must "have to become Gods, merely to seem worthy of the act of being God's executioners." In this passage and similar ones we see a foretaste of a radical autonomy and freedom, total responsibility for our actions, being, and selfhood, which reaches its peak in the atheistic existentialism of the late Jean-Paul Sartre: "We are condemned to freedom."

Who can predict the future? It could be that humanity will someday accept Nietzsche's vision, outgrow religion, and "come of age," standing on its own two feet as an autonomous adult. It could be argued that humankind would be better off with a purely moral faith, minus the religious underpinnings. And many people seem to live well with a purely rational morality. Furthermore, religion is not all sweetness and light. There is a dark side to religion, too—its bigotry, wars, "cleansings," intolerance. The Crusades, the Arab (Muslim)–Israeli (Jewish) conflict, the Protestant–Catholic violence in Northern Ireland, the Hindu–Muslim massacres on the Indian subcontinent should all give us pause before we celebrate religion as the highest civilizing, beneficent force.

Of course, alternative explanations of the origin of religion exist in abundance. Sigmund Freud, in *The Future of an Illusion,* said that religion is an illusion, a projection of the Father image. Children grow up thinking their parents, often their fathers, are godlike and very powerful. They stand in reverent awe of their father's grandeur and look to him for providential support. When they become teens, they realize that their fathers are also mortal and not especially powerful, but they still have this inclination to worship the kind of being that they revered as small children. Hence the projection on the empty heavens of the father image, thus worshipping a God made in their father's image. Religion, being illusory, would evaporate when people became autonomous, understood their primal urges, and became liberated from atavistic myths.[2]

Similarly, Karl Marx viewed religion as the misplaced longings of alienated people:

> Religion . . . is the self-conscious and self-feeling of the man who either has not yet found himself, or else (having found himself) has lost himself once more. But man is not an abstract being. . . . Man is the world of men, the State, society. This State, this society, produces religion, produces a perverted world consciousness, because they are a perverted world. . . . Religion is the sigh of the oppressed creature, the feelings of a heartless world, just as it is the spirit of unspiritual conditions. It is the opium of the people.
>
> The people cannot be really happy until it has been deprived of illusory happiness by the abolition of religion. The demand that the people should shake itself free of illusion as to its own condition is the demand that it should abandon a condition which needs illusion.[3]

Are Freud and Marx correct in treating religion as an illusion? The jury is still out on this. It could be that Freudianism and Marxism, both comprehensive worldviews and rivals to religious views, have the defect of imposing their own controversial assumptions onto religion. For example, why should one automatically assume religion is an illusion just because belief in God is (partially?) caused by our relation as children to our more powerful and benevolent parents? Could that not be the medium by which God prepares us for a trusting relationship with himself? Many would argue that Freudianism itself, together with his thesis on *The Future of an Illusion,* is the "illusion of the future," and Marxism has been criticized as a mistaken attempt to reduce all human experience to class struggle and economic conditions. You will have to decide the relative merits of these theories.

What is the truth about religion? We want to know if religion, or any particular one at least, is true. We want to assess the evidence and arguments for and against its claims in an impartial, judicious, open-minded manner. This is what I will endeavor to do in this book.

The key notion of most religions is the idea of a God, an all-powerful, benevolent, and providential being, who created the universe and all therein. Questions connected with the existence of God may be the most important that we can ask and attempt to answer. If God exists, then it is of the utmost importance that we come to know that fact and as much as possible about God and his plan. Implications follow that affect our understanding of the world and ourselves. If God exists, the world is not accidental, a product of mere chance and necessity, but a home which has been designed for rational and sentient beings, a place of personal purposefulness. We are not alone in our struggle for justice but are working together with One whose plan is to redeem the world from evil. Most important, there is Someone to whom we are responsible and to whom we owe absolute devotion and worship. Other implications follow for our self-understanding, such as the way we ought to live our lives and prospects for continued life after death. In short, if there is a God, we ought to do everything possible to discover this fact, including using our reason in the discovery itself or as a means to test the validity of claims of such a discovery.

On the other hand, it may be that a supreme, benevolent being does not exist. If there is no God, we want to know this, too. Whether we believe in God or not will make a difference in the way we view the universe and in the way we live.

Many people have lived well without believing in God. The French scientist Marquis de La Place, when asked about his faith, is reported to have replied, "I have no need of that hypothesis." But the testimony of humankind is against him. Millions have needed and been inspired by this notion. So great is the inspiration issuing from the idea of God that we could say that if God doesn't exist, the idea is the greatest invention of the human mind. What are all the world's works of literature, art, music, drama, architecture, science, and philosophy compared with this simple concept? To quote the philosopher Anthony Kenny:

> If there is no God, then God is incalculably the greatest single creation of the human imagination. No other creation of the imagination has been so fertile of ideas, so great an inspiration to philosophy, to literature, to painting, sculpture, architecture, and drama. Set beside the idea of God, the most original inventions of mathematicians and the most unforgettable characters in drama are minor products of the imagination: Hamlet and the square root of minus one pale into insignificance by comparison.[4]

The field of philosophy of religion documents the history of humanity's quest for a supreme being. Even if God does not exist, the arguments centering on this quest are interesting in their own right for their ingenuity and subtlety—even apart from their possible soundness. It may be argued that the Judeo-Christian tradition has informed our self-understanding to such a degree that it is imperative for every person who would be well informed to come to grips with the arguments and counterarguments surrounding its claims. Hence, if one rejects the assertions of religion, it is important to understand what is being rejected and why.

In this book I examine the major problems in philosophy of religion: whether a God exists, the significance of religious and mystical experience, the attributes of God, the problem of evil, miracles, survival after death, faith and reason, and the relationship between religion and ethics. I can only hope that the passion and vitality of the debate that has lasted over two thousand years will ignite your hearts and minds in coming to grips with these issues.

RATIONALITY

Philosophy of religion is a branch of philosophy itself, and philosophy has to do with providing reasons and arguments for particular hypotheses. Because the concept of reason or rationality will be our mode of assessing theses in this book, we should spend a short time explaining just what **rationality** is. Broadly speaking, rationality consists in supporting our hypotheses or beliefs with reasons. We can divide rationality into two distinct types: theoretical and practical. *Theoretical rationality* aims at procuring true—or well-justified—beliefs. *Practical rationality* aims at producing reason that will guide our actions to realize our goals. For example, theoretical reason might aim to discover which kinds of subatomic particles exist or whether there is life on other planets, whereas practical reasoning might engage in a cost–benefit analysis of whether the cost of seeking to find life outside the Earth is worth the heavy investment. We may characterize the difference between theoretical and practical reasoning by use of the concept of the *direction of fit*. Let S represent the subject and W the world (or reality). Then:

1. Theoretical reasoning: $S \leftarrow W$
2. Practical reasoning: $S \rightarrow W$

In theoretical reasoning, we try to let reality affect us so that our beliefs correspond to the facts, so that our beliefs are true. The direction of fit is from world to subject. In practical reasoning, we try to find reasons which will be action guiding, enabling us to change the world in conformity with our goals or desires. The direction of fit is from subject to world. In both kinds of reasoning, we desire to optimize our resources, to get the most for our efforts—either the most justified beliefs or the most satisfying results from our actions. We want the best supported beliefs about the world on the one hand and the best supported reasons for our actions on the other.

In this book I am mainly concerned with the matter of theoretical reasoning, seeking to discover whether reason supports religious hypotheses or their denials. In Chapters 9 and 10, however, I consider practical reasons for adopting religious hypotheses. The classic paradigm of such reasoning is Pascal's Wager, in which he urges us to do a cost–benefit analysis, concluding that believing in God is the best bet in life. The three types of theoretical reasoning—deductive reasoning, inductive reasoning, and abductive reasoning—are discussed in the following sections.

Deductive Reasoning

Philosophy is centered in the analysis and construction of **arguments.** We call the study of arguments *logic.* Let us devote a little time to the rudiments of logic. By argument I do not mean a verbal fight but a process of supporting a thesis (called the *conclusion*) with reasons (called *premises*). An argument consists of at least two declarative sentences (sometimes called **propositions**), one of which (the conclusion) logically follows from the others (the premises). The connection by which the conclusion follows from the premises is called an *inference:*

The Structure of an Argument

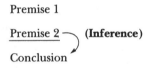

Premise 1

Premise 2 ⌐ **(Inference)**

Conclusion

A valid **deductive argument** is one that follows a correct logical form so that if the premises are true, the conclusion must also be true. If the form is not a good one, the argument is invalid. We say that a valid deductive argument preserves truth. It does so in much the same way as a good refrigerator preserves food. If the food is good, a good refrigerator will preserve it; but if the food is already spoiled, the refrigerator will not make it good. The same is true for the premises of a valid argument. If the statements are true and the form is correct, the conclusion will be true; but if the premises are not true, a valid argument will not guarantee a true conclusion.

A classic example of a valid argument is the following:

1. Socrates is a man.
2. All men are mortal.
3. Therefore ∴ Socrates is mortal.

To identify the form, let us look at conclusion 3 and identify the two major components: a subject (*S*) and a predicate (*P*). "Socrates" is the subject term, and "mortal" is the predicate term. Now return to the two premises and identify these two terms in them. We discover that the two terms are connected by a third term, "man" (or the plural "men"). We call this the *middle term* (M). The form of the argument is as follows:

1. S is M.
2. All M are P.
3. ∴ S is P.

This is an example of a valid deductive form. If premises 1 and 2 are true, we will always get a true conclusion by using this form. But notice how easy it would be to get an invalid form. Change the order of the second premise to read "All P are M." Let the first premise read "My roommate is a mammal" and the second premise read "All dogs are mammals." What do you get? The following:

1. My roommate, Sam Smith, is a mammal. (Premise)
2. Dogs are mammals. (Premise)
3. ∴ My roommate is a dog. (Conclusion)

Regardless of how badly you might treat your roommate, the argument has improper form and cannot yield a valid conclusion. It is *invalid*. Every argument is either valid or invalid. Just as a woman cannot be a little pregnant, an argument cannot be partly valid or invalid but must be completely one or the other. By seeking to find counterexamples for argument forms, we can discover which are the correct forms. (A full study of this would require a course in logic.)

But validity is not the only concept we need to examine. Soundness is also important. An argument can be valid but still unsound. An argument is sound if it has a valid form and if all its premises are true. If at least one premise is false, the argument is unsound. Here is an example of a sound argument:

1. If Mary is a mother, she must be a woman.
2. Mary is a mother (for she has just given birth to a baby).
3. ∴ Mary is a woman.

If Mary has not given birth, then premise 2 is false, and the argument is unsound.

Deductive arguments have the distinct asset of guaranteeing a true conclusion from true premises, but they do not really teach us anything new.

They only make what is implicit explicit. The only pure deductive argument I use is the ontological argument (Chapter 4), though most of the traditional arguments for and against the existence of God take on a deductive form—using inductive evidence to establish the premises. Inductive reasoning is discussed next.

Inductive Reasoning

Let us turn our attention to inductive reasoning. Unlike their counterpart, valid deductive arguments, **inductive arguments** are not truth preserving. That is, they do not guarantee that if we have true premises, we will obtain a true conclusion. They bring only probability; but in most of life, that is the best we can hope for. Thus, as Bishop Joseph Butler (1692–1752) said, "Probability is the guide of life." And the wise person, David Hume (1711–1776) argued, "proportions the strength of his belief to the strength of the evidence."* We usually do not speak of inductive arguments as valid or invalid or as sound or unsound but as strong or weak or as cogent or implausible. In inductive arguments, the premises are evidence for the conclusion or hypothesis. If the evidence for the conclusion is substantial, we call the argument a strong inductive argument; but if the evidence is weak, so is the argument as a whole. A typical inductive argument has the following form:

1. A_1 is a B.
2. A_2 is a B.
3. A_3 is a B.
4. So probably the next A we encounter (A_4) will also be a B.

For example, suppose that you are surrounded by four islands somewhere in the Pacific Ocean. You examine all the trees on three of the islands, but you cannot get to the fourth. Nevertheless, you might make some predictions on the basis of your experience on the first three islands. For example, you note that all the trees on islands A, B, and C are coconut trees. From this you predict that there will be coconut trees on island D and that probably only coconut trees will be found there. We often form generalizations on the basis of inductive reasoning, such as the laws of motion or gravitation. From making a number of observations of objects falling to Earth at specific acceleration and finding no counterinstances,

---

*Enquiry Concerning Human Understanding, Section x.

we generalize that all objects fall at a rate of 32.17 feet per second. For most purposes, inductive reasoning is more useful than deductive reasoning because it adds knowledge to our epistemic repertoire. The teleological argument for the existence of God (Chapter 3) makes use of this form of reasoning.

Abductive Reasoning

Deductive and inductive arguments are the two main types of reasoning. A lesser known type of reasoning, first formulated by the American philosopher Charles S. Peirce (1839–1914), is called abductive reasoning or "reasoning to the best explanation." Like inductive reasoning, **abduction** yields only probable truth. Whereas induction establishes general premises or probabilities about future occurrences, abduction provides explanatory hypotheses. It answers the question, Why is such and such the case? We can illustrate abductive reasoning with the following example of Sherlock Holmes's reasoning:

> The portly client puffed out his chest with an appearance of some little pride and pulled a dirty and wrinkled newspaper from the inside pocket of his greatcoat. As he glanced down the advertisement column, with his head thrust forward and the paper flattened out upon his knee, I took a good look at the man and endeavoured, after the fashion of my companion, to read the indications which might be presented by his dress or appearance.
>
> I did not gain very much, however, by my inspection. Our visitor bore every mark of being an average commonplace British tradesman, obese, pompous, and slow. He wore rather baggy gray shepherd's check trousers, a not over-clean black frock-coat, unbuttoned in the front, and a drab waistcoat with a heavy brassy Albert chain, and a square pierced bit of metal dangling down as an ornament. A frayed top-hat and a faded brown overcoat with a wrinkled velvet collar lay upon a chair beside him. Altogether, look as I would, there was nothing remarkable about the man save his blazing red head, and the expression of extreme chagrin and discontent upon his features.
>
> Sherlock Holmes's quick eye took in my occupation, and he shook his head with a smile as he noticed my questioning glances. "Beyond the obvious facts that he has at some time done manual labour, that he takes snuff, that he is a Freemason, that he has been in China, and that he has done a considerable amount of writing lately, I can *deduce* nothing else."
>
> Mr. Jabez Wilson started up in his chair, with his forefinger upon the paper, but his eyes upon my companion.
>
> "How, in the name of good-fortune, did you know all that, Mr. Holmes?" he asked. "How did you know, for example, that I did manual labour? It's as true as gospel, for I began as a ship's carpenter."

"Your hands, my dear sir. Your right hand is quite a size larger than your left. You have worked with it, and the muscles are more developed."

"Well, the snuff, then, and the Freemasonry?"

"I won't insult your intelligence by telling you how I read that, especially as, rather against the strict rules of your order, you use an arc-and-compass breastpin."

"Ah, of course, I forgot that. But the writing?"

"What else can be indicated by that right cuff so very shiny for five inches, and the left one with the smooth patch near the elbow where you rest it upon the desk?"

"Well, but China?"

"The fish that you have tattooed immediately above your right wrist could only have been done in China. I have made a small study of tattoo marks and have even contributed to the literature of the subject. That trick of staining the fishes' scales of a delicate pink is quite peculiar to China. When, in addition, I see a Chinese coin hanging from your watch-chain, the matter becomes even more simple."

Mr. Jabez Wilson laughed heavily. "Well, I never!" said he. "I thought at first that you had done something clever, but I see that there was nothing in it, after all."[5]

Philosophers appreciate Mr. Wilson's final remark, that Holmes's explanation makes so much sense that one wonders why one didn't think of it oneself. Holmes often chided Watson: "You see, but you do not observe." A good philosopher, like a good detective or scientist, observes while he or she sees.

There is, however, a significant inaccuracy in Holmes's description of what he does. He claims to be deducing the conclusions about Mr. Wilson from the telltale signs. Strictly speaking, he is doing no such thing. In deductive reasoning, if the form is correct and the premises are true, one cannot help but obtain a true conclusion, but such is *not* the case with Mr. Holmes's reasoning. For example, consider Wilson's arc-and-compass breastpin, which leads Holmes to conclude that Wilson is a Freemason. If the reasoning were deductive, the argument would go something like this:

1. Everyone wearing an arc-and-compass breastpin is a Freemason.
2. Mr. Wilson is wearing an arc-and-compass breastpin.
3. Therefore, Mr. Wilson is a Freemason.

Is this a sound argument? Of course not. Imagine that Mr. Wilson, who is not a Freemason, bought a similar arc-and-compass breastpin at a pawnshop and wore it, thinking it was a beautiful bit of Muslim design. In that case, premise 1 would be false. Not everyone wearing an arc-and-compass breastpin is a Freemason. Because it is possible that non-Freemasons wear that pin, the deductive argument is not sound.

What Holmes has really done is reason abductively, that is, reason to the best explanation of the facts. Like inductive reasoning, abduction does not guarantee the truth of the conclusions. Unlike induction, it is not simply about the probability of such and such being the case based on the evidence. Abductive reasoning attempts to offer explanations of the facts, why things are the way they are. The best explanation of Mr. Wilson's wearing the arc-and-compass breastpin is his belonging to the Freemasons. The best explanation of a child's having a fever and red spots is that she has the measles. The best explanation of the puddles outside is that it has recently rained.

The notion of the best explanation is fascinating in its own right. How do we discover the best explanation? What characteristics does it have? How do we rank various virtues of a good explanation? There are no definite answers to these questions, but it is generally agreed that such traits as predictability, coherence, comprehensiveness, simplicity, and fruitfulness of new ideas and research programs are among the main characteristics. If a theory helps us predict future events, that is a powerful weapon. If it coheres well with everything or nearly everything else that we hold true in the field, that lends support to it. If it is simpler than its rivals, if it demands fewer **ad hoc,** or auxiliary, hypotheses, that is a virtue. If it leads to new insight and discoveries, that is also a point in its favor. But what if explanatory theory A has more of one of these features and theory B more of another? Which should we prefer? There is no decision-making procedure to decide the matter with any finality. In a sense, abduction is educated guesswork or intuition. Counterevidence counts strongly against a hypothesis, so that if we can falsify our thesis, we have good reason to drop it; however, sometimes we can make adjustments in our hypothesis to accommodate the counterevidence.

Abduction has been neglected in philosophy, but it really is of the utmost importance. Consider the following questions: Why do you believe in God? Why do you believe in evolutionary theory? Why do you believe that there are universal moral principles? Why do you believe that all events are caused? In one way or another, the answer will probably be abductive: What you believe seems to you to be the best explanation among all the competitors of certain phenomena. In philosophy of religion we face the question, Given the fact of our world, what best explains its origin and continued existence? The **naturalist,** who believes that the world is simply a given or a brute fact, argues for a nonreligious explanation, whereas the theist seeks to provide a cumulative argument to the effect that the best explanation of the world's existence is a creator God. Abductive cumulative arguments are not accepted as valid forms of reasoning by every philosopher, but this seems to be an oversight. Such arguments are used in law courts every day to reason from circumstantial evidence to a conclusion. Even the theory of evolution has no better defense than a cumulative case based on fossil records, vestigial organs, **isotropic** animal structures, and the like. Criteria of good explanatory accounts are such qualities as predictability, simplicity, comprehensiveness, and coherence. The issue of the rationality of God's existence will probably be decided on the basis of abductive reasoning. Do the traditional arguments, including the argument from religious experience, point to a transcendent reality as the best explanation of why we are here, or does a nonreligious theory provide a better explanation? Keep this mode of reasoning in mind when examining the various topics and arguments in this book. I address this issue in the Conclusion.

We cannot live without reason. True, many animals seem to get on fine without deliberative reason, using instinct and experience. But human beings have evolved to the place at which reason is our guide to the complexities of life. Even the question, Why be rational? presumes a rational answer. No doubt we need not be rational all the time, but even determining when to let ourselves go, when to put ourselves on automatic pilot and trust our emotions or intuitions, is a matter for reason to decide. On a higher level, reason may advise us not to reason all of the time. We will play the piano better, play tennis better, swim better, and make love better if we don't overanalyze these activities while engaged in them. There is such a thing as the *paralysis of analysis*. But reason, using inductive processes, is exactly what tells us when to suspend active rational deliberative thinking. Although, as Hume pointed out, we cannot give a rational justification for induction, for we cannot argue from past observations to future contingencies, nevertheless, following the urgings of induction seems to be a reasonable course of action, a reliable process. Although induction and abduction offer us only probability where we desire certainty, no alternative to these forms of reasoning is available that gives satisfactory results in attaining information, in guiding our actions, or in justifying our beliefs. Try **anti-induction:** In all past occurrences in which people jumped off 50-story buildings, they were pulled down to Earth at a rate of about 32 feet per second and were killed; but anti-induction instructs us that nature's laws will change tomorrow and something different will happen—for example, we will fly or levitate. Although this is logically possible, it seems wiser to go with what has worked so well in the past. Evolution seems to have selected for using induction. Otherwise, we, as rational beings, would not have survived to the present time.

TERMINOLOGY

In this book I accept the standard theistic definition of God, as an Omnipotent (all-powerful), Omniscient (all-knowing), Omnibenevolent (all-good) being who is the creator of and providential sustainer of the universe. I ignore such questions as whether he is immutable (unchangeable) or whether he is Eternal (existing outside time) or simply Everlasting (existing in time forever, having neither a beginning nor an end, but still existing as a person who can change in time and act in time). There are difficulties with each option. If God is Eternal, outside of time, it is hard to understand how he can act on a temporal world, for action seems to imply a decision which takes time (an intention that precedes the act). But what is a timeless act? On the other hand, if God is in time, Everlasting, it raises questions about his beginning. We seem to be involved in an infinite regress. If God—in time—created the temporal world, what caused God? Most theologians reject the notion of *causa sui* (that God created himself out of nothing) as incoherent, though many accept the idea of *creatio ex nihilo* (that God created the universe out of nothing). Theologians say that God is *uncaused*, not *self-caused*. But the idea of God's everlastingness raises another problem, for it eliminates the unique status or necessity of God; if we can accept an everlasting Creator, why not simply accept an everlasting universe, which is a simpler hypothesis? Why appeal to the notion of God at all, if we can accept the idea that the universe is uncaused?

Some theists modify this standard definition by qualifying one of its properties. Some eliminate the attribute of Omnipotence (all-power), thereby explaining why evil exists—God can't prevent all evil. Some theologians eliminate his Omniscience (all-knowingness), thereby thinking to save man's free will. (Some argue that if God knows the future, then we are not free to do what we will because the future would be determined; but this is a non sequitur. Your knowing that I will die does not determine my death, but many theists hold to this idea and so give up the attribute of Omniscience.) **Deists,** such as Thomas Paine, Thomas Jefferson, and Benjamin Franklin, even give up the idea of Omnibenevolence (God's total providential goodness). God may have created the world, but he has done it as we might wind up a watch and then let it run down by its own power.

Other views of God include **Pantheism,** the idea, held by Advaitian Hindus, that God is Everything, the Whole. But if God is equally everything—both the living and nonliving—then it is hard to see that it matters what we do, for God remains intact regardless of whether I have killed my father or given aid to lepers. Pantheism should not be confused with **Panentheism,** the idea that God is in everything. Process theologians hold that the world or nature is God's body—God being an emergent property, much like our minds may be emergent properties based on brain processes. Among theists, a *monotheist* believes in only one God, a *polytheist* believes in more than one God.

In this book, **Atheism** (from the Greek "no God") stands for the view that no God or gods exist. **Agnosticism** (from the Greek "no knowledge [of God])" refers to those who claim there is insufficient evidence to decide the matter or that the probabilities for and against the proposition that God exists are roughly 50-50.

My plan is as follows. First I examine the traditional arguments for and against the existence of a God.

1. Cosmological arguments
2. Teleological arguments
3. Ontological arguments
4. Arguments from religious experience
5. The problem of evil

Then I turn to the possibility or actuality of Miracles. After this I examine the issue of immortality, especially in relation to personal identity, and then analyze the relationship between Faith and Reason. Can one be a rational believer? Need one believe in God or a particular religious creed in order to have religious faith? Finally, I consider the relationship between Religion and Ethics. Does morality depend on religion, or is morality autonomous? Put as the classic question, Does God love the Good because it is good, or is the Good good because God loves it?

Summary

In this chapter I have mainly discussed the ubiquity and importance of religion and have argued for the necessity of using reason in attaining and revising our beliefs. Finally, I have introduced some of the terminology that will be needed to understand the discussion in this book. Let us now begin with an examination of the major arguments for and against the existence of God.

Questions for Discussion

1. What are the primary functions of religion in society? Why do you think religion has played such an important role in human affairs? Discuss your answer.

2. Sigmund Freud said that religion is a projection of the father image. Children grow up thinking their parents, often their fathers, are godlike and very powerful. They stand in reverent awe of their father's grandeur and look to him for providential support. When they become teens, they realize that their fathers are also mortal and not especially powerful but retain this inclination to worship the kind of being that they revered as small children—hence the projection on the empty skies of the father image, thus worshipping a God. What do you think of Freud's account as an explanation of religious belief? How might a theist respond to it?

3. Explain the notion of rationality. What are the two main types of reasoning? What is a direction of fit and how does it relate to these forms of reasoning? Explain deductive, inductive, and abductive reasoning.

4. Do you believe that God exists or that theism lacks rational support? Explain your answer. Because most of this book will be about that question, I simply want you to begin to consider the evidence and how you might go about answering this question.

5. Some religious people denounce reason as antireligious. Evaluate this quote from the Protestant reformer Martin Luther.

> There is on earth among all dangers no more dangerous thing than a richly endowed and adroit reason, especially if she enters into spiritual matters which concern the soul and God. For it is more possible to teach an ass to read than to blind such a reason and lead it right; for reason must be deluded, blinded, and destroyed. Faith must trample underfoot all reason, sense, and understanding, and whatever it sees it must put out of sight, and wish to know nothing but the word of God.

For Further Reading

Hick, John. *Arguments for the Existence of God.* London: Macmillan, 1971. A clearly written, insightful examination of the central arguments.

Mackie, J. L. *The Miracle of Theism.* Oxford, England: Oxford University Press, 1982. A lively discussion of the proofs for the existence of God and other issues by one of the ablest atheist philosophers of our time.

Martin, Michael. *Atheism: A Philosophical Justification.* Philadelphia: Temple University Press, 1990. The most comprehensive English-language attack on theism. Clearly set forth.

Matson, Wallace. *The Existence of God.* Ithaca, N.Y.: Cornell University Press, 1965. A penetrating analysis of the arguments for and against the existence of God.

Peterson, Michael, William Hasker, Bruce Reichenbach, and David Basinger. *Reason and Religious Belief.* New York: Oxford University Press, 1991. A clearly written, helpful book from a theist point of view.

Pojman, Louis, ed. *Philosophy of Religion: An Anthology.* 3d ed. Belmont, Calif.: Wadsworth, 1998. A comprehensive anthology setting forth both sides of many issues.

Rowe, William. *Philosophy of Religion: An Introduction.* Belmont, Calif.: Wadsworth, 1978. A readable, reliable introductory work by a first-rate scholar.

Swinburne, Richard. *The Existence of God.* Oxford, England: Oxford University Press, 1979. Perhaps the most sustained and cogent defense of theism in the literature.

Wainwright, William J. *Philosophy of Religion.* Belmont, Calif.: Wadsworth, 1988. A careful, well-argued text from a theistic perspective.

Notes

1. L. D. Rue, "The Saving Grace of Noble Lies," at the AAAS, February 1991.
2. The question remains, Is Freud's *Future of an Illusion* true or merely the *Illusion Future?*
3. "Introduction to a Critique of Hegelian Philosophy of Right," in Karl Marx and Frederick Engels, *Collected Works* (London: Lawrence & Wishart, 1975).
4. Anthony Kenny, *Faith and Reason* (New York: Columbia University Press, 1983), 59.
5. Arthur Conan Doyle, *The Red-Headed League* (New York: Harper & Row, 1892).

2

COSMOLOGICAL ARGUMENTS

TRADITIONAL ARGUMENTS
FOR THE EXISTENCE OF GOD

C AN THE EXISTENCE OF GOD be demonstrated or made probable by
argument? The debate between those who believe that reason can
demonstrate that God exists and those who do not has an ancient lineage,
going back to Protagoras (ca. 450 B.C.) and Plato (427–347 B.C.). The
Roman Catholic Church has traditionally held that the existence of God is
demonstrable by human reason. The strong statement of the First Vatican
Council (1870) indicates that human reason is adequate to arrive at a state
of knowledge:

> If anyone says that the one and true God, our creator and Lord, cannot be
> known with certainty with the natural light of human reason by means of the
> things that have been made: let him be anathema.

Many others, including theists of various denominations, among them
Catholics, have denied that human reason is adequate to arrive at knowledge or to demonstrate the existence of God.

Arguments for the existence of God divide into two main groups: a posteriori and a priori arguments. An **a posteriori** argument is based on premises that can be known only by means of experience of the world (e.g., that
there is a world, that events have causes, and so forth). An **a priori** argument, on the other hand, rests on premises that can be known to be true
independently of experience of the world. One need only clearly conceive
of the proposition in order to see that it is true.

In this book I consider two types of a posteriori arguments for the existence of God and one a priori argument. The a posteriori arguments

are the cosmological argument and the teleological argument. The a priori argument is the ontological argument; I offer two forms of that argument type.

The question in this part of the book is, What, if anything, do the arguments for the existence of God establish? Do any of them demonstrate beyond reasonable doubt the existence of a supreme being or deity? Do any of them make it probable (given the evidence at hand) that such a being exists? That is, do they individually or collectively make a strong case for theism?

THE COSMOLOGICAL ARGUMENT

Asking religious people why they believe in God is likely to evoke something like this response: "Well, things just didn't pop up out of nothing. Someone, a pretty powerful Someone, had to cause the universe to come into existence. You just can't have causes going back forever. God must have made the world. Nothing else makes sense." The argument has a reputable pedigree, being embraced by the ancient Greeks Plato and Aristotle; the Arabic philosophers al Farabi, al Ghazali, and Averroës; the Jewish philosophers Maimonides and Spinoza; and the Christians Aquinas, Leibniz, Samuel Clarke, Richard Swinburne, and William Lane Craig.

All versions of the cosmological argument begin with the a posteriori assumptions that the universe exists and that something outside the universe is required to explain its existence. That is, it is **contingent,** depending on something outside of itself for its existence. That "something else" is logically prior to the universe. It constitutes the reason for the existence of the universe. Such a being is God.

One version of the cosmological argument is called the *First Cause* argument. From the fact that some things are caused, we can reason to the existence of a First Cause. A version of this argument was given by the Catholic monk St. Thomas Aquinas (1224–1274); his "second way" is based on the idea of causation:

> We find that there is among material things a regular order of causes. But we do not find, nor indeed is it possible, that anything is the cause of itself, for in that case it would be prior to itself, which is impossible. Now it is not possible to proceed to infinity in causes. For if we arrange in order all causes, the first is the cause of the intermediate, and the intermediate the cause of the last, whether the intermediate be many or only one. But if we remove a cause the effect is removed; therefore, if there is no first among causes, neither will there be a last or an intermediate. But if we proceed to infinity in causes there will be no first cause, and thus there will be no ultimate effect, nor any

intermediate causes, which is clearly false. Therefore it is necessary to suppose the existence of some first cause, and this men call God.[1]

The general outline, focusing on the second argument, goes something like this:

1. There exist things that are caused.
2. Nothing can be the cause of itself.
3. There cannot be an infinite regress of causes.
4. There exists an uncaused first cause.
5. The word *God* means uncaused first cause.
6. Therefore, God exists.

What can we say of this argument? Certainly, premise 1 is true—some things have causes. Science proclaims that the laws of physics are sufficient to explain all events in the universe. We generally believe that every event has a cause that explains why the event happened. Premise 2 also seems correct. Nothing can cause itself to come into existence (*causa sui*), for it would have to exist before it caused anything at all. To cause anything to happen implies that a thing has causal power, but nonexistent things have no power at all. Note that premises 2 and 4 do not contradict each other. There is nothing obviously incoherent about the idea that something or someone existed from eternity and so is uncaused, whereas there is something incoherent about the idea that something nonexistent caused itself to come into being.

The most controversial premise in this argument is premise 3: "There cannot be an infinite regress of causes." Why can't there be such a regress? As Hume noted, there is nothing logically impossible with the idea of an infinite regress, but it does seem counterintuitive. You might object that there are an infinite regress of numbers, so why can't there be an infinite regress of causes?

One response to this objection is that there is a significant difference between numbers and events and persons. Numbers are just abstract entities, whereas events and persons are concrete, temporal entities, the sort of things that need to be brought into existence. Numbers exist in all possible worlds. They are eternal. Napoleon, Mt. Everest, you, and I are not eternal but need a causal explanation. The child asks, "Mommy, who made me?" and the mother responds, "You came from my womb." The child persists, "Mommy, who made you and your womb?" The mother responds that she came from a fertilized egg in her mother's womb, but the child persists in the query until the mother is forced to admit that she doesn't know the answer or perhaps says, "God made the world and all that is in it." The mother assumes, as most of us do, that an infinite series is impossible. But some philosophers have challenged that assumption.

Recently, William Lane Craig has revived a medieval Islamic version of the cosmological argument, called the *Kalam Argument,* which argues in part against the proposition that the universe may consist of an actual infinite series of causes.[2] Craig argues that an actual infinity of events is absurd; therefore, the universe must have had a beginning in time. He formulates the argument this way:

1. An actual infinite number of events cannot exist.
2. A beginningless series of events in time entails an actual infinite number of things.
3. Therefore, a beginningless series of events in time cannot exist.

The first premise, "An actual infinite number of events cannot exist," is key to the argument, so we must give it special attention. Craig distinguishes between an actual infinite and a potential infinite. A potential infinite is a collection of things that increases in number toward infinity as a limit but never gets there. It is better called an *indefinite* number of things rather than an infinite. For example, one can subdivide any distance into a potential infinity of parts but never be able to reach an actual infinite number of parts. Such a potential infinity of parts is only an indefinite collection.

Craig considers, as support for his thesis, a thought experiment set forth by the German mathematician David Hilbert, called *Hilbert's Hotel.* Imagine a hotel with a finite number of rooms. Suppose, furthermore, that all the rooms are occupied. When a new guest, George, arrives, asking for a room, the manager responds, "Sorry, there are no vacancies." But now imagine that the hotel has an infinite number of rooms and that they are full. The manager now signs George in and puts George into room #1. He then moves Owen from room #1 to room #2, Tom from room #2 to room #3, Teresa from room #3 to #4, and so on to infinity. The result of this infinite series of changes is that George moves into room #1.

Surprisingly, according to Hilbert, no more people are in the hotel now than before George arrived. But how is this possible? It seems absurd.

But there is more. Now suppose that an infinity of new guests apply for rooms. The manager says that he can easily accommodate them all and proceeds to shift George from room #1 to room #2, Owen from room #2 to room #4, Tom from room #3 to room #6, and so on to infinity, always putting the former occupant into a room twice the number of his previous room. Because any natural number multiplied by two is always an even number, all the present guests are able to move into rooms with even numbers, leaving an infinite number of odd-numbered rooms for the infinite number of new guests. And yet, before the new guests arrived, all the rooms were occupied. And, amazingly, the number of guests in Hilbert's Hotel is the same as it was before the new guests were admitted.

The hotel is full, yet it has an infinite amount of vacancies. But this seems absurd. It's not possible to have a full hotel with an infinite number of vacant rooms. These absurdities indicate the impossibility of an infinite series of events, including an infinite regress of events or causes. Hence, it follows that the universe cannot have an infinite series of causes. Therefore, the universe must have had a beginning in time.

Supposing we accept this argument; what follows? That a divine (uncaused) being is the best hypothesis, explaining the origin of the universe? God may be one explanatory hypothesis to explain why the world came to be, but the question is, Does the First Cause argument, even if it is valid, give us a full-blown proof for the existence of God?

Consider: Does it rule out the possibility that this uncaused cause is matter itself? Does it prove that the First Cause still exists? There is a joke that God isn't dead, she's just moved to a better neighborhood. Could the Creator of this universe have moved off into a different, more satisfying neighborhood? Does the argument prove that just one Creator caused everything to come into being? Could there be many uncaused causes? Does the First Cause argument give any indication that the First Cause is benevolent, let alone omnibenevolent? Furthermore, why couldn't the world simply be eternal, a brute fact, itself an uncaused entity? Or maybe humans cannot understand the origin of the universe any more than we can understand how God can be self-sufficient. Before commenting further on these problems, let us examine a second form of the Cosmological Argument.

God may be one explanatory hypothesis, answering the question why the world came to be, but the question is, Does the First Cause argument, even if it is valid, give us a full-blown proof of the existence of God?

THE ARGUMENT FROM CONTINGENCY

Some philosophers believe that the English theologian and philosopher Samuel Clarke (1675–1729) has a superior version of the Cosmological Argument, called the *Argument from Contingency* (it may be helpful to read this passage out loud):

> There has existed from eternity some one unchangeable and independent
> being. For since something must needs have been from eternity; as hath
> been already proved, and is granted on all hands: either there has always
> existed one unchangeable and independent Being, from which all other

beings that are or ever were in the universe, have received their origin; or else there has been an infinite succession of changeable and dependent beings, produced one from another in an endless progression, without any original cause at all: which latter supposition is so very absurd, that tho' all atheism must in its account of most things terminate in it, yet I think very few atheists ever were so weak as openly and directly to defend it. For it is plainly impossible and contradictory to itself. I shall not argue against it from the supposed impossibility of infinite succession, barely and absolutely considered in itself; for a reason which shall be mentioned hereafter: but if we consider such an infinite progression, as one entire series of dependent beings; it is plain that this whole series of beings can have no cause from without, of its existence: because in it are supposed to be included all things that are or ever were in the universe: and it is plain it can have no reason within itself, of its existence; because no one being in this infinite succession is supposed to be self-existent or necessary (which is the only ground or reason of existence of any thing, that can be imagined within the thing itself), but every one dependent on the foregoing: and where no part is necessary; it is manifest the whole cannot be necessary; absolute necessity of existence, not being an outward, relative, and accidental determination; but an inward and essential property of the nature of the thing which so exists. An infinite succession therefore of merely dependent beings, without any original independent cause; is a series of beings, that has neither necessity nor cause, nor any reason at all of its existence, neither within itself nor from without: that is, it is an express contradiction and impossibility; it is a supposing something to be caused; and yet that in the whole it is caused absolutely by nothing: Which everyone knows is a contradiction to be done in time; and because duration in this case makes no difference, it is equally a contradiction to suppose it done from eternity: And consequently there must on the contrary, of necessity have existed from eternity, some one immutable and independent Being.[3]

Clarke, like Aquinas before him, identifies this independent and necessary being with God. We are dependent or contingent beings. Reducing it to the bare bones, the argument from contingency goes like this:

1. Every being that exists is either contingent or necessary.
2. Not every being can be contingent.
3. Therefore, there exists a necessary being on which the contingent beings depend.
4. A necessary being on which all contingent beings exist is what we mean by "God."
5. Therefore, God exists.

A necessary being is self-existing and independent and has the explanation of its existence in itself, whereas contingent beings do not have the reason for their existence in themselves but depend on other beings and ultimately on a necessary being.

The argument from contingency has one advantage over the First Cause argument. While the First Cause may have ceased to exist, the necessary being must still exist as that which supports all else that is. It cannot have ceased to be or to have "moved to a better neighborhood." The world is like a set of chains that are supported in midair. You can trace the links of the chain backward, but somewhere there has to be a being sufficient to sustain the whole chain of dependent beings, and that is a necessary or independent Being, God. We are confident that we and every object in the world is contingent, but if we are so, there must be a necessary (noncontingent) reality.

But the argument is not without problems. The weak link occurs between premises 2 and 3. From the fact that not every being is contingent or dependent, it does not follow that there must be one necessarily existing independent being. The mistake in this inference is called the *Fallacy of Composition,* whose form is the following:

1. Every member of the collection of dependent beings is accounted for by some explanation.
2. Therefore, the collection of dependent beings is accounted for by one explanation.

Premise 2 does not follow from premise 1 because every member of the collection can be explained by some other member of the collection (just in case the collection is infinitely large) or by several different explanations rather than just one.

Consider these illustrations of the fallacy. First,

1. Every human being has a mother.
2. Therefore, every human being has the same mother.

That is, one woman and only one woman has had all the children who have ever been born. Second,

1. Every sailor loves a girl.
2. Therefore, some girl—say, Sally—is loved by every sailor.

It is absurd to believe that there is just one mother in the world or that every sailor loves the same girl, Sally. But, just as it is absurd to infer from the fact that every sailor loves someone that there is just one girl who is loved, so it is illicit to infer from the fact that every contingent fact needs to be grounded in a noncontingent fact that there is just one noncontingent or necessary being who explains all the contingent ones. Why couldn't there be many necessary beings? Or, returning to the chain metaphor mentioned earlier, why couldn't there be many individual chains held by various necessary beings?

But other problems are present. Some of the same ones that haunted the First Cause argument still trouble the argument from contingency. Is the necessary being good or omnibenevolent? Is it even personal? Could this originating and sustaining necessary being be matter itself? Theists maintain that God, a necessary being, is a self-existent eternally brute fact (not needing further explanation). But why could not the universe itself be a self-existent eternally brute fact, needing no other explanation?

Although the cosmological arguments have problems, it may be precipitous to say that they are without any probative value at all. Perhaps they contribute in a modest but significant way to a total or cumulative case for the existence of God. For there is a mystery to be accounted for.

Imagine that you're hiking in the mountains above tree line when you spy a glowing translucent sphere, twenty feet in diameter, sitting on the trail just ahead. What would your reaction be?[4] Wonder, no doubt. "How did this get here?" you ask yourself. Suppose that your hiking companion says, "No one lugged it way up here. It just happened by sheer chance." Would you be satisfied with that answer? I wouldn't, for I'd want to know the explanation for the translucent sphere, and merely being told that it happened by chance doesn't constitute a good explanation. If we venture beyond the city with its fog and lights which block out the heavens and gaze up into the spacious starry skies, contemplate the vast expanse of the heavens, and then consider the mystery of the subatomic world of neutrons, electrons, protons, positrons, mesons, and so forth, do we not have a mystery more wonderful than a twenty-foot glowing translucent sphere? Shouldn't the universe, life, and, especially, consciousness cause a sense of deep wonder within? Do we take this mystery for granted simply because we are used to it? Should we not sit like little children before the wonder of the universe and ask fundamental questions?

But even if the answer to these questions is affirmative, we may still ask whether God is the only answer to these perplexing mysteries. Does God constitute a good explanation for the universe? Couldn't we go on to ask, Who caused God? Does the answer that God is eternal and uncaused satisfy us any better than saying that the universe itself just is eternal or that matter is uncaused and eternal?

The theist may claim, as an anonymous reviewer has, that this way of putting things misses the point. The whole point of the cosmological argument is that because the universe is contingent, it is the kind of entity that requires an explanation, but because God is necessary, He does not. But how do we know that the universe is contingent and not a necessary being, an eternal brute fact?

But consider some corroborating evidence from modern astronomy. In the early part of this century, many astronomers assumed that the universe was stationary—in a steady state. But in 1929 an astronomer named Edwin Hubble noticed that light from distant galaxies was redder than it should be under the prevailing theory. Hubble and other astronomers hypothesized that the increasing red light was evidence for the fact that the universe was expanding, was growing apart. He likened the expansions to a balloon with buttons on its surface. As the balloon is inflated, the buttons move farther apart, as well as farther from their original source. Astronomers soon inferred, working backward, that at some point in the distant past the entire universe was contracted down to a single point, called *singularity*, from which it exploded and quickly expanded, an event now referred to as the *Big Bang*. Astronomers calculate that the Big Bang occurred some 15 billion years ago. Here is how a group of astronomers describe the event:

> The universe began from a state of infinite density. Space and time were created in that event and so was all the matter in the universe. It is not meaningful to ask what happened before the *Big Bang*, any more than it is meaningful to ask what is north of the North Pole. Similarly it is not sensible to ask where the *Big Bang* took place. The point-universe was not an object isolated in space. It was the entire universe, and so the only answer can be that the *Big Bang* happened everywhere.[5]

It seems, then, that the primordial universe is reducible to an extensionless point, which somehow exploded from "nothing." This feature is so analogous to the traditional Christian doctrine *creatio ex nihilo* (creation from nothing, an idea that seems to conflict with the ancient Greek dictum, "out of nothing comes nothing") that Christian theologians embrace the theory of the Big Bang as evidence for the Biblical story of creation. If the Big Bang is likened to an explosion, who or what caused it? The theist's answer is: God. God as the creator of the cosmos makes more sense and is more in line with contemporary cosmology than any other hypothesis. Given the existence of the world and what we know of contemporary cosmology, the hypothesis of a Creator Eternal God who creates the universe in time makes sense.

The cosmological arguments seek to answer these questions: Why is there a universe at all? Why is there something and not just nothing? Why are we here? Some philosophers reject these questions as meaningless because we have no basis for answering them. They point out that if there was nothingness, we wouldn't be here to ask these questions. Other philosophers agree that they are valid questions but that the proper answer to them is, " I don't know the answer to why we're here, if there is a correct explanation, and what's more, I don't know anyone else who does." The religious person offers the existence of a personal, completely good Creator as the answer to those questions. But unless he or she has more evidence than simply the cosmological argument, that answer will be an extraordinary leap in logic. The cosmological argument may lead us to accept that the world was created in time and it may offer a hint of a divine creation, but more needs to be added before we can have the God of theism. But perhaps other arguments can supplement it and together produce a cumulative case for theism. I examine other arguments and also consider the possibility of a cumulative case in the Conclusion of this book.

Summary

The cosmological argument attempts to answer the question, Why is there a universe at all? It offers at least two types of arguments: the First Cause argument, which rejects as incoherent the notions of an uncaused cause and an infinite regress; and the argument from contingency, which argues from the idea that there are contingent beings to the necessity of an independent or necessary being. Two weaknesses of cosmological arguments are that they don't provide us with a personal or benevolent God, nor do they rule out the possibility that the universe is itself eternal, a brute fact. Nevertheless, the argument raises an important question about the explanation of the universe, which religion seeks to answer satisfactorily.

Questions for Discussion

1. The current view of physicists and astronomers is that the universe came into being about 15 or 16 billion years ago when an extensionless point exploded in the Big Bang. From this explosion, the universe swiftly expanded and is still doing so. Does the Big Bang theory support theism or does it offer an alternate account of the origin of the universe to the religious account? Can the Big Bang itself be viewed as a contingent event? Can we ask what caused the Big Bang? What do you think is the explanation of the Big Bang?

2. Sometimes it is argued that the cosmological argument unwarrantedly assumes that an infinite regress is impossible and that we need a First

Cause. Does science accept the possibility of an infinite regress of causes? Or is the idea of a Big Bang itself an attempt to stop the regress?

3. Is the theist's answer that God is the explanation for the universe really a better explanation than the nontheist's claim that the universe itself is eternal or that matter is uncaused and eternal?

4. Examine Craig's argument against an actual infinite regress of events. Is it compelling? Explain.

5. Is the question, Why is there something rather than nothing? a meaningful question? Does it point to a personal explanation of the universe?

For Further Reading

Craig, William. *The Cosmological Argument from Plato to Leibniz.* New York: Barnes & Noble, 1980. A good survey of the history of the argument.

Gale, Richard. *On the Nature and Existence of God.* Cambridge, England: Cambridge University Press, 1992. Chapter 7 is an excellent discussion of the argument.

Harrison, Jonathan. *God, Freedom and Immortality.* Aldershot, England: Ashgate, 1999. Now perhaps the most comprehensive and clearly written English-language attack on theism, especially Part 2.

Hick, John. *Arguments for the Existence of God.* London: Macmillan, 1971. A clearly written, insightful examination of the central arguments.

Mackie, J. L. *The Miracle of Theism.* Oxford, England: Oxford University Press, 1982. A lively discussion of the proofs for the existence of God and other issues by one of the ablest atheist philosophers of our time, especially Chapter 5.

Martin, Michael. *Atheism.* Philadelphia: Temple University Press, 1990. A comprehensive and clearly written English-language attack on theism.

Peterson, Michael, William Hasker, Bruce Reichenbach, and David Basinger. *Reason and Religious Belief.* New York: Oxford University Press, 1991. A clearly written, helpful book from a theist point of view.

Pojman, Louis, ed. *Philosophy of Religion: An Anthology.* 3d ed. Belmont, Calif.: Wadsworth, 1998. A comprehensive anthology, setting forth both sides of many issues. It contains the relevant selections from Aquinas, Edwards, Rowe, Craig, and Draper.

Rowe, William. *The Cosmological Argument.* Princeton, N.J.: Princeton University Press, 1971. A thorough and penetrating study.

Rowe, William. *Philosophy of Religion: An Introduction.* Belmont, Calif.: Wadsworth, 1978. A readable, reliable introductory work by a first-rate scholar.

Swinburne, Richard. *The Existence of God.* Oxford, England: Oxford University Press, 1979. Perhaps the most sustained and cogent defense of theism in the literature.

Wainwright, William J. *Philosophy of Religion.* 2d ed. Belmont, Calif.: Wadsworth, 1998. A careful, well-argued text from a theistic perspective.

Notes

1. Thomas Aquinas, *Summa Theologica,* trans. Laurence Shapcote (London: Benziager, 1911).

2. William Lane Craig, *Reasonable Faith* (Wheaton, Ill.: Crossway Books, 1984). See also his *The Cosmological Argument from Plato to Leibniz* (New York: Barnes & Noble, 1980).

3. Samuel Clarke, *A Demonstration of the Being and Attributes of God,* Part 2 (1705).

4. Richard Taylor, in his *Metaphysics* (Englewood Cliffs, N.J.: Prentice-Hall, 1983), first set forth this illustration.

5. J. R. Gott et al. "Will the Universe Expand Forever," *Scientific American* (March 1976): 65.

3

TELEOLOGICAL ARGUMENTS

THE TELEOLOGICAL ARGUMENT for the existence of God is our second a posteriori argument. It begins with the premise that the world exhibits intelligent purpose or order and concludes that there either must be or probably is a divine intelligence, a supreme designer to account for the observed or perceived intelligent purpose or order. Although the argument was first cited in Plato and in Cicero, we find an expression of the argument in the Hebrew Bible (the Psalms):

> The heavens declare the glory of God; and the firmament showeth his handiwork. Day unto day uttereth speech, and night unto night showeth knowledge. There is no speech nor language where their voice is not heard. Their line is gone out through all the earth. (Psalm 19)

PALEY'S ARGUMENT

William Paley (1743–1805) gives the clearest sustained treatment of the argument in *Natural Theology* (1802), in which he offers his famous "watch" argument. It begins as follows:

> In crossing a heath, suppose I pitched my foot against a stone, and were asked how the stone came to be there: I might possibly answer, that for any thing I knew to the contrary, it had lain there for ever: nor would it perhaps be very easy to shew the absurdity of this answer. But suppose I had found a watch upon the ground, and it should be inquired how the watch happened to be in that place. I should hardly think of the answer which I had before given, that, for any thing I knew, the watch might have always been there. Yet why should not this answer serve for the watch as well as for the stone? Why is it not as admissible in the second case, as in the first?

For this reason, and for no other, namely, that when we come to inspect the watch, we perceive (what we could not discover in the stone) that its several parts are framed and put together for a purpose, e.g., that they are so formed and adjusted as to produce motion, and that motion so regulated as to point out the hour of the day; that, if the different parts had been differently shaped from what they are, of a different size from what they are, or placed after any other manner, or in any other order, than that in which they are placed, either no motion at all would have been carried on in the machine, or none that would have answered the use that is now served by it. This mechanism being observed, the inference is inevitable, that the watch must have had a maker. That there must have existed, at some time, and at some place or other, an artificer or artificers, who formed it for the purpose which we find it actually to answer; who comprehended its construction, and designed its use.

Every indication of contrivance, every manifestation of design, which existed in the watch, exists in the works of nature; with the difference, on the side of nature, of being greater and more, and that in a degree which exceeds all computation.[1]

Paley argues that just as we infer an intelligent designer to account for the purpose-revealing watch, we must analogously infer an intelligent grand designer to account for the purpose- revealing world: "Every indication of contrivance, every manifestation of design, which existed in the watch, exists in the works of nature; with the difference, on the side of nature, of being greater and more, and that in a degree which exceeds all computation." The skeleton of the argument looks like this:

1. Human artifacts are products of intelligent design. (Purpose)
2. The universe resembles these human artifacts.
3. Therefore ∴ The universe is (probably) a product of intelligent design. (Purpose)
4. But the universe is vastly more complex and gigantic than a human artifact.
5. Therefore ∴ There probably is a powerful and vastly intelligent designer who designed the universe.

HUME'S CRITIQUE

Ironically, Paley's argument was attacked even before he had set it down, for David Hume (1711–1776) had already written his famous *Dialogues Concerning Natural Religion* (published posthumously in 1779), which constitutes the classic critique of the teleological argument. Paley seems to have been unaware of it. In it, the natural theologian Cleanthes debates the orthodox believer Demea and the skeptic or critic Philo, who does most of the serious arguing.

Hume, through Philo, attacks the argument from several different angles. First, he argues that the universe is not sufficiently like the productions of human design to support the argument. As Philo puts it,

> But can you think, Cleanthes, that your usual phlegm and philosophy have been preserved in so wide a step as you have taken, when you compare to the universe, houses, ships, furniture, machines; and from their similarity in some circumstances infer a similarity in their causes? . . . But can a conclusion, with any propriety, be transferred from the parts to the whole? Does not the great disproportion bar all comparison and inferences? From observing the growth of a hair, can we learn anything concerning the generation of a man?[2]

Hume claims that we cannot argue from the parts to the whole, but is he correct? If I observe green leaves on all of the trees in the forests of the Catskill Mountains in New York and the Uinta Mountains of Utah and make the same observation that all the leaves are green in the rain forests of Brazil and the Republic of the Congo, as well as the leaves on the trees around Lake Baikal in eastern Russia and the lakes of New Zealand, can't I make an inductive inference about the color of the leaves on the rest of the trees in the world?

When is it and when is not legitimate to reason from the parts to the whole? If all we have are a few instances that point to a common conclusion (like our green leaves on the trees case), we have a *weak* inductive argument, though one that grows stronger each time a new piece of confirming evidence is forthcoming. But until it is well confirmed, we should not put too much weight on our slight experience.

Hume's second objection is that the analogy fails because we have no other universe with which to compare this one, which would be necessary in order to decide if the universe was designed or simply developed on its own. As Charles Sanders Peirce (1839–1914) put it, "Universes are not as plentiful as blackberries." Because there is only one of them, we have no standard of comparison by which to judge it. Paley's answer to this would be that if we can find one clear instance of purposiveness in nature, we have a sufficient instance enabling us to conclude that there is probably an intelligent designer. Paley and Cleanthes thought that the eye provided such a clear example of purposiveness: "Consider, anatomize the eye, survey its structure and contrivance, and tell me from your own feeling, if the idea of a contriver does not immediately flow in upon you with a force like that of sensation."[3] Do you agree with Cleanthes here? Hume rejects this reasoning as sliding over strong objections, especially that there are no universes with which to compare this one.

But the theist may object that Hume misses the point of the argument from analogy. If the analogy comes close enough to what it is compared with, the conclusion is probable. Notice how the argument from analogy works.

We have an object O_1 and want to determine whether it has a property P_1. We note that it has other properties in common with objects O_2, O_3, and so on:

O_1, O_2, O_3 . . . all have P_2, P_3, and P_4.
Then we discover that O_2, O_3, . . . all have P_1, the property in question.
So we infer that *probably* O_1 also has P_1.

Suppose I am interested in buying a certain kind of Ford automobile. I reason that other Fords of this kind that I or my acquaintances have owned have served us very well; thus I reason that this Ford, which I am contemplating, will probably serve me well.

Or suppose I want to determine whether the mushroom (O_1) that I have just pulled up from the ground is edible (P_1). I note that it is similar in shape, color, and consistency (P_2, P_3, P_4) to other mushrooms (O_2, O_3, . . .) that turned out to be edible (P_1). Thus I infer that probably this mushroom (O_1) is edible (P_1).

Similarly, this world resembles man-made machines (O_2, O_3, . . .), so it probably has the property (P_1) of having an intelligent designer.

Hume, however, points out a problem with such reasoning from analogy. To the extent that the universe resembles a man-made artifact, to that extent God becomes finitized or limited, we become guilty of **anthropomorphism**—the tendency to humanize God:

> Now, Cleanthes, said Philo, with an air of alacrity and triumph, mark the consequences. First, by this method of reasoning, you renounce all claim to infinity in any of the attributes of the Deity. For, as the cause ought only to be proportioned to the effect, and the effect, so far as it falls under our cognizance, is not infinite; what pretensions have we, upon your suppositions, to ascribe that attribute to the Divine Being? You will still insist, that, by removing him so much from all similarity to human creatures, we give in to the most arbitrary hypothesis, and at the same time weaken all proofs of his existence.[4]

However, if we go the other way and say that the universe is much vaster than and different from anything (in order to save the infinity of God), the analogy breaks down. For then the necessary likeness becomes attenuated:

Anthropomorphism ◄————————————► Infinity
(*Analogy works but God limited*)   (*Analogy breaks down*)

In other words, the analogy tends to diminish God's power and infinity, while emphasizing these infinite attributes tends to undermine the argument from design.

Following up on this last point, Hume offers a third criticism of the analogy argument. The analogy leads us to infer the existence of a grand anthropomorphic designer, a human writ large, who has all the properties that we have:

> And why not become a perfect Anthropomorphite? Why not assert the deity or deities to be corporeal, and to have eyes, a nose, mouth, ears, etc.? Epicurus maintained, that no man had ever seen reason but in a human figure; therefore the gods must have a human figure. And this argument, which is deservedly so much ridiculed by Cicero, becomes, according to you, solid and philosophical.[5]

Hume's final objection is that the so-called design of the universe seems to be flawed with evil and inexactness, so that we should consistently infer that the designer is imperfect or not terribly intelligent or no longer interested in his work of bygone years. Perhaps there are a plurality of designers. We will examine this objection in Chapter 6 on the problem of Evil.

Hume makes several other points against the design argument. The universe resembles in some ways an animal and in other ways a plant, in which case, claims Hume, the argument fails because it depends on our seeing the world as a grand machine rather than as an animal or plant. Do you agree with Hume here?

Hume also points out that the universe might well be the result of mere chance. However, he agrees that the hypothesis of a designer is not completely useless, just very weak and uninformative:

> In a word, Cleanthes, a man who follows your hypothesis is able, perhaps, to assert or conjecture that the universe sometime arose from something like design: But beyond that position he cannot ascertain one single circumstance, and is left afterwards to fix every point of his theology by the utmost license of fancy and hypothesis. This world, for aught he knows, is very faulty and imperfect, compared to a superior standard; and was only the first rude attempt of some infant deity who afterwards abandoned it, ashamed of his lame performance. [Or] it is the work only of some dependent, inferior deity, and is the object of derision to his superiors. [Or] it is the production of old age and dotage in some superannuated deity; and ever since his death has run on at adventures, from the first impulse and active force which it received from him.[6]

THE DARWINIAN OBJECTION

A modern objection to the argument, one that was anticipated by Hume, is that based on Darwinian evolution, which has altogether undermined the notion of teleological explanation. Charles Darwin (1809–1882), in his *Origin of the Species* (1859), observed that the process of development from simpler living organisms to more complex ones took place gradually over many centuries through an apparently nonpurposive process of trial and error, of natural selection and survival of the fittest. As Julian Huxley (1887–1975) put it, the evolutionary process results immediately and automatically from the basic property of living matter—that of self-copying, but with occasional errors. Self-copying leads to multiplication and competition; the errors in self-copying are what we call mutations, and mutations will inevitably confer different degrees of biological advantage or disadvantage on their possessors. The consequence will be differential reproduction down the generations—in other words, natural selection.[7]

What is significant about Darwinian evolution is that it provides a nonpurposive (nonteleological) alternative to the classical notion that the universe must have been created for a purpose. Chance and the laws of motion and matter, not purpose, give rise to the universe, its order and regularity, including life and the evolution of purposive beings such as Homo sapiens. We are animals who have been selected for our ability to reason and attain our purposes. Evolution selected us, it seems, to have purposes, to act on them, and to see purpose in our projects. That sense of purpose spills over from our local projects to the universe, so that it seems natural to see ourselves as the outcome of a purposive creation.

As important as Darwin's contribution is in offering us an alternative model with respect to biological development, it doesn't altogether destroy the argument from design, for the theist can still argue that the process of natural selection is the *way* an ultimate designer is working out his purpose for the world. The argument from design could still be used as an argument to the best explanation, as an abductive argument.

The Oxford University philosopher Richard Swinburne, a modern Cleanthes, rejects all deductive forms of arguments for the existence of God but in their place sets a series of inductive arguments: versions of the cosmological argument, the teleological argument, the argument from religious experience, and others. Although none of these alone proves the existence of God or shows it to be more probable than not, each adds to the probability of God's existence. Together they constitute a cumulative case in favor of theism. There is something crying for an explanation: Why does this grand universe exist? Together the arguments for God's existence provide a plausible explanation of the existence of the universe, of why we are here, of why there is anything at all and not just nothing.[8]

Swinburne's arguments are set in terms of confirmation theory. He distinguishes arguments that are *P*-inductive (where the premises make the conclusion probable) from those that are *C*-inductive (where the premises confirm the probability of the conclusion or make it more probable than it otherwise would be, although not showing the conclusion to be more probable than not). An illustration of a P-inductive argument would be a regularity in nature. We have found that in every experiment performed the inverse square law of attraction acts between bodies. Therefore, there is overwhelming evidence that it will act on the next falling object. An illustration of a C-inductive argument would be: Every instance of finding another white swan makes the proposition that most swans are white more probable than it was. The cosmological and teleological arguments are, according to Swinburne, good C-inductive arguments. They make the hypothesis that a Creator-Designer God caused the universe to come into being more likely than it would have been without these arguments. Because there is no counterargument to theism and religious experience offers "considerable evidential force" in favor of theism, the cumulative effect is "sufficient to make theism over all probable."[9]

Whether and how the cumulative case for theism can be made is a task I must leave for you, but a common objection to it is the "ten leaky buckets" argument. The objector claims that the theist is using several bad arguments to make a cumulative case, much as one would try to carry water by putting it into ten leaky buckets. Ten leaky buckets won't hold water any more than one leaky bucket will.

The counterobjection to this objection is that the ten leaky buckets will hold water better than one leaky bucket if the buckets are put inside one another and the leaks of each bucket are covered by the base of the one below it. Similarly, although not a set of arguments that offers full proof, the case for theism may be better than rival explanatory theory.

Perhaps we will be in a better situation to evaluate the case for and against theism after we have considered the other arguments in this part of the book.

Summary

The teleological argument proceeds from the perceived orderly process in the world and argues to the conclusion that such orderly processes must have an orderer or designer. It is unreasonable to suppose that the incredible intricacy of the world and its apparent conformity to laws are just the product of chance. Nevertheless, there are several problems with the argument, among these being the tendency toward anthropomorphism and our inability to make intercosmic comparisons.

Questions for Discussion

1. Evaluate the teleological argument for yourself. What does it indicate about the origins of the universe? Is the hypothesis of a designer plausible? Or can the process of chance and necessity account for the orderliness we perceive?

2. Assess Richard Swinburne's idea of a cumulative case for the existence of God. Is this a good use of abductive argument? Is the case for the existence of God like a case in civil law in which both sides try to assemble the evidence in a way that best supports their side of the issue?

3. It is sometimes objected that the "ten leaky buckets" argument begs the question for theism because the metaphor suggests that a composite arrangement of the buckets (and so the arguments) very likely can be made to hold water (demonstrate the existence of God). Evaluate this criticism.

4. Sometimes the objector to the teleological argument claims that the orderliness of the universe must be taken as a given, not as something to be accounted for, because if there were no orderliness, we could not even comment on the fact. Swinburne argues by analogy that this objection misses the point:

> Suppose that a madman kidnaps a victim and shuts him in a room with a card-shuffling machine. The machine shuffles ten packs of cards simultaneously and then draws a card from each pack and exhibits simultaneously ten cards. The kidnapper tells the victim that he will shortly set the machine to work and it will exhibit its first draw, but that unless the draw consists of an ace of hearts from each pack, the machine will simultaneously set off an explosion which will kill the victim, in consequence of which he will not see which cards the machine drew. The machine is then set to work, and to the amazement and relief of the victim the machine exhibits an ace of hearts drawn from each pack. The victim thinks that this extraordinary fact needs an explanation in terms of the machine having been rigged in some way. But the kidnapper, who now reappears, casts doubt on this suggestion. "It is hardly surprising," he says, "that the machine draws only aces of hearts. You could not possibly see anything else. For you would not be here to see anything at all, if any other cards had been drawn." But of course the victim was right and the kidnapper is wrong. There is indeed something extraordinary in need of explanation in ten aces of hearts being drawn. The fact that this peculiar order is a necessary condition of the draw being perceived at all makes what is perceived

no less extraordinary and in need of explanation. The teleologist's starting-point is not that we perceive order rather than disorder, but that order rather than disorder is there.[10]

Evaluate Swinburne's claim about the legitimacy of looking for an explanation for the orderliness in the universe. Does his way of stating the matter help the theist?

For Further Reading

Hume, David. *Dialogues Concerning Natural Religion,* 1779. A classic critique of the teleological argument.

Mackie, J. L. *The Miracle of Theism.* Oxford, England: Oxford University Press, 1982. A lively discussion of the proofs for the existence of God and other issues by one of the ablest atheist philosophers of our time.

Martin, Michael. *Atheism: A Philosophical Justification.* Philadelphia: Temple University Press, 1990. Chapters 5 and 13 contain a strong expression of the atheist's position.

McPherson, Thomas. *The Argument from Design.* London: Macmillan, 1972. A good introduction to several forms of the argument.

Pojman, Louis, ed. *Philosophy of Religion: An Anthology.* 3d ed. Belmont, Calif.: Wadsworth, 1998. A comprehensive anthology setting forth both sides of many issues.

Swinburne, Richard. "The Argument from Design." *Philosophy* 43 (1968).

Swinburne, Richard. *The Existence of God.* Oxford, England: Oxford University Press, 1979. Perhaps the most sustained and cogent defense of theism in the literature.

Notes

1. William Paley, *Natural Theology* (1802).
2. David Hume, *Dialogues Concerning Natural Religion* (1779).
3. Ibid.
4. Ibid.
5. Ibid.
6. Ibid.
7. Julian Huxley, *Evolution as Process* (New York: Harper & Row, 1953), 4.
8. Richard Swinburne, *The Existence of God* (Oxford, England: Oxford University Press, 1979).
9. Ibid.
10. Ibid.

4

ONTOLOGICAL ARGUMENTS

AN ANALYSIS OF ANSELM'S ARGUMENT

THE ONTOLOGICAL ARGUMENT for the existence of God is the most intriguing of all arguments for theism. It is one of the most remarkable arguments ever set forth. First set forth by Anselm (1033–1109), Archbishop of Canterbury in the eleventh century, the argument has continued to puzzle and fascinate philosophers ever since. Let the testimony of the agnostic philosopher Bertrand Russell (1872–1970) serve as a typical example here:

> I remember the precise moment, one day in 1894, as I was walking along Trinity Lane [at Cambridge University where Russell was a student], when I saw in a flash (or thought I saw) that the ontological argument is valid. I had gone out to buy a tin of tobacco; on my way back, I suddenly threw it up in the air, and exclaimed as I caught it: "Great Scott, the ontological argument is sound!"[1]

The argument is important for two reasons: It claims to be an a priori proof for the existence of God, and it is the primary locus of such philosophical problems as whether *existence* is a property and whether the notion of *necessary existence* is intelligible. Furthermore, it has special religious significance because it is the only one of the traditional arguments that clearly concludes to the necessary properties of God—that is, his Omnipotence, Omniscience, Omnibenevolence, and other properties that make God great.

Although there are many versions of the ontological argument and multiple interpretations of some of these, most philosophers agree on the essential form of Anselm's version in the second chapter of his *Proslogium*. Anselm believes that God's existence is so absolutely certain that only a fool would doubt or deny it. Yet he desires understanding to fulfill his faith:

And so, Lord, do thou, who dost give understanding to faith, give me, so far as thou knowest it to be profitable, to understand that thou art as we believe; and that thou art that which we believe. And indeed, we believe that thou art a being than which nothing greater can be conceived. Or is there no such nature, since the fool hath said in his heart, there is no God? (Psalms 14:1). But at any rate, this very fool, when he hears of this being of which I speak— a being than which nothing greater can be conceived—understands what he hears, and what he understands is in his understanding; although he does not understand it to exist. For, it is one thing for an object to be in the understanding, and another to understand that the object exists. When a painter first conceives of what he will afterwards paint, he has it in his understanding, but he does not yet understand it to be, because he has not yet painted it. But after he has made the painting, he both has it in his understanding and he understands that it exists, because he has made it. Hence, even the fool is convinced that something exists in the understanding, at least, than which nothing greater can be conceived. For, when he hears of this, he understands it. And whatever is understood, exists in the understanding. And assuredly that, than which nothing greater can be conceived, cannot exist in the understanding alone. For, suppose it exists in the understanding alone: then it can be conceived to exist in reality; which is greater. Therefore, if that, than which nothing greater can be conceived, exists in the understanding alone, the very being, than which nothing greater can be conceived, is one, than which a greater can be conceived. But obviously this is impossible. Hence, there is no doubt that there exists a being, than which nothing greater can be conceived, and it exists both in the understanding and in reality.[2]

Anselm's reasoning may be treated as a reductio ad absurdum argument. That is, it begins with a supposition S (suppose that the greatest conceivable being exists in the mind alone) that is contradictory to what one desires to prove. One then goes about showing that S added to other certain or self-evident assumptions, A_1 and A_2, yields a **contradiction,** which in turn demonstrates that the contradictory of S must be true. Anselm's argument goes like this:

1. Suppose that the greatest conceivable being (GCB) exists in the mind alone (and not in reality). (S)
2. Existence in reality is greater than existence in the mind alone. (A_1)
3. We can conceive of a GCB that exists in reality as well as in the mind. (A_2)
4. Therefore ∴ There is a being that is greater than the greatest conceivable being. (from premises 1, 2, and 3)
5. But this is impossible, for it is a contradiction.
6. Therefore ∴ It is false that a GCB exists in the mind alone and not in reality (from premises 1 and 5).

So a greatest conceivable being must exist in reality as well as in the mind. This being is, by definition, God.

Questions immediately arise. Is existence a perfection, so that we can say that it is better to exist than not to exist? Or is such locution nonsense because you can't compare existing things with nonexisting ones? Does some possible entity become greater by becoming actual?

Anselm's contemporary, Gaunilo, sets forth the first objection to Anselm's argument (entitled "On Behalf of the Fool"). Accusing Anselm of "pulling rabbits out of hats," he tells the story of a delectable lost island, one that is more excellent than all lands. Because it is better that such a perfect island exists in reality than simply in the mind alone, this Isle of the Blest must necessarily exist. Anselm's reply is that the analogy fails, for unlike the greatest possible being, the greatest possible island can be conceived as not existing.

Is Gaunilo correct? Some philosophers say no because, simply, some properties do and some properties don't have intrinsic maximums. No matter how wonderful you make the Isle of the Blest, we can conceive of a more wonderful island. The greatness of islands is like the greatness of numbers in this respect. There is no greatest natural number, for no matter how large the number you choose, we can always conceive of one twice as large. On the other hand, the properties of God seem to have intrinsic maximums. For example, we can define perfect knowledge this way. For any proposition, an Omniscient being knows whether it is true or false. An Omnipotent being can do anything that is logically possible. An Omnibenevolent being will always do what is right in terms of maximizing the good.

A second criticism of the ontological argument was lodged by Immanuel Kant (1724–1804), who accused the proponent of the argument of defining God into existence. "Being" is not a "real predicate" like "red" or "six feet tall" or "rational." Here is the relevant passage:

> "Being" is obviously not a real predicate; that is, it is not a concept of something which could be added to the concept of a thing. It is merely the positing of a thing, or of certain determinations, as existing in themselves. Logically, it is merely the copula of a judgment. The proposition, "God is omnipotent" contains two concepts, each of which has its object—God and omnipotence. The small word "is" adds no new predicate, but only serves to posit the predicate in its relation to the subject. If, now, we take the subject (God) with all its predicates (among which is omnipotence), and say "God is," or "There is a God," we attach no new predicate to the concept of God, but only posit the subject in itself with all its predicates, and indeed posit it as being an object that stands in relation to my concept. The content of both must be one and the same; nothing can have been added to the concept, which expresses merely what is possible, by my thinking its object (through

the expression "it is") as given absolutely. Otherwise stated, the real contains no more than the merely possible. A hundred real thalers [i.e., German money] do not contain the least coin more than a hundred possible thalers. For as the latter signify the concept, and the former the object and the positing of the object, should the former contain more than the latter, my concept would not, in that case, express the whole object, and would not therefore be an adequate concept of it. My financial position is, however, affected very differently by a hundred real thalers than it is by the mere concept of them (that is, of their possibility). For the object, as it actually exists, is not analytically contained in my concept, but is added to my concept (which is a determination of my state) synthetically; and yet the conceived hundred thalers are not themselves in the least increased through thus acquiring existence outside my concept. By whatever and by however many predicates we may think a thing—even if we completely determine it—we do not make the least addition to the thing which we further declare that this thing is. Otherwise, it would not be exactly the same thing that exists, but something more than we had thought in the concept; and we could not, therefore, say that the exact object of my concept exists. If we think in a thing every feature of reality except one, the missing reality is not added by my saying that this defective thing exists.[3]

Kant claims that Anselm makes the mistake of treating "existence" or "being" as a first-order predicate like "blue" or "great," as though I could go to the bank and withdraw $100 on the basis of having the concept of owning $100. When you say that a check for $100 is equivalent to one hundred single dollars, you are describing the properties of the check; when you predicate the idea with the concept of *existence,* you haven't added a new property to the idea of $100. You are simply saying that the concept is exemplified. Similarly, when you say that the castle is blue, you are adding a property (viz., blueness) to the idea of a castle; but when you say that the castle *exists,* you are not adding anything to the concept of a castle, only saying that the concept is exemplified or instantiated. You are taking a possible property (*B*) and affirming that it is exemplified (*A*), claiming that it is actual.

   (A) First-order property (actual)
   (B) Nonexisting property (possible)

We might say that "real" predicates or properties are first-order properties, but the idea of existence is a second-order property, which asserts something about the status of possible properties. In Anselm's argument, "existence" is treated as a first-order predicate that adds something to the concept of an entity, making it *greater.* This, according to Kant and those who follow him, is the fatal flaw in the argument.

Here is another way to make this point. Consider the table on which you are writing and abstract from it all its properties except *existence*. That is, imagine that you could leave it existing without all the other properties: its color, shape, substance, function, and so forth. What would be left? Existence alone. But what is the difference between existence alone and nothing at all?

Existence is an odd kind of "property" that has no *meaning* without first-order properties. This is why we label it a second-order property. It tells us whether the other properties are actualized or exemplified.

If *existence* is not a real property, it is not a perfection either, as René Descartes thought. Suppose that Lisa and Jane each wrote down the qualities of a perfect husband. Here are their lists:

Lisa's List	*Jane's List*
intelligence	intelligence
devotion	devotion
kindness	kindness
attractiveness	attractiveness
sense of humor	sense of humor
moral integrity	moral integrity
good health	good health
existence	

Lisa's and Jane's lists are identical except for the quality of *existence* on Lisa's list. But is Lisa's list really better? Not at all. She has misunderstood the purpose of the list, which is to set forth the qualities an ideal existing husband would have. It's another matter whether these qualities are exemplified in an actual man.

If existence were a perfection, we could define things into existence simply by building the concept of existence into the definition. Suppose we define a "unicorn" as a horse with horns. No unicorns exist. But suppose we defined a "unicorn" as a unicorn that exists. So unicorns must exist because unicorns exist by definition. But, of course, this is just a verbal trick. We cannot define things into existence. This is the point of Kant's criticism.

Although Kant's criticism may work against the standard version of the ontological argument, some philosophers—namely, Charles Hartshorne, Norman Malcolm, and William Lawhead—argue that Anselm had a second version of the argument, based on *necessary* existence. They contend that although existence itself may not be a property or a perfection, necessary existence is. The second version of the ontological argument, as set forth by Lawhead, goes like this:

1. It is possible that God exists.
2. God must be conceived as being the greatest possible being.
3. The greatest possible being must be a necessary being.
4. The existence of a necessary being must be either (a) impossible, (b) merely possible (contingent), or (c) necessary.
5. We can exclude (a), for it cannot be impossible for a necessary being to exist. There is no contradiction in the concept of a necessary being.
6. Nor can it be (b), that it is a mere possibility that God exists, for such existence would be (i) dependent and (ii) happenstance, and such a being could not be God.
7. Therefore ∴ A necessary being necessarily exists. That is, God exists.

Has this new improved version of the ontological argument proved that God exists? The argument is valid (it has a proper form). Is it sound? Consider the premises. Are they all true? Premise 1 seems right. Even most atheists acknowledge that it is logically possible that God exists. Premise 2 seems correct. God must be thought to be unsurpassably great: Omnipotent, Omniscient, Omnibenevolent, and so forth. Premise 3 also seems right. It cannot just be an accident that God exists, otherwise his existence needs an explanation. What caused it? A greatest possible being is not contingent or a mere outcome of luck but must necessarily exist, as premises 4 and 5 argue. So it would seem that a necessary being must necessarily exist.

God exists! This, if it is true, is a momentous discovery.

Have we really proved that God exists? Well, there are two objections you might consider. The first is that the same argument can be used to prove the existence of an all-powerful devil. We define a devil as the worst possible being:

1. It is possible that the devil exists.
2. The devil must be thought as the worst possible being.
3. The worst possible being must be a necessary being.
4. The existence of a necessary being must be either (a) impossible, (b) merely possible (contingent), or (c) necessary.
5. We can exclude (a), for it cannot be impossible for a necessary being to exist. There is no contradiction in the concept of a necessary being.
6. Nor can it be (b), that it is a mere possibility that the devil exists, for such existence would be (i) dependent and (ii) happenstance, and such a being could not be the devil.

7. Therefore ∴ A worst possible being must necessarily exist. That is, the devil exists.

Because it seems contradictory to suppose a best possible being and a worst possible being both exist, for they could not both be all-powerful, something must be wrong with this form of the argument.

Some argue that we can argue only for the greatest possible being and not for a worst possible one because all other qualities of the devil would be good ones (e.g., knowledge, power, and presence). But proponents of the devil argument would argue, following Kant, that the only intrinsically good quality is the good will, so that all other virtues turn out to be vice-enhancing. If this is correct, the devil argument seems valid.

There is a second objection to Anselm's second argument. The argument still defines things into existence, only this time it defines things into necessary existence. Suppose we list all the triangles ever drawn and someone argues that it is necessary that a greatest possible triangle exists:

1. It is possible that the perfect triangle exists.
2. The perfect triangle must be thought as the best possible triangle.
3. The best possible triangle must be a necessary being.
4. Something that necessarily exists must exist.
5. Therefore ∴ The greatest possible triangle must exist.

But something seems absurd about this argument. There is no reason to believe that such a thing really does exist. Furthermore, couldn't we use the concept of necessary existence to define other things into existence? Consider Lisa's and Jane's ideas of an ideal husband. When Lisa argues that her ideal is better than Jane's because hers (Lisa's) contains the concept of existence, Jane can shoot back, "But mine contains the property of *necessary existence,* so my notion of a husband is better." Of course, some would argue that the idea of necessary existence does not apply to such innately contingent beings as husbands, but the question for you to consider is, Why?

Suppose that these two criticisms fail to dislodge Anselm's second version of the ontological argument; have we then proved that God exists? I don't think so. What we have done is something interesting but less than a proof. An opponent could still attack the first premise and say that, although it may not be obvious at first sight, it really is not possible that God exists. The reason is that the argument really gives us only two choices: either God *necessarily exists* or *necessarily does not exist.* Because we do not know which to choose on the basis of the concept of necessary being alone, we may suppose that, given the lack of other evidence, God's existence is impossible. Or, perhaps more prudently, we may remain agnostic.

So the ontological argument, at best, does not prove that God exists. It shows that it is reasonable to believe that he exists. However, even that may be too generous. Perhaps it is simply that it is not altogether foolish to believe that a necessary being exists. It is a difficult question.

But there is one more version of the ontological argument we must consider, that put forth by Alvin Plantinga.

THE MODAL VERSION
OF THE ONTOLOGICAL ARGUMENT

One of the most ingenious versions of the ontological argument has been set forth by Alvin Plantinga.[4] Plantinga gets around Kant's criticism that *existence* is not a real property by interpreting the argument in modal terms (*possibility, possible worlds,* and *necessity*). He follows Hartshorne in holding that God's existence cannot be merely contingent but must be necessary— that is, *maximal greatness* must be exemplified in every possible world. A possible world is one that is logically possible—it does not contain contradictory states of being (like round squares). The argument goes like this:

1. To say that it is possible that there is a God is to say that there is a possible world in which God exists.
2. To say that God necessarily exists is to say that God exists in every possible world.
3. God is necessarily perfect (i.e., *maximally excellent*).
4. Since God is necessarily maximally excellent, he is maximally excellent in every possible world.
5. If God is maximally excellent in every possible world, he must exist in every possible world, from which it follows that God exists.
6. God is also necessarily *maximally great*. To be maximally great is to be perfect or *maximally excellent* in every possible world.
7. Therefore, 'it is possible that there is a God' means that there is a possible world which contains God, that God is *maximally great,* and that God exists in every possible world and is consequently necessary.
8. God's existence is at least possible.
9. Therefore ∴ by 7, God exists.

What should we say about this argument? It is formally valid, but is it sound (i.e., are its premises true)? The first worry is the concept of a *possible world.* Only the actual world exists—possible worlds don't exist. They are not places we can visit, so no God exists in a possible world, let alone a maximally perfect God—any more than David Copperfield exists, in spite of being a character in one of Dickens's novels.

To say that you might have constructed a colonial house or a ranch-type house instead of the simple bungalow that you actually built doesn't mean that your colonial house exists in another possible world and your ranch-type house exists in still another possible world. Those houses don't exist at all. They were only possibilities in your mind (or blueprints in your files) that you never actualized. You can't live in your colonial house or your ranch-type dwelling; only your bungalow exists. You can no more live in your colonial or ranch-type houses than you can pay your tuition with Monopoly money.

Even if we waive the objection to possible worlds, all that Plantinga's modal version of the ontological argument shows is that if there is a God, he must be perfect; but this does not prove that God exists.

But if I am right that possible worlds don't exist, then God can't exist in one either, so Plantinga hasn't proved that God exists. At the very best, he has shown that God might exist—or that it is not contrary to reason that maximal greatness is exemplified. But it is not surprising that it is not contrary to reason that maximal greatness is exemplified, because Plantinga defines God as maximal excellence that is instantiate in every possible world. But that seems to be defining God into existence, the very thing at which Kant's criticism is aimed. Plantinga claims that he has avoided Kant's criticism that existence is not a real property with his (Plantinga's) modal categories such as *necessary existence,* but this seems mistaken, for necessary existence is still a type of existence, no more a real property than existence itself. So we must conclude that Plantinga's version of the ontological argument fails like all the others we have examined. You simply cannot define God into existence.

Summary

The ontological argument is an a priori argument for the existence of God, which attempts to establish the necessity of the existence of God through an understanding of the concept of existence or necessary being. Its strength is that it provides one with an idea of an adequate God, one who is maximally powerful and benevolent ("a greatest possible being"). Although it is difficult to assess in all its multifarious ramifications, no version has been completely successful in proving the existence of God. On the other hand, the argument may lend a measure of plausibility to the idea of the existence of a maximally powerful and benevolent being. The issue is controversial.

Questions for Discussion

1. Review the two versions of the ontological argument discussed in this chapter. How telling are Gaunilo's and Immanuel Kant's criticisms? Does Anselm misunderstand the concept of "being," as the critics claim?

2. Is it greater to exist than not to exist, as Anselm argues? Or is the term *greater* used ambiguously or wrongly here?

3. Could an argument similar to Anselm's be used to prove that a perfectly powerful devil exists as the supreme being and creator of the universe? In their article "An Ontological Argument for the Devil" (*Monist* 54, 1970), David and Marjorie Haight put forth such an argument:

1. I have a concept of something than which nothing worse can be conceived.
2. If that "something" did not actually, or in fact, exist, it would not be "that than which nothing worse could be conceived," because something could always be conceived to be much worse, viz. something that actually exists.
3. The "greatest something" we shall call the Devil.
4. Therefore, the Devil exists.

Evaluate this argument.

For Further Reading

Gale, Richard. *On the Nature and Existence of God.* Cambridge, England: Cambridge University Press, 1991. Chapter 6 contains an excellent discussion of this argument.

Mackie, J. L. *The Miracle of Theism.* Oxford, England: Oxford University Press, 1982. A lively discussion of the proofs for the existence of God and other issues by one of the ablest atheist philosophers of our time.

Martin, Michael. *Atheism: A Philosophical Justification.* Philadelphia: Temple University Press, 1990. One of the most comprehensive and clearest English-language attacks on theism.

Plantinga, Alvin. *God, Freedom, and Evil.* New York: Harper & Row, 1974. Part 2 contains a brilliant contemporary defense of the argument. Reprinted in Pojman (below).

Plantinga, Alvin, ed. *The Ontological Argument from St. Anselm to Contemporary Philosophers.* Garden City, N.Y.: Doubleday, 1965. A good anthology on the subject.

Pojman, Louis, ed. *Philosophy of Religion: An Anthology.* 3d ed. Belmont, Calif.: Wadsworth, 1998. A comprehensive anthology, setting forth both sides of many issues. It contains William Rowe's modal version of the ontological argument and J. N. Findlay's "God's Existence Is Necessarily Impossible."

Notes

1. Bertrand Russell, *Autobiography of Bertrand Russell* (New York: Little, Brown, 1967).
2. St. Anselm, *Proslogium,* trans. S. W. Deane (La Salle, Ill.: Open Court, 1903) (slightly edited).
3. Immanuel Kant, *Critique of Pure Reason,* trans. J. Meiklejohn (New York: Colonial Press, 1900), 335–336.
4. See *God, Freedom, and Evil* (New York: Harper & Row, 1974). Reprinted in *Philosophy of Religion,* 3d ed., ed. Louis Pojman (Belmont, Calif.: Wadsworth, 1998).

5

THE ARGUMENT FROM RELIGIOUS EXPERIENCE

There was not a mere consciousness of something there, but fused in the central happiness of it, a startling awareness of some ineffable good. Not vague either, not like the emotional effect of some poem, or scene, or blossom, or music, but the sure knowledge of the close presence of a sort of mighty person, and after it went, the memory persisted as the one perception of reality. Everything else might be a dream, but not that.[1]

The Ego has disappeared. I have realized my identity with Brahman and so all my desires have melted away. I have arisen above my ignorance and my knowledge of this seeming universe. What is this joy I feel? Who shall measure it? I know nothing but joy, limitless, unbounded! The treasure I have found there cannot be described in words. The mind cannot conceive of it. My mind fell like a hailstone into that vast expanse of Brahman's ocean. Touching one drop of it, I melted away and became one with Brahman. Where is this universe? Who took it away? Has it merged into something else? A while ago, I beheld it—now it exists no longer. Is there anything apart or distinct from Brahman? Now, finally and clearly, I know that I am the Atman [the soul identified with Brahman], whose nature is eternal joy. I see nothing, I hear nothing, I know nothing that is separate from me.[2]

ENCOUNTERS WITH GOD

THE HEART OF RELIGION is and always has been experiential. Encounters with the supernatural, a transcendent dimension, the Wholly Other are at the base of every great religion. Abraham hears a Voice that calls him to leave his family in Haran and venture out into a broad unknown, thus becoming the father of Israel. Abraham's grandson Jacob wrestles all night with an angel and is transformed, gaining the name

"Israel," "prince of God." While tending his father-in-law's flock, Moses is appeared to by "I am that I am" (Yahweh) in the burning bush and ordered to deliver Israel out of slavery into a land flowing with milk and honey. Isaiah has a vision of the Lord "high and exalted, and the train of his robe filled the temple" of heaven. In the New Testament, John, James, and Peter behold Jesus gloriously transformed on the Mount of Transfiguration and are themselves transformed by the experience. After the death of Jesus, Saul is traveling to Damascus to persecute Christians when he is met by a blazing light and hears a Voice, asking him why he is persecuting the Lord.[3] Changing his name to Paul, he becomes the leader of the Christian missionary movement. The Hindu experiences the Atman (soul) as Brahman (God), "That art Thou," or beholds the glories of Krishna. The Advaitian Hindu merges with the One, as a drop of water merges with the vast ocean. The Buddhist merges with Nirvana or beholds a vision of Buddha.[4] Allah reveals his holy word, the Koran, to Mohammed. Joan of Arc hears voices calling on her to save her people, and Joseph Smith has a vision of the angel Moroni, calling him to do a new work for God.

Saints, mystics, prophets, ascetics, and common believers of every creed, of every race, in every land, and throughout recorded history have undergone esoteric experiences that are hard to explain but impossible to dismiss as mere nonsense. There appear to be common features linking these otherwise disparate experiences to one another, resulting in a common testimony to this Otherness, a *consensus mysticum*. Rudolf Otto characterizes the religious (or "numinal," spiritual) dimension in all of these experiences as the *mysterium tremendum et fascinans*.[5] Religion is an unfathomable mystery, *tremendum* ("to be trembled at"), awe-inspiring, and *fascinans* ("fascinating"), magnetic. To use a description from Søren Kierkegaard, religious experience is a "sympathetic antipathy and an antipathetic sympathy" before a deep unknown.[6] Like looking into an abyss, it both repulses and strangely attracts.

AN ANALYSIS OF RELIGIOUS EXPERIENCE

What, then, is the problem with religious experience? If I say that I hear a pleasant tune, and you listen and say, "Yes, I hear it now too," we have no problem; but if you listen carefully and don't hear it, you might well wonder whether I am really hearing sounds or only imagining that I am. Perhaps we could bring in others to check out the matter. If they agree with me, well and good; but if they agree with you and don't hear the sounds, then we have a problem. Perhaps we could bring in an audiometer to measure the decibels in the room. If the meter confirms my report, then it is simply a case of my having better hearing than you and the rest of the witnesses; but if the meter doesn't register at all, assuming that it is in working order, then we would have good evidence that I am only imagining the sounds. Perhaps I need to change my claim and say, "Well, I seem to be hearing a pleasant tune."

One problem is that religious experience is typically private. You have the sense of God forgiving you or an angel speaking to you, but I, who am in the same room with you, neither hear nor see nor feel anything unusual. You are praying and suddenly feel transported by grace and sense the unity of all reality. I, who am sitting next to you, wonder at the strange expression on your face and ask you if something is wrong. Perhaps your brain is experiencing an altered chemical or electrical state?

Yet religious experiences of various types have been reported by numerous people, from dairymaids such as Joan of Arc to mystics such as St. Theresa of Avila and St. John of the Cross. They cannot be simply dismissed without serious analysis.

There are two levels of problem here: (1) To what degree, if any, is the subject of a religious experience justified in inferring from the psychological experience (the subjective aspect) to the existential or ontological reality of that which is the object of the experience (the objective aspect)? (2) To what degree, if any, does the cumulative witness of those undergoing religious experience justify the claim that there is a God or transcendent reality?

Traditionally, the argument from religious experience has not been one of the "proofs" for God's existence. At best, it has confirmed and made existential what the proofs conveyed with icy logic. Some philosophers, such as C. D. Broad (1887–1971) and the contemporary philosophers Richard Swinburne and Gary Gutting, believe that the common experience of mystics is strong justification or evidence for all of us for the existence of God.[7] Others, such as William James (1842–1910), believe that religious experience is sufficient evidence for the subject himself or herself for the existence of a divine reality but only constitutes a possibility for the nonexperiencer. That is, religious experience grants us only weak justification. Religious skeptics, such as Walter Stace (1886–1967) and Bertrand Russell (1872–1970), doubt this and argue that a subjective experience by itself is never warrant for making an existential claim (of an object existing outside oneself). It is a fallacy to go from the psychological experience of X to the reality of X.

There are two main traditions regarding religious experience. One, which we can call "mystical," posits the unity of all reality or the unity of the subject with its object (the mystic is absorbed in God, becomes one with God, etc.). The second type of religious experience can be called simply "religious experience" in order to distinguish it from the mystical. It does not conflate the subject with the object but is a numinal (Divine)experience wherein the believer (or subject) experiences the presence of God or an angel or Christ or the Holy Spirit, either speaking to or appearing to the experient or forgiving him or her. While in prayer, believers often experience a sense of the presence of God or the Holy Spirit.

Now, there are many psychological explanations of religious experience that cast doubt on its validity. One of the most famous is the Freudian interpretation. Sigmund Freud said that it was the result of the projection of the father image within oneself. The progression goes like this. When you were a child, you looked on your father as a powerful hero who could do everything, meet all your needs, and overcome the normal obstacles that hindered your way at every step. When you grew older, you sadly realized that your father was fallible and very finite, indeed, but you still had the need of the benevolent, all-powerful father. So subconsciously you projected your need for that long-lost parent onto the empty heavens and invented a god for yourself. Because this is a common phenomena, all of us who have successfully "projected daddy onto the big sky" go to church or synagogue or mosque or whatever and worship the illusion on our favorite holy day. But it is a myth. The sky is empty, and the sooner we realize it, the better for everyone.

This is one explanation of religious experience and religion in general. It is not a disproof of God's existence, simply a hypothesis. Even if it is true psychologically that we tend to think of God as a powerful and loving parent, it could still be the case that the parental relationship is God's way of teaching us about himself—by analogy.

In his classic on the subject, *Varieties of Religious Experience* (1902), William James describes what he considers the deepest kind of religious experience, mystical experience, a type of experience that transcends our ordinary, sensory experience and that cannot be described in terms of our normal concepts and language. It is "ineffable experience." The experient realizes that the experience "defies expression, that no adequate report of its content can be given in words. It follows from this that its quality must be directly experienced; it cannot be imparted or transferred to others."[8] And yet it contains a **noetic** quality, a content. It purports to convey truth about the nature of reality, namely, that there is a unity of all things and that that unity is spiritual, not material. It is antinaturalistic, pantheistic, and optimistic. Two other characteristics are predicated to this state. Mystical states are transient—that is, they cannot be sustained for long—and they are passive—that is, the mystic is acted on by divine deliverance, grace. We can prepare ourselves for the experience, but it is something that happens to us, not something that we do.

James is cautious about what can be deduced from mystical experience. Although mystical states are and ought to be absolutely authoritative over the individuals to whom they come, "no authority emanates from them which should make it a duty for those who stand outside of them to accept their revelations uncritically." But their value is that they provide us a valid alternative to the "non-mystical rationalistic consciousness, based on understanding and the senses alone. They open out the possibility of other orders of truth, in which, so far as anything in us vitally responds to them, we may freely continue to have faith."

Broad goes even further than James. In his book *Religion, Philosophy, and Psychical Research* (1930), he likens the religious sense to an ear for music. There are a few people on the negative end who are spiritually tone deaf and a few on the positive end who are the founders of religion, the Bachs and Beethovens. In between are the ordinary followers of religion, who are like the average listener to music, and above them are the saints, who are likened to those with a very fine ear for music.

The chief difference is that religion, unlike music, says something about the nature of reality. Is what it says true? Does religious experience lend any support to the truth claims of religion? Is religious experience veridical, and are the claims about "the nature of reality which are an integral part of the experience, true or probable?" Broad considers the argument from mystical agreement:

1. There is an enormous unanimity among the mystics concerning the spiritual nature of reality.
2. When there is such unanimity among observers as to what they take themselves to be experiencing, it is reasonable to conclude that their experiences are veridical (unless we have good reason to believe that they are deluded).
3. There are no positive reasons for thinking that mystical experiences are delusive.
4. Therefore, it is reasonable to believe that mystical experiences are veridical.

The weak premise is 3, for there is evidence that mystics are neuropathic or sexually repressed. Broad considers these charges, admits some plausibility in them, but suggests that they are not conclusive. Regarding the charge of neuropathology, he urges that "one might need to be slightly *cracked* in order to have some peep-holes into the super-sensible world"; with regard to sexual abnormality, it could simply be the case that no one who was "incapable of strong sexual desires and emotions could have anything worth calling religious experience."

His own guarded judgment is that, given what we know about the origins of religious belief and emotions, there is no reason to think that religious experience is "specially likely to be delusive or misdirected," so that religious experience can be said to offer us strong justification for a transcendent reality.

Gutting develops Broad's strong-justification thesis further, arguing that religious experience "establishes the existence of a good and powerful being concerned about us, and [this] justifies a central core of religious belief."[9] On this basis, he argues that the essential validity of religion is vindicated. However, like Broad, he finds that this sort of justified belief "falls far short of the claims of traditional religions" so that detailed religious accounts are nearly as suspect as nonreligious accounts. "The heart of true religious belief is a realization that we have access to God but only minimal reliable accounts of his nature and relation to us." Gutting develops three criteria that veridical religious experiences must meet: They must be repeatable, must be experienced by many in many diverse climes and cultures, and must issue forth in morally better lives.

But in arguing for the strong-justification thesis, Gutting seems to me to have gone too far. A strong justification makes it rationally obligatory for everyone to believe in the conclusion of an argument, in this case, that God exists. A weak justification only provides rational support for those who have an "of-God" experience (or already accept the worldview that made such experiences likely). Gutting believes that he has given a strong justification for religious belief, sufficient to establish the existence of God, but there are reasons to suppose that the argument from religious experience offers, at best, only weak justification.

A CRITIQUE OF THE STRONG-JUSTIFICATION THESIS

Three criticisms of the strong-justification thesis follow:

1. Religious experience is too amorphous and disparate for us to generalize from in the way Gutting would have us do. That is, there are many varieties of religious experiences, which seem mutually contradictory or vague, so that it is not clear whether we can give the proper criteria necessary to select "of-God" experiences as veridical or having privileged status.

2. Justification of belief in the veridicality of religious experience is circular, so that the belief in it will rest on premises that are not self-evident to everyone. In effect, all assessment of the veridicality of such experience depends on nonuniversal background beliefs.

3. When taken seriously as a candidate for veridical experience, religious experience has the liability of not being confirmed in the same way that perceptual experience is. That is, although religious experience may sometimes be veridical, it cannot be checked as ordinary perceptual experience can, nor can we make predictions on account of it. This indicates that it cannot be used as an argument for the existence of God in the way that Gutting uses it. Let us look closer at these counterarguments.

Religious Experience Is Amorphous and Varied

Religious experience is amorphous and too varied to yield a conclusion with regard to the existence of God. Consider the various types of religious experiences, most of which can be documented in the literature:

1. S senses himself absorbed into the One, wherein the subject–object distinction ceases to hold.
2. One senses the unity of all things and that she is nothing at all.
3. The Buddhist monk who is an atheist senses the presence of the living Buddha.
4. One senses the presence of God, the Father of our Lord Jesus Christ.
5. The Virgin Mary appears to S (in a dream).
6. The Lord Jesus appears to Paul on the road one afternoon, though no one else realizes it but him.
7. One senses the presence of Satan, convincing him that Satan is the highest reality.
8. Achilles is appeared to by the goddess Athene, whom he believes to be descended from Zeus's head. She promises that he will win the battle on the morrow.
9. Allah appears to S and tells him to purify the land by executing all infidels (e.g., Jews and Christians), whose false worship corrupts the land.
10. A guilt-ridden woman senses the presence of her long-deceased father, assuring her that he has forgiven her of her neglect of him while he was aging and dying.
11. A mother senses the presence of the spirit of the river, telling her to throw back her deformed infant because it belongs to the river and not to her.
12. One senses the presence of the Trinity and understands how it could be that the three persons are one God, but he cannot tell others.

13. One senses the presence of the **demiurge** who has created the universe but who makes no pretense to be omnipotent or omnibenevolent.

14. An atheist senses a deep infinite gratitude for the life of his son without in the least believing that a god exists (the philosopher George Nakhnikian's personal example).

15. An atheist has a deep sense of nothingness in which she is absolutely convinced that the universe has manifested itself to her as a deep void.

The problem for those who would strongly justify the practice of religious experience (that is, show that we are rationally obligated to believe the content of the experience) is to differentiate the valid interpretations from the invalid. Which of these experiences are valid? That is, do any of these guarantee the truth of the propositions contained in the experience? For the believer or experient, each is valid for him or her, but why should the non-experient accept any of these reports? And why should the experient continue to believe the content of the report himself after it is over and after he notes that there are other possible interpretations of it or that others have had mutually contradictory experiences? It would seem that they cancel each other out. Note the disparity of different types of "nonphysical" or religious experiences in the preceding list. There is not even any consensus that there is one supreme being who is benevolent. Experiences 1 through 3 do not involve a divine being at all. Contrary to what Gutting says about the virtual universality of god experiences, the branches of Buddhism and Hinduism (in experiencing Nirvana) have religious experiences without experiencing a god. Furthermore, experience 7 supposes that the supreme being is evil, and experience 13 denies omnibenevolence. Experiences 14 and 15 have all the self-authenticating certainty of a religious experience but involve a conviction that no god exists. Do we understand how to distinguish genuine religious experiences from "spiritually" secular ones like experience 14? Why should we believe that the testimony of "of-God" experients is veridical, but not the other types (e.g., 1, 3, 7, 9, 11, 13, and 15) that are inconsistent with it? The very private nature of religious experience should preclude our being hasty in inferring from the psychological state to the reality of the object of the experience.

Gutting recognizes the diversity of religious experiences but fails to realize how troublesome this is for his thesis. He tries to find a core in these experiences to the effect that there is a "good and powerful non-human being who cares about us."[10] Gutting admits that we can't derive very much from "of-God" experiences, only that there is a being who is more powerful than we are, very powerful and very good. But even if his argument were to show this, would it be sufficient as a definition of "God"? What would be the difference between this and experience 13, Plato's finite demiurge, or experience 10, the guilt-ridden woman's sense of her father, who presumably was both mentally and physically more powerful than she (he was Arthur Conan Doyle, a genius and pugilist)? How would this show that there is a God, whom we should worship? How would this differ from ancestor worship or polytheism? Or a visitor from outer space? All of these could be "powerful, good, nonhuman and caring for us." Why should we prefer the "of-God" experiences to the "of-a-supreme-Devil" experiences? Gutting rejects the notion of self-authentication as the guarantee for the veridicality of these religious experiences,[11] but, if this is so, how does the experient tell the difference between the nonhuman being who cares for her and one who only pretends to care? And how does one reidentify the being who has appeared to him in a nonsensory form?

The Argument from Religious Experience Is Circular

Justification of belief in religious experience is circular, so that the belief in it will rest on premises that are not self-evident to everyone. If I am right about the difficulties in singling out "of-God" experiences from other deeply felt experiences, it would seem that we can only justify belief in the content of religious experience through circular reasoning, by setting forth hypothetical assumptions that we then take as constraints on the experience itself. For example, we suppose that God's ways are mysterious and beyond finding out, and so we are ready to accept our fellow believer's testimony of a deep "of-God" experience. A polytheist in East Africa already believes that the hippopotamus-god appears to women with deformed children in dreams, asking for them back, and so credits his wife with a veridical experience when she reports that she has had such an encounter in a dream.

It would seem, then, that whether or not our interpretations of religious experience are justified depends on our background beliefs and expectations. Our beliefs appear to form a network, or web, in which all our beliefs are variously linked and supported by other beliefs. Some beliefs (call them "core beliefs"—e.g., my belief that 2 + 2 = 4, or that I seem to see a computer monitor, or that there are other minds, or that I am not now dreaming) are more centrally located and interconnected than other beliefs. If our core beliefs fall, our entire noetic structure is greatly affected, whereas some beliefs are only loosely connected to our noetic structure (e.g., my belief that the Yankees will win the pennant this year or that it is better to have an IBM PC computer than a TRS 80). Similarly, religious people and nonreligious people often have fundamentally different propositions at or near the center of their noetic structure. The religious person already is predisposed to have theistic-type religious experiences,

whereas the nonreligious person is not usually so disposed (in the literature, Christians have visions of Jesus, Hindus of Krishna, Buddhists of Buddha, ancient Greeks of Athene and Apollo, etc.). If you had been brought
up in a Hindu culture, wouldn't you be more likely to have a Hindu religious experience than a Christian type? Would there be enough in common for you to decide that both really converged to a common truth?

All experiencing takes place within the framework of a worldview. Certain features of the worldview may gradually or suddenly change in importance, thus producing a different total picture, but there is no such thing
as neutral evaluation of the evidence. As we have noted, what we see
depends to some degree on our background beliefs and expectations. The
farmer, the realtor, and the artist looking at the same field do not see the
same field. Neither do the religious person and the atheist see the same
thing when evaluating other people's religious experience.

It might be supposed that we could agree on criteria of assessment in
order to arrive at the best explanatory theory regarding religious experience, and there are, of course, competing explanations. There are Freudian, Marxian, and naturalist accounts that, suitably revised, seem to be as
internally coherent as the sophisticated theist account. For one account to
win our allegiance, it would be necessary for that account to win out over
all others. To do this, we would have to agree on the criteria to be met by
explanatory accounts. But it could turn out that there are competing criteria, so that theory A would fulfill criteria 1 and 2 better than theories B
and C; but B would fulfill criteria 3 and 4 better than the others, whereas C
might have the best overall record without best fulfilling any of the criteria.
It could be a close second in all of them. At this point, it looks as if the very
formulation and preference of the criteria of assessment depend on the
explanatory account that one already embraces. The theist may single out
self-authentication of the "of-God" experience, but why should that convince the atheist who suspects that criterion in the first place? It seems that
there is no unambiguous, noncircular consensus of a hierarchy of criteria.

Gutting is confident of a core content that would be experienced (1)
repeatedly, (2) by many, and (3) in such a way that the experiencers will be
led to live better moral lives.[12] But why should this convince a naturalist
who already has a coherent explanation of this phenomena? Plato's "noble
lie" (a lie that is useful to achieve social harmony), recently advocated by
the scientist Dr. Loyal Rue (see Chapter 1) presumably would have had the
same effect, but it still was a lie. Even if we took a survey and discovered
that the "of-God" experiences were common to all people, what would that
in itself prove? We might still have grounds to doubt its veridicality. As
Richard Gale notes, mere unanimity or agreement among observers is not
a sufficient condition for the truth of what is experienced:

Everybody who presses his finger on his eyeball will see double, everybody who stands at a certain spot in the desert will see a mirage, etc. The true criterion for objectivity is the Kantian one: An experience is objective if its contents can be placed in a spatiotemporal order with other experiences in accordance with scientific laws.[13]

Gale may go too far in limiting objectivity to that which is accessible to scientific laws, but his negative comments about unanimity are apposite.

Let me illustrate this point in another way. Suppose Timothy Leary had devised a psychogenic pill that had this result: Everyone taking it had a "deep religious experience" exactly similar to that described by the Western theistic mystics. Would this be good evidence for the existence of God? Perhaps some would be justified in believing it to be. We could predict the kinds of religious experience atheists would have on taking the pill. But suppose, further, that on taking two of the same pills, everyone had a deep religious experience common only to a remote primitive tribe: sensing the presence of a pantheon of gods, one being a three-headed hippopotamus who created the lakes and rivers of the world but didn't care a bit about people. The fact that there was complete agreement about what was experienced in these states hardly by itself can count for strong evidence for the truth of the existential claims of the experience. It would be likely that theists would have taken the experience to be veridical until they had a double dosage, and it would be likely that the tribespeople would have believed the double dosage to be veridical until they took a single dosage. Doesn't this indicate that it is our accepted background beliefs that predispose us to accept or reject that which fits or doesn't fit into our worldview?

Religious Experience Cannot Be Confirmed

When taken seriously as a candidate of veridical experience, religious experience fails in not being confirmable in the same way that perceptual experience is. There is, however, one criterion of assessment that stands out very impressively in the minds of all rational people (indeed, it is one of the criteria of rationality itself) but that is unduly ignored by proponents of the argument from religious experience, such as Gutting. It is the Achilles' heel (if anything is) of those who would place too much weight on religious experience as evidence for the content of religion. This is the complex criterion of checkability-predictability (I link them purposefully). The chemist who says that Avogadro's law holds (i.e., equal volumes of different gases, at the same temperature and pressure, contain an equal number of molecules) predicts exactly to what degree the inclusion of certain gases will increase the overall weight of a gaseous compound. Similarly, if, under normal circumstances, we heat water to 100°C, we can predict that it will boil. If you doubt my observation, check it out yourself. After suitable experiment, we see these propositions confirmed in such a way as to leave little room for doubt in our minds about their truth. After studying some chemistry, we see that they play a role in a wider network of beliefs that are mutually supportive. Such perceptual beliefs force themselves on us.

This notion of predictability can be applied to social hypotheses as well. For instance, an orthodox Marxist states that if her theory is true, capitalism will begin to collapse in industrialized countries. If it doesn't, we begin to doubt Marxism. Of course, the Marxist may begin to revise her theory and bring in ad hoc hypotheses to explain why what was expected didn't occur, but the more ad hoc hypotheses she has to bring to bear in order to explain why the general thesis isn't happening, the weaker the general thesis itself becomes. We come to believe many important propositions through experiment, either our own or those of others whom we take as authoritative (for the moment at least). With regard to authority, the presumption is that we could check out the propositions in question if we had time or need to do so.

How do we confirm the truth of religious experience? Does it make any predictions that we could test now in order to say, "Look and see, the fact that X occurs shows that the content of religious experience is veridical"? How do we check on other people's religious experiences, especially if they purport to be nonsensory perceptions?

The checkability factor is weak in Gutting's account. He claims that we have a duty to believe simply on the report of others, not on the basis of our own experience or of any special predictions that the experient would be able to make. But, if the Bible is to be believed, this wasn't always the case, nor should it be today. We read in 1 Kings 18 that to convince the Israelites that Yahweh, and not Baal, was worthy of being worshipped, Elijah challenged the priests of Baal to a contest. He proposed that they prepare a bullock and call on Baal to set fire to it. Then he would do the same with Yahweh. The priests failed but Elijah succeeded. Convincing evidence! Similarly, at the end of Mark, we read of Jesus telling his disciples that "signs shall follow them that believe; In my name shall they cast out devils; they shall speak with new tongues; They shall take up serpents; and if they drink any deadly thing, it shall not hurt them; they shall lay hands on the sick, and they shall recover" (Mark 16:17–18). I once read of a sect in Appalachia who followed this principle and fondled poisonous snakes. Funerals outnumbered miracles. Some believers doubt whether this text is authentic, and others seek to explain it away (e.g., "Jesus only meant his apostles and was referring to the apostolic age"), but if a religion were true, we might well expect some outward confirmation of it, such as we find in Elijah's actions at Mt. Carmel or in Jesus' miracles. The fact that religious experience isn't testable and doesn't yield any nontrivial predictions surely makes it less reliable than perceptual experience.

Not only does religious experience not usually generate predictions that are confirmed, but it sometimes yields false predictions. An example is an incident that happened to me as a student in an evangelical Christian college. A group of students believed that the Bible is the inerrant Word of God and cannot contain an untruth. Now the Gospel of Matthew 18:19 records Jesus as saying that "if two of you shall agree on earth as touching anything that they shall ask, it shall be done for them of my Father which is in heaven," and Matthew 17:20 tells of faith being able to move mountains: "Nothing shall be impossible for you." Verses in Mark confirm this, adding that God will answer our prayer if we pray in faith and do not doubt. So, one night several believers prayed through the entire night for the healing of a student who was dying of cancer. We prayed for her in childlike faith, believing that God would heal her. As morning broke, we felt the presence of God among us, assuring us that our prayer had been answered. As we left rejoicing and were walking out of the room, we received the news that the woman had just died.

It is interesting to note that none of the participants lost faith in God over this incident, though I for one was traumatically shaken by it. Some dismissed it as one of the mysteries of God's ways, others concluded that the Bible wasn't to be taken literally, and still others concluded that they hadn't prayed hard enough or with enough faith. But, as far as the argument for the veridicality of the content of religion is concerned, this failure has to be taken as part of the total data. How it weighs against empirically successful prayers or times when the content of the experience was confirmed, I have no idea, and I don't think Gutting has either. But, unless we do, it is hard to see how the argument from religious experience could be used as strong evidence for the existence of God to anyone else except those who had the experiences. As James concludes about mystical states (one form of religious experience), whereas those having the experience have a right to believe in their content, "no authority emanates from them which should make it a duty for those who stand outside of them to accept their revelations uncritically."

Let me close with an illustration of what might be a publicly verifiable experience of God, one that would be analogous to the kind of perceptual experience by which we check scientific hypotheses. What if tomorrow morning (8:00 A.M. CST) there were a loud trumpet call and all over North America people heard a voice speak out, saying, "I am the Lord, your God, speaking. I have a message for you all. I am deeply saddened by the violence and lack of concern you have for one another. I am calling on all nations to put aside nuclear weapons and to stop burning dangerous fossil fuels. I will give a leading environmental scientist (Dr. J. Walker) the formula for producing an efficient, low polluting fuel. At the same time I replenish the depleted ozone layer and help scientists with a cure for AIDS. This message is being delivered to over one hundred locales at different times today. I want you to know that I will take all means necessary to clean up the environment and prevent a nuclear war and punish those nations and businesses who persist on the mad course on which they are now embarked. I love each one of you. A few signs will confirm this message. Later today, while speaking to Israel and the Arab states, I will cause an island, which is intended as a homeland for the Palestinians, to appear west of Lebanon in the Mediterranean. I will also cause the Sahara Desert to become fruitful in order to provide food for the starving people in the sub-Sahara. But I will have you know that I will not intervene often in your affairs. I'm making this exception simply because it is an emergency situation."

Imagine that all over the world the same message is conveyed during the next 24 hours and the predictions fulfilled. Would your religious faith be strengthened by such an event? The question is, Why don't religious experiences like this happen? If there is a God, why does he or she seem to hide from us? Why doesn't God give us more evidence? I leave this question for you to reflect on.

Summary

Religious experience is at the core of the religious life. Throughout the ages, in virtually every culture, people have reported deeply religious, even mystical, experiences that have confirmed their beliefs and added meaning to their lives. Yet problems surround the phenomena because there are discrepancies between accounts, because they tend to be amorphous and varied, and because they seldom are verified.

Questions for Discussion

1. To what degree, if any, is a person who has a religious experience (of God) justified in inferring the existence of God? Should he or she seriously consider that the experience might be delusionary? How can one tell the difference between veridical and delusionary experiences?

2. Suppose that we agree with William James that the subject of a deep religious experience is justified in believing it to be veridical: How much

should this influence the rest of us who have not had such an experience to accept the content of his or her experience?

3. What do you make of the criticism that religious experiences are too amorphous and varied to yield conclusions with regard to the existence of God?

4. What do you make of the criticism that belief in religious experience tends to be circular so that the belief in it will rest on premises that are not self-evident to everyone?

5. What do you make of the criticism that religious experience is not a good candidate for veridical experience because, unlike perceptual experience, it cannot be verified?

For Further Reading

Alston, William. *Perceiving God*. Ithaca, N.Y.: Cornell University Press, 1991. An important work on the epistemology of religious experience.

Gale, Richard. *On the Nature and Existence of God*. Cambridge, England: Cambridge University Press, 1991. Chapter 8 contains a penetrating critique.

Gutting, Gary. *Religious Belief and Religious Skepticism*. Notre Dame, Ind.: University of Notre Dame Press, 1982. A well-argued contemporary discussion.

Harrison, Jonathan, *God, Freedom, and Immortality*. Aldershot, England: Ashgate, 1999, especially Chapter 10.

James, William. *The Varieties of Religious Experience*. New York: Modern Library, 1902. This marvelous treatise is the definitive work on the subject.

Otto, Rudolf. *The Idea of the Holy*, translated by J. Harvey. Oxford, England: Oxford University Press, 1923. A classic study on religious experience.

Pojman, Louis, ed. *Philosophy of Religion: An Anthology*. 3d ed. Belmont, Calif.: Wadsworth, 1998. Part 2 contains several important articles.

Swinburne, Richard. *The Existence of God*. Oxford, England: Oxford University Press, 1979. Contains an important discussion of religious experience.

Wainwright, William. *Mysticism*. Madison: University of Wisconsin Press, 1981. A comprehensive and sympathetic study of mysticism.

Notes

1. William James, *The Varieties of Religious Experience* (New York: Modern Library, 1902), 63.

2. Shankara's *Crest Jewel of Discrimination,* trans. Swami Prabhavandanda (New York: Mentor Books, 1970), 103–104.

3. "Now as he journeyed, Saul approached Damascus, and suddenly a light from heaven flashed about him. And he fell to the ground and heard a voice saying to him, 'Saul, Saul, why do you persecute me?' And he said, 'Who are you,

Lord?' And he said, 'I am Jesus whom you are persecuting; but rise and enter the city, and you will be told what you are to do.' The men traveling with him stood speechless, hearing the voice but seeing no one. Saul arose from the ground; and when his eyes were opened, he could see nothing; so they led him into Damascus" (Acts 9).

4. Here is an illustration of Buddhist meditation:

> Of one who has entered the first trance the voice has ceased; of one who has entered the second trance reasoning and reflection have ceased; of one who has entered the third trance joy has ceased; of one who has entered the fourth trance the inspiration and expiration have ceased; of one who has entered the realm of the infinity of space the perception of form has ceased; of one who has entered the realm of the infinity of consciousness the perception of the realm of the infinity of space has ceased; of one who has entered the realm of nothingness the perception of the realm of the infinity of consciousness has ceased. (Samyutta-Nikaya 36:115, in *Buddhism in Translation,* ed. Henry C. Warren. New York: Atheneum, 1973, 384.)

5. Rudolf Otto, *The Idea of the Holy* (Oxford, England: Oxford University Press, 1958).

6. Søren Kierkegaard, *The Concept of Dread* (Princeton, N.J.: Princeton University Press, 1939).

7. C. D. Broad, *Religion, Philosophy, and Psychical Research* (London: Routledge & Kegan Paul, 1930); Richard Swinburne, *The Existence of God* (Oxford, England: Clarendon Press, 1979); Gary Gutting, *Religious Belief and Religious Skepticism* (Notre Dame, Ind.: University of Notre Dame Press, 1982).

8. James, op. cit., 371. Here is another testimony reported by James:

> I remember the night, and almost the very spot on the hilltop, where my soul opened out, as it were, into the Infinite, and there was a rushing together of the two worlds, the inner and the outer. I stood alone with Him who had made me, and all the beauty of the world, and love, and sorrow, and even temptation. I did not seek Him, but felt the perfect unison of my spirit with His. The darkness held a presence that was all the more felt because it was not seen. I could not any more have doubted that He was there than that I was. I felt myself to be, if possible, the less real of the two. (p. 67)

9. Gutting, op. cit.

10. Ibid., 113.

11. Ibid., 145.

12. Ibid., 152.

13. Richard Gale, "Mysticism and Philosophy," *Journal of Philosophy* (1960).

6

THE PROBLEM OF EVIL

Is he willing to prevent evil, but not able? Then he is impotent.
Is he able, but not willing? Then he is malevolent.
Is he both able and willing? Whence then is evil?

—EPICURUS'S PARADOX

THE MYSTERY OF EVIL

WHY IS THERE EVIL IN THE WORLD? Why do bad things happen to good people? "The whole earth is cursed and polluted," says Philo in David Hume's (1711–1776) famous dialogue on natural religion. He continues:

> A perpetual war is kindled among all living creatures. Necessity, hunger, want, stimulate the strong and courageous; fear, anxiety, terror agitate the weak and infirm. The first entrance into life gives anguish to the new-born infant and to its wretched parent; weakness, impotence, distress attend each stage of that life, and it is, at last, finished in agony and horror. Man is the greatest enemy of man. Oppression, injustice, contempt, contumely, violence, sedition, war, calumny, treachery, fraud—by these they mutually torment each other, and they would soon dissolve that society which they had formed were it not for the dread of still greater ills which must attend their separation.[1]

In Fyodor Dostoevsky's (1821–1881) *The Brothers Karamazov,* Ivan relates the following story to his religious brother Alyosha. There was an aristocratic Russian general who had two thousand serfs and hundreds of hunting dogs. One day an eight-year-old serf boy threw a stone in play and hurt the paw of the general's favorite hound. "Why is my favorite lame?" the general inquires. He is told that the boy threw a stone that hurt the dog's paw. "So you did it!" the general exclaimed and ordered the boy taken away from his mother and kept shut up all night. Early the next morning, the general came out on horseback with his hounds, servants, and huntsmen all mounted, ready for a hunt. The eight-year-old boy is summoned from his cell, undressed. He shivers in the cold, numb with terror. "Make him run," commands the general. The boy runs. "At him!" yells the general, and he sets the pack of one hundred hounds loose. The hounds catch him and tear the boy to pieces before his mother's eyes.

Ivan cannot accept a world where such incidents occur. No amount of utility can justify the torture of a child. He cannot accept God's entrance ticket:

> And so I hasten to give back my entrance ticket, and if I am an honest man I am bound to give it back as soon as possible. . . . Tell me yourself, I challenge you. Imagine that you are creating a fabric of human destiny with the object of making men happy in the end, giving them peace and rest at last, but that it was essential and inevitable to torture to death only one tiny creature—that baby beating its breast with its fist, for instance—and to found that edifice on its unavenged tears, would you consent to be the architect on those conditions? Tell me, and tell me the truth.[2]

We have been looking at arguments in favor of God's existence. The agnostic and atheist usually base their case on the alleged unsoundness of the arguments for God's existence. But they have one arrow in their own quiver, an argument for disbelief. It is the problem of evil. From it the "atheologian" (one who argues against the existence of God) hopes either to neutralize any positive evidence for God's existence based on whatever in the traditional arguments survives their criticism or to demonstrate that it is unreasonable to believe in God. We will examine ways in which moral and natural evil are thought to provide evidence against the existence of a wholly good, omnipotent God, including the argument from evolution, which provides an alternative explanatory account of evil. We shall also consider the two main defenses against the argument from evil: the free-will defense and the theodicy defense. But first let us examine the core argument from evil against the existence of God.

THE ARGUMENT FROM EVIL

The problem of evil arises because of the paradox, cited at the beginning of this chapter, presented by an omnibenevolent, omnipotent deity allowing the existence of evil. The Judeo-Christian tradition has affirmed these three propositions:

1. God is all-powerful (including omniscient).
2. God is perfectly good.
3. Evil exists.

But if God is perfectly good, why does he allow evil to exist? Why didn't he create a better world, if not with no evil, then at least with substantially less evil than in this world? Many have contended that this paradox, first schematized by Epicurus (341–270 B.C.), is worse than a paradox. It is an implicit contradiction, for it contains premises that are inconsistent with one another. They argue something like the following:

4. If God (an all-powerful, omniscient, omnibenevolent being) exists, there would be no (or no unnecessary) evil in the world.
5. There is evil (or unnecessary evil) in the world.
6. Therefore ∴ God does not exist. To see whether they are right, let us review each of the basic propositions that generate the paradox.

Proposition 1: God is all-powerful.

"God is all-powerful" has been a cornerstone of Christian theology since the early centuries of the Church. Although it is debatable whether one can show that the biblical writers had such a strong concept (or whether the exact formulation is derived from a Platonic and Aristotelian metaphysics), most Judeo-Christian theologians have seen it as entailed by any adequate view of deity. Some philosophers and theologians, such as John Stuart Mill, William James, Alfred North Whitehead, Charles Hartshorne, and John Cobb, have relinquished this attribute of omnipotence to get God "off the hook" with regard to evil. They accept a *limited* God. God is perfectly good and the greatest possible being, but not omnipotent or omniscient. He cannot do many things, nor does he know the future. They argue that if God knew the future, we would not be free to act, for his knowledge would determine the future. I think this is fallacious, for the epistemic domain does not affect ontological ones. My knowing that you will decide not to cheat on a test when you get a chance does not determine your decision not to cheat. Similarly, God could simply know how we will use our free will. Because he exists in eternity beyond time, it seems reasonable to suppose that he knows what we regard as the future without causing it. But these philosophers, called *process philosophers*, suppose that God's knowledge is somehow determining, so that it is reasonable to relinquish the claim of omniscience. God, like other finite beings, is still learning. But because he is neither all-powerful or all-knowing, he cannot eliminate all evil from the world. God simply does the best he can. Does this argument work? Many think that this is too desperate a move. Other critics point out that, even if God is not all-powerful, he certainly must be exceedingly powerful (and knowledgeable), and, if so, he should have been able to prevent evil (or most of the evil) in the world. On the other hand, if he is not so powerful, why do we call him "God" rather than "demiurge" and worship, instead, the *ideal* of moral goodness? This is not to say that such process theologians and philosophers do not have a case but that their case may not be any better than some of the alternative solutions. Many will find it too radical altogether.

Finally, when theists speak of God being omnipotent, they usually mean that God can do anything that is logically possible. God cannot make a stone heavier than he can lift, will that he never existed, or make $2 + 2 = 5$. This will be important with regard to the defense of theism from the charge of the atheologian.

Proposition 2: God is perfectly good.

The Judeo-Christian, Muslim, and Hindu traditions all subscribe to the doctrine of complete divine benevolence. Take the property of benevolence from God, and what is the difference between God and a supreme devil? If mere power constitutes God's essence, why should we love and worship him? We might fear him, but he would hardly deserve our adoration or love. No, it is not mere power or knowledge but his complete goodness, his omnibenevolence, that makes God worthy of our worship. God cannot do evil and still remain God. All the major religions—Hinduism, Islam, Judaism, and Christianity—agree on this point. As the Psalmist exclaims, "Oh that men would praise the Lord for his goodness, and for his wonderful works to the children of men" (Psalms 107).

Proposition 3: There is evil.

"There is evil" may be denied by some Eastern religions, which view it as an illusion, but the Judeo-Christian tradition has always taken it as a fundamental datum to be overcome, if not explained. Suffering and pain, disease and death, cruelty and violence, rape and murder, poverty and natural havoc have all been viewed as the enemy of the good. The millions of humans who have starved to death or died victims of torture, bloody battle, and brutal wars, the myriads who have been abandoned, abused, and aborted all testify to the tragedy of the human condition: Evil exists in abundance.

Generally, Western thought has distinguished between two types of evil: moral and natural. *Moral evil* covers all those bad things for which humans are morally responsible. *Natural evil,* or *surd (irrational) evil,* stands for all those terrible events that nature does of her own accord—for example, hurricanes, tornadoes, earthquakes, volcanic eruptions, and natural diseases, which bring suffering to humans and animals. However, some defenses of theism affirm that all evil is essentially moral evil. Here the devil is brought in as the cause of natural evil.

Sometimes students argue that evil is logically necessary for the good, so God could not remove all evil without removing all good. Evil is the necessary counterpart to goodness, as the tail of a coin is the necessary complement of the head of a coin. Without evil, there could not be good. This seems fallacious reasoning. A property need not have an actual opposite in order to exist, though we might not be able to appreciate the good without some contrasting experiences. First of all, Christian and Muslim doctrine has always taught that no evil exists in heaven, which is the paradigm of perfect goodness, so goodness apparently can exist without evil in these traditions. But even if we waive this point and concede the contrast to the counterpart theorist, this doesn't get him very far. For God could equip us with enormous imaginative powers, so that we can imagine great evil without really experiencing it. So although some people may not be able to appreciate the good without some evil, evil is not necessary to the good.

Let us turn to the two main defenses against the argument from evil. The first is the free-will defense.

THE FREE-WILL DEFENSE

The main defense of theism in the light of evil is the free-will defense, going back as far as St. Augustine (354–430) and receiving modern treatment in the works of John Hick, Alvin Plantinga, and Richard Swinburne. The free-will defense adds an additional premise (3A) to Epicurus's paradox in order to show that propositions 1 through 3 are consistent and not contradictory:

Proposition 3A: *It is logically impossible for God to create free creatures and guarantee that they will never do evil.*

Because it is a good thing to create free creatures who are morally responsible agents, there is no assurance that they will not also do evil. Free agency is so important that it is worth the price of the evil it may cause or permit. As Plantinga puts it:

> God has actualized a possible world A containing significantly free creatures (angels, human beings, other kinds, what have you) with respect to whose actions there is a balance of good over evil (so that A on balance is a very good world); some of these creatures are responsible for moral and natural evil; and it was not within God's power to create significantly free creatures with respect to whose actions there would be a better balance of good over evil than that displayed in A.[3]

Imagine that God viewed an infinite set of possible worlds. In some of them, he saw humans as not sinning but also not free. In some he saw humans as free and doing less evil than in this world, but he chose to create this world with its enormous amount of good and evil. Perhaps he could have created other worlds with more good or less evil, but he could not create a world with a lesser proportion of good over evil than this one has, and no world he could have created could have a better proportion of good over evil. This world, though not perfect, is the best an omnipotent, omnibenevolent God could do.

This defense assumes a libertarian view of freedom of the will. That is, humans are free to choose between good and evil acts. They are not caused (though they may be influenced) to do one deed rather than the other, but rather they are causally underdetermined. Given two identically similar situations with identical causal antecedents, an agent could do act A at one time and act B at the other. This view is opposed to determinism, as well as compatibilism (a view that tries to reconcile freedom of action with determinism). If you are committed to compatibilism or determinism, the free-will defense will not be effective against the argument from evil. The theologian Marilyn McCord Adams thinks that the free-will defense overestimates the level of free agency in humans. She holds that humans have diminished agency before God, analogous to a small child's ability to act freely against an adult, so that humans cannot be held responsible for the amount and quality of evil.[4]

Many philosophers go even further than Adams and argue that metaphysical libertarianism is unsupported by any sound arguments. Every event in the world, including every action, is either the product of cause or chance. If the event is the result of mere chance, it is not a deliberative act for which we can be held accountable. On the other hand, if it is the effect of prior causes, we are not fully or strongly responsible for it—though we could be said to be responsible in a weak sense (we did the deed voluntarily).

If this is sound, then the problem with the free-will defense discussion is that the same arguments against libertarian freedom can be used to undermine or diminish divine agency. The crucial argument against libertarian free will and responsibility consists in a dilemma:

1. To be really free and responsible for our actions, we must be the cause of what we are (our states of mind).
2. No one is the cause of one's self. Not even God is *causa sui.*
3. So no one is really free and responsible.

As far as I can see, no one has explained what free will is (how it functions), let alone how it is possible. Roderick Chisholm calls it a mysterious *miracle.* Compatibilism, a form of *soft determinism,* toward which Adams seems to lean, may well be successful in reconciling determinism and responsibility, but this is not the robust kind of freedom needed for the free-will defense. The fact that I voluntarily do X makes me only the *proximate,* but not the *ultimate,* cause of X. Even my attitude of voluntariness is determined. But if God does not create himself, he is not free to do otherwise than he does. His actions are as causally determined as ours. Either he acts out of his basic character for determining reasons or he acts in an arbitrary manner. Either way, he is not omnipotent in the robust way the orthodox tradition supposes. Is there a way between the horns of this dilemma?

To return to the main issue, the proponent of the free-will defense claims that all moral evil derives from creature freedom of the will. But what about natural evil? How does the theist account for it? There are two different ways. The first one, favored by Plantinga and Stephen Davis, is to attribute natural evil to the work of the devil and his angels. Disease and tornadoes are caused by the devil and his minions. The second way, favored by Swinburne and Hick, argues that natural evil is part and parcel of the nature of things: a result of the combination of deterministic physical laws that are necessary for consistent action and the responsibility given to humans to exercise their freedom.

THE THEODICY DEFENSE

Whereas the free-will defense is concerned to show that Epicurus's original argument from evil is not decisive and that the problem of evil does not prove that God does not exist, the **theodicy** defense, first set forth by the German idealist Gottfried Wilhelm Leibniz (1646–1716), goes even further and argues that all evil will contribute to the greater good, so that this world, despite appearances, is the *best of all possible worlds.* The most prominent proponent of the theodicy defense is the British theologian John Hick.

Hick's thesis is particularly interesting because he endeavors to put forth a full-scale justification for God's permitting the evil in the world. Why does God allow natural evil and not normally intervene in either natural or moral evil? Hick answers: in order that human beings, as free responsible agents, may use this world as a place of "soul making," which involves the spiritual perfection of our character and persons. The skeptic errs in complaining about the recalcitrant structure of the world because he or she makes the assumption that God created humanity as a completed creation. The skeptic mistakenly thinks:

> that God's purpose in making the world was to provide a suitable dwelling-place for this fully-formed creature. Since God is good and loving, the environment which he has created for human life to inhabit is naturally as pleasant and comfortable as possible. The problem is essentially similar to that of a man who builds a cage for some pet animal. Since our world, in fact, contains sources of hardship, inconvenience, and danger of innumerable kinds, the conclusion follows that this world cannot have been created by a perfectly benevolent and all-powerful deity.[5]

Hick, drawing on the work of the second-century theologian Irenaeus, argues that humanity was made in the *image,* but not the *likeness,* of God. Incomplete beings, we must aim at full and perfect likeness. Our world, with all its rough edges and obstacles, "is the sphere in which this second and harder stage of the creative process is taking place."

Suppose that the world were a paradise, without the possibility of suffering, pain, and death. In that case, we would not be seriously accountable for our deeds:

> No one could ever injure anyone else; the murderer's knife would turn to paper or his bullets to thin air; the bank safe, robbed of a million dollars, would miraculously become filled with another million dollars; fraud, deceit, conspiracy, and treason would somehow always leave the fabric of society undamaged. . . . The reckless driver would never meet with disaster. There would be no need to work, since no harm could result from avoiding work; there would be no call to be concerned for others in time of need or danger, for in such a world there could be no real needs or dangers.[6]

Our present ethical concepts would not apply in such a safe "playpen paradise"; concepts like courage, honesty, love, benevolence, and kindness would make no sense because no one could do any harm, nor would there be need for heroism or saintliness. Such a world would certainly promote pleasure, but it would be wholly inadequate for character development. But our world is not such a hedonistic romper room. It is a place where we must take full responsibility for our actions, for they have serious consequences. It is a place where we can and should develop our characters into the full likeness of God.

PROBLEMS WITH THE THEODICY DEFENSE

I will leave it to you to analyze Hick's challenging argument fully, but a few questions are in order. First, if this world with "the heartache, and the thousand natural shocks that flesh is heir to"[7] is useful for suffering, couldn't a world with less suffering and evil than this one be adequate for the task? Were Auschwitz, My Lai, and Buchenwald and the torture chamber really necessary for soul building? While in training, astronauts are allowed to make mistakes, but built-in feedback mechanisms correct their mistakes before disaster sets in, while allowing the trainees to learn from their mistakes. Couldn't God have given us free will, allowed us to learn from our mistakes, and still constructed a world in which feedback mechanisms prevented the kind of monstrous disasters that occur around the world every day? Hick's theodicy may overestimate human capacity to use evil for good. It also seems inefficient. Why could God not aid us in our soul building without resorting to horrendous evils, perhaps in the way that astronauts are trained? A good teacher can educate and help build character without resorting to torture and brutality.

With or without the free-will defense, many philosophers maintain that the problem of evil still persists. Some, like J. L. Mackie and William Rowe, contend that the burden of proof is on the theist to explain why God does not intervene in the suffering of the world. If, by the mere pressing of a button, I could have caused Hitler to have had a heart attack before starting World War II, I would have been obliged to do so. Why did God not intervene in 1939 and prevent the evil of World War II, including the Holocaust? Why didn't he intervene in the event, described by Dostoevsky, in which the mad general set his hounds on the eight-year-old boy? Why does he not intervene in the sufferings of millions all over the world? Perhaps some evil is impossible to prevent, but why is there so much of it? Couldn't an all-knowing God have foreseen the evil in this world and created one in which people do not commit the amount of evil that occurs in our world? Couldn't he have seen another possible world in which humans are free but do much better than we do? Couldn't he have created a world with less natural evil, with less gratuitous pain in humans and animals? Couldn't an all-powerful, all-knowing deity do better than this? We could formulate the argument this way:

1. A morally good being will eliminate evil as much as possible unless he has good reason to allow it.
2. If there is evil in the world, God must have a good reason to allow it.
3. There is evil in the world.
4. Therefore ∴ God must have a good reason for allowing evil.

But the atheologian points out that even if God has such a reason, unless he communicates it to us, we are not in the epistemic position to appreciate that reason, and hence in no position to believe that he has a sufficient reason to allow seemingly gratuitous evil. If God does not intervene in human and animal suffering, don't we have grounds to suspect that he doesn't exist, doesn't care, or is severely limited? Or perhaps God is not omnibenevolent, but only partly good and partly bad? If this is sound, the problem of evil seems to be a strong argument against belief in the God of classical theism.

Of course, theists counter each of these objections. Some, we have noted, maintain that God is not all-powerful but limited in what he can do. Others argue that it is simply a mystery why God, although all-powerful, doesn't intervene to prevent more evil than he does. How do we know that he hasn't prevented much more evil than there is? Or perhaps in heaven there will be due recompense for the suffering here on Earth. Perhaps the lesson of evil is to show us just how serious our moral responsibilities are. Why blame God for evil, when it is we humans who are producing it?

With regard to natural evil (e.g., genetic deformities, diseases, earthquakes, and volcanic eruptions that kill innocent people), the theist argues that this is simply part of an orderly process of nature. The laws of nature are necessarily such that the good is interconnected with the bad. The same rain that causes one farmer's field to germinate floods and ruins another farmer's field. Although there are, no doubt, limits to the amount of evil God will allow, he cannot constantly intervene without eroding human responsibility or the laws of nature. Where those limits of evil are, not one of us can know. And yet we wonder. Couldn't an all-powerful God have created a better world than this, a world with a significantly greater proportion of good over evil?

Finally, theists argue that in heaven God will thank us for enduring the evil we have suffered and compensate us for it. The lame will walk with special ability and the blind see with acuity. This thesis rests on the coherence and plausibility of the notion of survival in an afterlife. We will examine the topic of personal identity and immortality in Chapter 8. I must leave you to deliberate on how the debate should continue, but there is one more argument from evil that we should consider before leaving the topic—that is the argument from evolution.

EVOLUTION AND EVIL

As we saw in Chapter 3 when discussing the argument from design, theists may have good reason to fear evolutionary theory and support creationist accounts of the origin of life and human beings, for evolution proposes a radical alternative paradigm to a theistic, purposive creation. This point can now be employed to undermine theism with regard to evil. Evolution holds that evil is not the result of Satan's sin or Adam's fall or human misuse of free will but rather the consequence of the species developing adaptive strategies that tend to be accompanied by pain, suffering, unhappiness, and conflicts of interest, the major categories of evil. It is our evolution first from nonsentient to sentient beings that enables us to experience pain. Pain serves as a warning mechanism, but extreme contingencies can utilize the capacity for no protective reason. The sensation of pain may cause us to withdraw our hand from a fire, but being immolated in a burning building or funeral pyre serves no warning purpose at all and seems entirely gratuitous. Much of our physical suffering is simply the failure of evolution's adaptive strategies. For example, bipedalism, the ability to walk upright on two limbs, enables "higher" primates, including humans, to free up their forelimbs for other purposes, like grasping and thrusting, but it incurs several liabilities—including the loss of speed of its quadrupedal ancestors, an imbalanced vertebral column, which increases the likelihood of lower back pain, troublesome birth pangs, and even stomach problems and herniation, as the center of balance shifts and more pressure is placed on the abdominal region. On a more local scale, sickle-shaped red blood cells are adaptive in areas in which malaria is rampant, but where it is not, they are lethal: Children born with sickle-cell anemia have only one-fifth the chance of other children of surviving to maturity. Similarly, human aggression may be adaptive in hunting and defending oneself against predators, but in social groups, in the face of conflicts of interest, it tends to be maladaptive, causing suffering, injury, and death. Use of reason is necessary for social cooperation and coexistence, but the instincts of our ancestor species are more reliable and efficient. Reason leads to institutions such as morality and law, which are necessary for civilization but create their own liabilities in terms of guilt, shame, litigation, and frustration. No lion deliberates as to whether he should kill an antelope or copulate with an available lioness, nor are his forays followed by guilt or remorse. He enjoys his conquests without worrying about whether he has violated antelope rights. He simply follows his instincts and usually gets away with it.

The point is not that we should go back to the state of the "noble savage." We couldn't, even if we tried. The point I'm trying to make is that each evolutionary adaptive strategy tends to incur a loss of some other virtue or capability, and this is what accounts for evil. What we call evil is simply part of the natural evolutionary process, which, as Tennyson pointed out, "is red in tooth and claw."* Much, if not most, of moral or man-made evil is the "unintended" result of nature's making us creatures with insatiable wants but limited resources and sympathies.

This evolutionary account of the origins of evil fits within the broader framework of human biology and animal ethology. To that extent it is confirmable by scientific research, whereas the religious accounts of the origin of evil have less impressive credentials. How do we recreate or confirm the record of the fall of Adam and Eve? The naturalistic account holds that we don't need myths or dogmas about the fall or original sin. Simply investigating evolutionary processes of adaptation is sufficient as an explanation for our greatest problems. Evil has a biological basis, being simply the inextricable concomitant of characteristics that served an adaptive function.

The theist has responses to this account of evil. She may either reject evolution in favor of a creationist account or absorb the evolutionary account within a theistic framework. The first strategy seems a lost cause, because evolution is supported by all we know about animal biology and genetics. The second strategy is more promising, but it is haunted by problems of explaining why God wasn't more efficient and benevolent in developing the species. Couldn't he have avoided the waste (sacrificing the millions of less fit individuals and species) and done things more benevolently—for example, made carnivorous animals herbivores and so avoided the predator–prey cycle of death and destruction?

So the problem of evil persists in haunting theism, and theists continue to devise strategies to ward off the attacks. On which side do the best reasons lie?

Summary

The problem of evil has to do with three propositions that, at first glance, seem incompatible: God's benevolence, God's omnipotence, and evil in

---

*Tennyson, *In Memorium*, LVI.

the world. Why did an all-powerful and omnibenevolent God permit evil in the first place, and, once established, why did he not eliminate it? The theist generally replies that it is better that God creates free beings who sin but who can be redeemed than for God to create a paradise in which only automatons mechanically do good. John Hick provides a second argument in terms of evil being necessary for soul building, so that humans may perfect themselves by developing into full spiritual beings, into the likeness of God. The skeptic objects to both of these proposals, arguing that it is implausible to suppose that an all-powerful, omnibenevolent God couldn't do better than make a world with this much evil in it.

Finally, we noted how an evolutionary explanation of the origins of evil competes with a theological account. Not Adam's fall but the evolution of the species is the best explanation of evil in the world.

Questions for Discussion

1. Go over the argument from evil against the existence of God. How cogent is it? Does the fact of evil or the amount of evil in the world count against the hypothesis that God exists? Explain your answer.

2. Does John Hick's account of soul making successfully answer the skeptic on why there is so much natural and moral evil? How would Hick meet the objection that God is "overdoing it" with Auschwitz and torture chambers?

3. What do you make of the suggestion that God is limited and is either not all-knowing or all-powerful and thus is not ultimately responsible for the amount of evil in the world? Does this view solve the problem of evil? Or does it merely extinguish the notion of a sovereign deity?

4. Some Christians, such as Marilyn McCord Adams, argue that part of the solution to the problem of evil is the incarnation (of God in Christ) and crucifixion, wherein God himself suffers horrendous evil, thus identifying with us in our suffering. How comforting is this thought?

5. Examine the evolutionary account of the origins and present reality of evil. Does it make more sense than theistic accounts? How should theists respond? By denial, accommodation, or surrender? Explain your answer.

For Further Reading

Adams, Marilyn McCord. *Horrendous Evils and the Goodness of God.* Ithaca, N.Y.: Cornell University Press, 1999. A comprehensive and illuminating contemporary treatment of the problem of horrendous evil.

Anders, Timothy. *The Evolution of Evil.* Open Court Books, 1994. A good account of the thesis set forth at the end of this chapter defending an evolutionary explanation of evil.

Hick, John. *Evil and the God of Love.* New York: Harper & Row, 1977. Contains the account of the theodicy discussed in this chapter.

Lewis, C. S. *The Problem of Pain.* London: Geoffrey Bles, 1940. A clear and cogent defense of theism.

Mackie, J. L. *The Miracle of Theism.* Oxford, England: Oxford University Press, 1982. Chapter 9 is an insightful, well-argued essay from an atheist's perspective.

Martin, Michael. *Atheism.* Philadelphia: Temple University Press, 1990. A comprehensive critique of theist arguments regarding the problem of evil. See especially Chapters 14–17.

Plantinga, Alvin. *God, Freedom, and Evil.* New York: Harper & Row, 1974. A clear, cogent account of the free-will defense from a theist perspective.

Pojman, Louis, ed. *Philosophy of Religion: An Anthology.* 3d ed. Belmont, Calif.: Wadsworth, 1998. Contains important readings in this area.

Swinburne, Richard. *The Existence of God.* Oxford, England: Oxford University Press, 1978. Chapter 11 contains a careful defense of theism against the charges of the skeptic.

Symons, Donald. *The Evolution of Human Sexuality.* New York: Oxford University Press, 1979.

Williams, George. *Adaptation and Natural Selection: A Critique of Some Current Evolutionary Thought.* Princeton, N.J.: Princeton University Press, 1966.

Notes

1. David Hume, *Dialogues Concerning Natural Religion* (1779). Section reprinted in *Philosophy of Religion: An Anthology,* 3d ed., ed. Louis Pojman (Belmont, Calif.: Wadsworth, 1998).

2. Fyodor Dostoevsky, *The Brothers Karamazov,* trans. Constance Garnett (Heinemann, 1912).

3. Alvin Plantinga, *The Nature of Necessity* (Oxford, England: Clarendon Press, 1974), 164–193.

4. Marilyn McCord Adams, *Horrendous Evils and the Goodness of God* (Ithaca, N.Y.: Cornell University Press, 1999), Chapter 1.

5. John Hick, *Philosophy of Religion* (Englewood Cliffs, N.J.: Prentice-Hall, 1963), 45.

6. Ibid.

7. William Shakespeare, *Hamlet,* Act III, scene I, ll. 62–63.

7

MIRACLES

So that, upon the whole, we may conclude, that the Christian Religion not only was at first attended with miracles, but even at this day cannot be believed by any reasonable person without one. Mere reason is insufficient to convince us of its veracity: And whoever is moved by Faith to assent to it, is conscious of a continued miracle in his own person, which subverts all the principles of his understanding, and gives him a determination to believe what is most contrary to custom and experience.

—DAVID HUME

WHAT ARE MIRACLES?

WHAT ARE MIRACLES? Are they possible? How should we define a *miracle?* Do they occur?

Every major religion includes a record of miraculous events. Examples of miracles fill the pages of the Bible: the ten plagues visited on the Egyptians and the parting of the Red Sea as the Israelites seek to escape from Egyptian bondage, the raining of manna for the Israelites in the Sinai Desert, Balaam's ass speaking, the resurrection of the witch of Endor to appear to Saul, the sun and moon standing still for a day in the Book of Joshua, Jesus turning water into wine, the raising of Lazarus, and the resurrection and ascension of Jesus Christ. In the Hindu tradition Krishna, the incarnate deity, is born of a virgin in Matura, India, and in the Muslim tradition Mohammed rises into heaven from Jerusalem.

We begin with our first question: What are miracles? Should miracles be defined as violations of the laws of nature? This is how David Hume defines the concept of *miracle:*

A miracle is a violation of the laws of nature; and as a firm and unalterable experience has established these laws, the proof against a miracle, from the very nature of the fact, is as entire as any argument from experience can possibly be imagined. Why is it more than probable, that all men must die; that lead cannot, of itself, remain suspended in the air; that fire consumes wood, and is extinguished by water; unless it be, that these events are found agreeable to the laws of nature, and there is required a violation of these laws, or in other words, a miracle to prevent them? Nothing is esteemed a miracle, if it ever happen in the common course of nature.[1]

A miracle is a violation of a law of nature, and a *law of nature* is a process whereby certain types of events are (absent intervention) always followed by a definite kind of other event. For example, the law of gravitation entails that within the Earth's gravitational zone objects will fall downward toward Earth at an acceleration of 32.17 feet per second, and we have no record of a counterinstance to this.

This notion of a miracle as a violation of a law of nature has been disputed on the basis of the contention that in the Bible, which is the witness to the most significant alleged miracles in the Judeo-Christian tradition, there is no concept of nature as a closed system of law. For the biblical writers, miracles signify, in the words of R. H. Fuller, simply an "extraordinary coincidence of a beneficial nature."[2]

This view is proposed by R. F. Holland in his article "The Miraculous," in which the following story is illustrative:

> A child riding his toy motor-car strays on to an unguarded railway crossing near his house and a wheel of his car gets stuck down the side of one of the rails. An express train is due to pass with the signals in its favor and a curve in the track makes it impossible for the driver to stop his train in time to avoid any obstruction he might encounter on the crossing. The mother coming out of the house to look for her child sees him on the crossing and hears the train approaching. She runs forward shouting and waving. The little boy remains seated in his car looking downward engrossed in the task of pedaling it free. The brakes of the train are applied and it comes to rest a few feet from the child. The mother thanks God for the miracle; which she never ceases to think of as such, although, as she in due course learns, there was nothing supernatural about the manner in which the brakes of the train came to be applied. The driver had fainted, for a reason that had nothing to do with the presence of the child on the line, and the brakes were applied automatically as his hand ceased to exert pressure on the control lever. He fainted on this particular afternoon because his blood pressure had risen after an exceptionally heavy lunch during which he had quarreled with a colleague, and the change in blood pressure caused a clot of blood to be dislodged and circulate. He fainted at the time when he did on the afternoon in question because this was the time at which the coagulation in his blood stream reached the brain.[3]

Was this a miracle, or was it not? It is, if we define miracles in Fuller's biblical sense. It is not if we define them in an interventionist sense, as a divine violation of the laws of nature. We can certainly understand the woman's feeling on the matter, and perhaps in some mysterious way God had "allowed" nature to run its course so that the little boy would be saved. Perhaps we need not be overly exclusionary but say that if there is a God, each sense is valid: the weaker sense of an extraordinary coincidence and the stronger sense of a violation of the laws of nature. Nonetheless, what is philosophically interesting, as well as controversial, with regard to miracles is the stronger sense, that of a violation of the laws of nature by a divine force. It is this sense of miracles that we consider in this part of our work.

HUME'S CRITIQUE OF MIRACLES

The most celebrated article ever written on miracles is by David Hume. In Section 10 of *An Enquiry Concerning Human Understanding* he sets forth an argument against belief in miracles that provoked a lively response in his time and continues to be the subject of vigorous dispute up to the present day. Let us analyze it briefly.

Hume begins his attack on miracles by appealing to the biases of his Scottish Presbyterian readers. He tells of a marvelous proof that Dr. Tillotson devised against the Roman Catholic doctrine of transubstantiation, the doctrine that the body and blood of Christ are present in Holy Communion. Tillotson argues that because the evidence of the senses is of the highest rank and because it is evident that it must diminish in passing through the original witnesses to their disciples, the doctrine of transubstantiation is always contrary to the rules of reasoning and opposed to our sense experience.

1. Our evidence for the truth of transubstantiation is less than the evidence of our senses. (Even for the apostles this was the case, and their testimony must diminish in authority in passing from them on to their disciples).
2. A weaker evidence can never destroy a stronger. (That is, we are not justified in believing the weaker evidence over the stronger.)
3. Therefore, we are not warranted in believing in transubstantiation. (Even if the doctrine of transubstantiation were clearly revealed in the Scriptures, it would be against the rule of reason to give our assent to it.)

No doubt Hume's Scottish Protestant readers were delighted with such a piercing refutation of the Papist doctrine of transubstantiation. But the mischievous Hume now turns the knife on his readers, applying the argument to Protestant Christianity's doctrine of miracles. He begins his argument with a definition of the rational person: "A wise person always proportions one's belief to the evidence." One has an enormous amount of evidence for the laws of nature, so that any testimony to the contrary is to be seriously doubted. Although miracles, as violations of the laws of nature, are not logically impossible, we are never justified in believing in one.

The skeleton of the argument contained in the reading goes something like this:

1. One ought to proportion one's belief to the evidence.
2. Sense perception is generally better evidence than testimony (if for no other reason than that valid testimony is based on another's sense experience).
3. Therefore, when there is a conflict between sense experience and testimony, one ought to believe according to sense perception.
4. Sense perception does not reveal any miracles to us (but rather the presumption of natural law prevails).
5. Therefore, we are never justified in believing in miracles, but we are justified in believing in the naturalness of all events.

Although Hume concedes that miracles are theoretically possible, he argues that the case against them is so cogent and comprehensive that we are never warranted in believing that they occur. His main argument is from the regularity of nature. Because we have had innumerable instances confirming the law of nature, the probability for events to conform to it must be enormous. And because we have enormous evidence in favor of the uniformity of nature, every testimony of a miracle must be weighed against that preponderance and be found wanting. On the probability scale the likelihood of a miracle happening will virtually always be outweighed by the law of nature. But what if we believe that we personally have beheld a miracle? Aren't we justified in believing one in that case? No, for given the principle of induction (that every time we pursue an event far enough, we discover it to have a natural cause), we are still not justified in believing the event to be a miracle. Rather, we ought to look further (far enough) until we discover the natural cause. The only exception to this rule (or "proof" against miracles) is if it would be even more miraculous for a miracle not to have occurred: "That no testimony is sufficient to establish a miracle, unless the testimony be of such a kind, that its falsehood would be more marvelous, than the fact, which it endeavors to establish; and even in that case there is a mutual destruction of argument, and the superior only gives us an assurance suitable to that degree of force, which remains, after deducting the inferior." The best we can hope for seems to be an agnostic standoff in the matter.

But even to make a belief in a miracle minimally rational, certain criteria would have to be fulfilled: (1) A sufficient number of witnesses of (2) good sense and education and (3) integrity and reputation would have to testify to a (4) public performance of the incident. Hume offers several putative examples of such cases; for example, a case reported by Cardinal de Retz of a one-legged doorkeeper in Saragossa in Aragon, who regained his missing limb after having holy oil rubbed on the stump. Although the Cardinal and many others witnessed this with their own eyes, Hume applauds the Cardinal for rejecting the validity of the episode. His rational trust in the laws of nature outweighed even his perception in this instance.

Hume continues his argument: Humans have such a positive tendency to believe the marvelous and mysterious that one should be suspicious of reports of miracles. Furthermore, miracle reports are discredited by being related mainly among primitive people.

> It forms a strong presumption against all supernatural and miraculous relations, that they are observed chiefly to abound among ignorant and barbarous nations; or if a civilized people has ever given admission to any of them, that people will be found to have received them from ignorant and barbarous ancestors, who transmitted them with that inviolable sanction and authority, which always attend received opinions. When we peruse the first histories of all nations, we are apt to imagine ourselves transported into some new world; where the whole frame of nature is disjointed, and every element performs its operations in a different manner, from what it does at present. Battles, revolutions, pestilence, famine, and death, are never the effect of those natural causes, which we experience. Prodigies, omens, oracles, judgments, quite obscure the few natural events, that are intermingled with them. But as the former grow thinner every page, in proportion as we advance nearer the enlightened ages, we soon learn, that there is nothing mysterious or supernatural in the case, but that all proceeds from the usual propensity of mankind towards the marvelous, and that, though this inclination may at intervals receive a check from sense and learning, it can never be thoroughly extirpated from human nature.

In sum, then, not only is the weight of evidence (given the significance of a law of nature) virtually always against the likelihood of a miracle, but the accompanying circumstances also add confirmation to the thesis that we are virtually never justified in believing one has occurred.

REPLIES TO HUME

One of the most vigorous critics of Hume has been Richard Swinburne of Oxford University. Swinburne inquires first whether there could be evidence that a law of nature had been violated and second whether there could be evidence that the violation was due to a god. To satisfy the first inquiry, we would have to have good reason to believe that an event has occurred contrary to the predictions of a law that we had good reason to believe to be a law of nature; and, furthermore, we would have to have good reason to believe that events similar to the event would not occur in circumstances similar to those of the original. Here Swinburne distinguishes between situations in which we do and in which we do not have sufficient circumstantial evidence to warrant our attributing the anomalous event to the work of an invisible deity.[4] The circumstantial evidence must be strong before we are justified in believing that an event is a genuine miracle—for example, the case of Elijah's calling on Yahweh to send fire and consume his offering on Mt. Carmel (1 Kings 18). Such an event would be sufficiently analogous to normal human agency to justify our believing that a divine being caused it. But all this supposes that we do have some independent evidence for the existence of a divine being in the first place, which justifies our seeing anomalous events as genuine miracles. Accordingly, we cannot view the topic of miracles in isolation, apart from our whole comprehensive system of beliefs. If we think we have evidence for the existence of a providential deity, then miracles will seem likely. The big question for religious people is why they don't happen today—or why they don't occur with the frequency one might expect from a benevolent God. But, for all we know, they may occur more often than we expect. We may simply not have "eyes to see and ears to hear" the wonders of providential action. On the other hand, the evidence we do have may not be adequate to believe miracles do occur, which is no proof that they don't.

In *The Miracle of Theism,* the late J. L. Mackie of Oxford University, a man who loved Hume and exemplified his thought, argues that in practice the evidence for miracles will never be very great. The argument is epistemological, not ontological.[5] That is, although miracles may be logically possible (and may indeed have occurred), we are never justified in believing in one. The concept of a miracle is a coherent one, but, Mackie argues, the double burden of showing both that the event took place and that it violated the laws of nature will be extremely hard to lift, for "whatever tends to show that it would have been a violation of natural law tends for that very reason to make it most unlikely that it actually happened." Correspondingly, the deniers of miracles have two strategies of defense. They may argue that the event took place but wasn't a violation of a law of nature (the event simply followed an unknown law of nature); or they can admit that if the event had happened, it would indeed have been a violation of a law of nature, but for that reason "there is a very strong presumption against its having happened, which it is most unlikely that any testimony will be able to outweigh."

Are Hume and Mackie correct that we are never justified in believing that a miracle occurred? One way out might be to adopt Holland's weak sense of miracle and argue that God guides nature in some way to produce seemingly marvelous events. So the resurrection of Jesus Christ would not be a violation of a law of nature but an instance of a rare combination of intersecting laws. One problem with this strategy is that it still seems to require a God to manipulate the laws—breaking the normal cause–event relationship—so that on a different level a violation of the laws still occurs. But if God does perform miracles, shouldn't we be able to give evidence for them? For example, the Christian Scriptures make certain predictions about miraculous happenings. For example, Jesus is reported by Mark's Gospel as saying that if believers "drink poison," it will not harm them (Mark 16:17–18). We could test this by giving poison (arsenic, cyanide, etc.) to believers and observing whether they are harmed. Actually, a religious group in Kentucky, believing such passages (including taking up poisonous snakes), has tested these predictions. According to the report I've received, their numbers have dwindled.

Perhaps Swinburne's broader strategy of interpreting a miracle within the framework of a wider metaphysical system is more promising. If we already have good reason to believe that a providential God exists, then we might expect that the same Power who created the laws of nature can intervene in overriding them. So our background assumptions are relevant in determining whether we are justified in believing a miracle took place. Of course, the theist will be circumspect in concluding that such-and-such an event is a divine intervention, but given suitable evidence, it may turn out that in some instances it would be more miraculous for the testimony of witnesses to be false than for a miracle to have occurred. Perhaps we have to look at the cases individually: What is the evidence that Jesus Christ, or Lord Krishna, was born of a virgin or rose from the dead? Or that they are God incarnate? Of course, even if there is a case that both Christ and Krishna are miraculous incarnations, so long as the truth claims of the religions are mutually exclusive, they would cancel each other out epistemically. But, if one believes in a pluralist revelation by God, the two miracles might be complementary, not contradictory.

Perhaps a more troubling question for theists who believe in miracles is, Why don't miracles happen more often? Is it our blindness that prevents us from seeing them all around us or our unbelief that prevents them from occurring more frequently—or both?

Questions for Discussion

1. Examine the quotation by Hume at the beginning of this chapter. What does Hume mean by saying that the Christian religion cannot be believed without a miracle? Is he correct?

2. Examine Hume's argument against miracles. Do you agree with him? Do you think miracles are possible? If so, are we ever justified in believing an event is a miracle?

3. Examine Holland's story at the beginning of this chapter. Does it describe a miracle or a mere lucky coincidence?

4. Do you think miracles still occur? Examine Hume's four necessary conditions for the justification of belief that a miracle occurred. Does the resurrection of Christ fulfill them? Does any other alleged miracle meet these conditions?

5. Is prophecy a miracle? Is one form of miracle God's revealing the future to his disciples, the prophets?

6. Here is the testimony of a friend of mine.

> When I, as a young Christian mystic, was attending a Christian college in the eastern United States, I believed in miracles. But for our lack of faith, we could walk on water and say to the mountains, "Be thou removed to a closer place to me," and it would be so. Every Thursday after dinner, we had Testimony Time in which students would get up and relate what God had done for them that week or make a request for prayer. One Thursday at Testimony Time, Bill, a disabled married student with several children, got up to request prayer that God would perform a miracle on his behalf, sending him several thousand dollars to pay next semester's tuition, enabling him to continue to prepare for the ministry.
>
> I prayed for Bill that night, and as I did so I heard in my heart the Spirit of God, commanding me to withdraw from the bank all the hard-earned money—money I had worked for in a factory in order to pay my tuition next semester—and place it anonymously in Bill's mailbox. The Voice of the Lord assured me that a miracle would happen to me, so that the tuition money would appear in my mailbox before tuition was due. So I obediently went to the bank the next day and withdrew all my funds, placing them in an envelope which I addressed to Bill.
>
> Next Thursday during Testimony Time, Bill was ecstatically leaping out of his crutches, praising God for the miracle of his tuition money. "God gave me exactly the amount I needed!" "Amen" and "Praise the Lord"

were shouted into the air throughout the dining hall. Some said it was proof of the mighty providential power of God, and irrefutable evidence of His existence.

In a month or so, tuition for the Spring semester came due. I was certain that the tuition money would appear in my mailbox, and came to it every morning without success. On the day that the tuition was due, I opened my mailbox, fully believing that the funds would be there for me. I put my hand in the box and pulled something out—a *Time* magazine. That moment I was converted from Mysticism to Rationalism. It was my crucial experiment. As far as I could see, miracles don't occur. (Personal communication)

Evaluate this incident. Does the nonoccurrence of a miracle provide evidence against miracles? If God exists, why might he have omitted to perform a miracle? Explain your answer.

For Further Reading

Broad, C. D. "Hume's Theory of the Credibility of Miracles." *Proceedings of the Aristotelian Society* 17 (1916–17). An insightful critique of Hume.

Flew, Antony. "Miracles." In *Encyclopedia of Philosophy*, edited by Paul Edwards. New York: Macmillan, 1966. A good survey of the problem, containing a Humean version of the attack on miracles.

Geisler, Norman L. *Miracles and Modern Thought*. Grand Rapids, Mich.: Zondervan, 1982. A clearly written apology for an evangelical position that comes to terms with major philosophical opponents. Valuable for its terse analyses, though tending to oversimplify the opposition.

Holland, R. F. "The Miraculous." *American Philosophical Quarterly* 2 (1965): 43–51. An elaborate study and defense of the possibility of miracles, containing important conceptual distinctions.

Lewis, C. S. *Miracles*. New York: Macmillan, 1947. A cogently and clearly argued defense of miracles.

Mackie, J. L. *The Miracle of Theism*. Oxford, England: Oxford University Press, 1982, especially Chapter 1.

Nowell-Smith, Patrick. "Miracles." In *New Essays in Philosophical Theology*, edited by Antony Flew and Alasdair MacIntyre. London: Macmillan, 1955. Attacks the concept of miracles as unscientific and, as such, incoherent.

Rowe, William. *Philosophy of Religion*. Belmont, Calif.: Wadsworth, 1978. A lucid introductory discussion of the overall problem.

Smart, Ninian. *Philosophy and Religious Truth*. London: SCM, 1964. A defense of miracles against the charge that they are unscientific.

Swinburne, Richard. *The Concept of Miracle*. London: Macmillan, 1970. A development of the ideas discussed in this chapter.

Notes

1. David Hume, *Enquiry Concerning Human Understanding* (1748), Section 10.
2. R. H. Fuller, *Interpreting the Miracle* (London: 1968), p. 8.
3. R. F. Holland, "The Miraculous," *American Philosophical Quarterly* 2 (1965).
4. Richard Swinburne, "The Possibility of Miracles," *American Philosophical Quarterly* (1965). Reprinted in *Philosophy of Religion,* ed. Louis Pojman (Belmont, Calif.: Wadsworth, 1998).
5. J. L. Mackie, *The Miracle of Theism* (Oxford, England: Oxford University Press, 1982) especially Chapter 1.

8

PERSONAL IDENTITY
AND IMMORTALITY

D O WE SURVIVE OUR DEATHS or is death the final curtain—after
which we rot?

Before we can understand the arguments for life after death, we need
to understand what personal identity is. We begin with an analysis of the
relevant concepts.

PART ONE: PERSONAL IDENTITY

Suppose you wake up tomorrow in a strange room. There are pictures of
unfamiliar people on the light blue walls. The furniture in the room is very
odd. You wonder how you got here. You remember being in the hospital
where you were dying of cancer. Your body was wasting away, and your
death was thought to be a few days away. Your physician, Dr. Matthews, had
kindly given you an extra dose of morphine to kill the pain. "This can't be,"
you think, noting that the date on the calendar is April 1, "for yesterday was
January 2nd." Not quite your normal, alert self, you try to take this all in.
"Where have I been all this time?" Suddenly, you see a mirror. You reel
back in horror, for it's not your body that you spy in the glass but a large
woman's body. Your color has altered, and, if you're male, so has your sex.
You have more than doubled your previous normal weight and look 25
years older. You feel tired, confused, and frightened and can scarcely hold
back tears of dismay. Soon a strange man, about 45 years of age, comes
into your room. "I was wondering when you would waken, Maria," he says.
"The doctor said that I should let you sleep as long as possible, but I didn't
think that you would be asleep two whole days. Anyway, the operation was

a success. We had feared that the accident had ended your life. The children and I are so grateful. Jean and John will be home in an hour and will be so happy to see you awake. How do you feel?"

"Can this be a bad joke, an April Fool's prank?" you wonder. "Who is this strange man, and who am I?" Unbeknownst to you, Dr. Matthews needed a living brain to implant in the head of Mrs. Maria Martin, mother of four children, who had been in a car accident. After arriving at the hospital, her body was kept alive by technology, but her brain was dead. Your brain was in excellent shape but lacked a healthy body. Maria Martin's body was intact but needed a brain. Being an enterprising brain surgeon, Dr. Matthews saw his chance of performing the first successful brain transplant. Later that day, Matthews breaks the news of your transformation to you. He congratulates you on being the first human to survive a brain transplant and reminds you, just in case you are not completely satisfied with the transformation, that you would have been dead had he not performed the operation. Still dazed by the news, you try to grasp the significance of what has happened to you. You wonder whether you would not be better off dead. The fact that the operation was a success is of little comfort to you, for you're not sure whether you are you!

The problem of personal identity is one of the most fascinating in the history of philosophy. It is especially complicated because it involves not one but at least three, and possibly four, philosophical questions. What is it to be a person? What is identity? What is personal identity? How is survival possible given the problems of personal identity? Let us look briefly at each of these first three questions. (Part Two discusses the fourth question.)

WHAT IS IT TO BE A PERSON?

What is it that sets us human beings off as having special value, as being entities with serious moral rights? What characteristics must one have to have high moral value? The Judeo-Christian tradition generally defines personhood in terms of our ability to reason and make moral choices. Writing within the Judeo-Christian tradition, the English philosopher John Locke (1632–1704) said that a person is defined as "a thinking intelligent being, that has reason and reflection, and can consider itself as itself, the same thinking thing, in different times and places; which it does only by that consciousness which is inseparable from thinking, and as it seems to me, essential to it." That is, our ability to reason, introspect, and survey our memories and intentions sets us apart from the animals as being of greater value. The view may be challenged by the materialist who says that it is really our brain (or our brain and our body) that defines our personhood. It is the fact that we have a more developed brain that sets us apart from other animals. We are, of course, conscious beings. Although we do not understand how consciousness works, the physicalist believes that consciousness is a function of the brain. David Hume (1711–1776) argued that the notion of a self or soul is very likely a fiction. "I" am merely a bundle of perceptions. There is consciousness of a continuing succession of experiences but not of a continuing experiencer. This view is compatible with the physicalist view of personhood.

How do we decide what it is that makes us valuable? Perhaps self-consciousness is a necessary or minimal condition, but is it a sufficient one? Are primates and other mammals persons? The subject is a difficult philosophical problem whose solution will likely depend on wider metaphysical and theoretical considerations. But if the question of personhood is a difficult problem, the question of identity is no less so.

WHAT IS IDENTITY?

At first glance, this sounds like an absurdly simple question. Identity is the fact that everything is itself and not another. In logic, the law of identity—the formula $A = A$—formally states the definition. But we are not interested in a formal definition of mere identity but in identity *over time*, or reidentification (sometimes this is referred to as *numerical identity*). What is it to be the same thing over time? Suppose that you go to an automobile dealership in order to buy a new car. You see several blue Fords parked side by side. They resemble one another so much that you cannot tell them apart. They are the same type of car and are exactly similar to one another. Suppose you pick one out at random and buy it. Your car is different from the other blue Fords, even though you couldn't tell the difference between them. A year passes, and your blue Ford now has 20,000 miles on it and a few scratches. Is it the same car that you originally bought? Most of us would probably agree that it is. The changes have altered but not destroyed its identity as the blue car that you bought and have driven 20,000 miles.

What does your blue Ford have that causes it to be the same car over the period of one year? A common history, continuity over time. The car is linked by a succession of spatiotemporal events from its origins in Detroit to its present place in your driveway. This distinguishes it from all other Fords that were ever built, no matter how similar they appear. So we might conclude that *continuity over time* is the criterion of identity.

But immediately we find problems with this criterion. The Rio Grande dries up in places in New Mexico every summer, only to reappear as a running river in the early spring. Is the Rio Grande the same river this year as it was last? There isn't any continuity over time of water flowing over the riverbed. Perhaps we can escape the problem by saying that by "river" we really mean the riverbed that must hold running water sometimes but need not always convey it. Does this solve the problem?

Consider another counterexample: The Chicago White Sox are playing the New York Yankees in Yankee Stadium in late April. The game is called in the fifth inning with the Yankees leading 3–2. Shortly afterward, there is a baseball strike, and all players take to the picket lines while a new set of players comes up from the minor leagues to fill their positions. The "game" is continued in Chicago in August with a whole new set of players on both sides. The White Sox win, and the game decides who wins the division pennant. Suppose the Yankee shortstop, who had been a philosophy major in college, protests that this hybrid game must not count and that a new game must be played in its stead. He argues that because there was no continuity between the two segments of the "game," because not even one of the same players played in both halves, the two segments cannot count as constituting one and the same baseball game. Does the shortstop have a point? Should the Yankee manager accept his argument and appeal the game to the commissioner of baseball? Should the commissioner call for a new game? Why, or why not?

The most perplexing problem with regard to the notion of "sameness" or identity over time is illustrated by the ancient tale of Theseus's ship. Suppose you have a small ship that is in need of some repairs. You begin (at time t_1) to replace the old planks and material one by one with new planks and material. After one year (time t_2), the ship is completely made up of different material. Do you have the same ship at t_2 as you had at t_1? If not, at what point did it (call it *Theseus 2*) become a different ship? (See the figure below.)

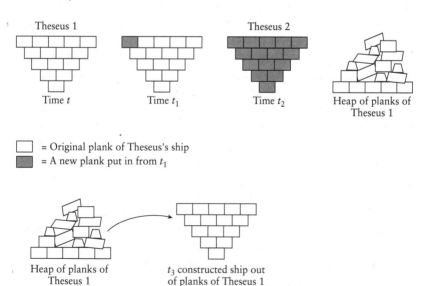

Theseus 1

Theseus 2

Time t Time t_1 Time t_2 Heap of planks of Theseus 1

☐ = Original plank of Theseus's ship
■ = A new plank put in from t_1

Heap of planks of Theseus 1 t_3 constructed ship out of planks of Theseus 1

People disagree as to whether Theseus's ship has changed its identity. Suppose that you argue that it is the same ship with which you started, for it had a continuous history over time and therefore is the same ship. But now suppose that your friend takes the material discarded from *Theseus 1* and reconstructs that ship (call it *Theseus 3*). Which ship is now Theseus's ship? There is the continuity of the ship between *Theseus 1* and *2* but continuity of material between *Theseus 1* and *3*. Which type of continuity should be decisive here? If it worries you that there was a time when the material of *Theseus 1* was not functioning as a ship, we could alter the example and suppose that as the planks were taken from *Theseus 1* they were transferred to another ship, *Argos,* to replace the *Argos*'s planks; the result was a ship that contained every board and nail from the original *Theseus* (call this transformed *Argos Theseus 4*). Which is now the original *Theseus?* (See the figure below.)

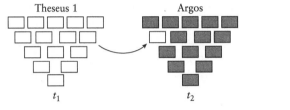 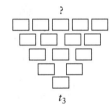

Theseus 1	Argos	?
t_1	t_2	t_3
The process begins of replacing the planks on *Argos* with those of *Theseus.*		The process of replacing planks on *Argos* completed.

Does there not seem something puzzling about the notion of identity? Now we must take the two puzzling concepts, *personhood* and *identity,* and combine them.

WHAT IS PERSONAL IDENTITY?

What is it to be the same person over time? Are you the same person that you were when you were 1 year old or even 16 years old? John Locke held that mental characteristics (ability to reflect or introspect) constitute personhood. Personal identity is indicated by the successive memories that the person has had, the continuity over time of a set of experiences that were remembered. We can call this the psychological states criterion of personal identity. The main competitor of this view is the brain criterion of personal identity, although some philosophers hold to a body criterion. Let us examine each of these briefly.

The *psychological states criterion* holds that our memories constitute our identity over time. You are the same person now that you were at 10 years of age because you have a continuous set of memories that contains all the memories that you had at age 10 plus others that continued after that year. Can you detect any problems with this view? Consider the following. In the first place, our memories are not continuous in our consciousness. When we sleep, we cease to have memories at all. During partial amnesia, do we cease to be who we are? Thomas Reid (1710–1796), questioning Locke's theory of personhood, argued that there is a problem of transitivity with regard to memories. Suppose there is a gallant officer who at age 25 years is a hero in a battle and who remembers getting a flogging in his childhood. Later, at age 65, he recalls the heroic deed done at age 25 but cannot recall the flogging. If he cannot remember the flogging, is he the same person he was when he did remember it? Can Locke answer Reid?

What about the phenomenon of split personalities and multiple personalities? The most famous of these is Sybil, who allegedly expressed 16 different personalities with 16 different sets of memories. According to a psychological states account, would we have to say that one body contains (or is associated with) 16 persons? Are there different persons inside each of us, expressed by different "sides" of our personalities?

Sometimes a person expresses apparent memories of events that occurred in distant times and to different "persons." Is the body of the contemporary being possessed by another person? If your friend suddenly starts reminiscing about the Battle of Waterloo and the beautiful Empress Josephine, has Napoleon suddenly come alive in your friend's body? This would truly be a case of reincarnation! But what if two of your friends came to you with the same "foreign" memories? Your friend Bill recites in great detail the events of the Battle of Waterloo and describes in minute detail the wardrobe of the Empress Josephine. Then, shortly after, your friend Joyce describes similar events and details that she could not possibly have read in books. If memory constitutes the criterion for personal identity, then Bill is Napoleon and Joyce is Napoleon. But if they both are Napoleon, then Bill is Joyce. Because Bill is Joyce's husband, he is married to himself!

Furthermore, on this account, what is to prohibit complete soul flow, a different person inside you each day? How do you know that the soul that is remembering today is the same soul that remembered yesterday? You might object that this couldn't be the case because you have the same body, but that objection won't work, because the body has nothing to do with the psychological states criterion. If you think that the body is important, this might be an indication that the memory criterion is inadequate on its own and depends on a physical body for continuity.

The *body criterion* has difficulties, one of which is the fact that even though the body can undergo radical changes, we would still want to call the person the same person. Almost all the cells in our body change every seven years. Do we become a new person every seven years? Or think of the story at the beginning of this chapter in which Dr. Matthews transplants your brain into Maria Martin's body. Despite these physical changes, wouldn't you still be you?

This suggests a third criterion, the *brain criterion* of personal identity. Our memories are contained within our brain, so we might want to say that having the same brain constitutes the same person. But this has difficulties, which are brought out by the Oxford University philosopher Derek Parfit. It is well known that if the corpus callosum (the great band of fibers that unites the two hemispheres of the brain) is cut, two different centers of consciousness can be created. When either side of the cerebral cortex of the brain is destroyed, the person can live on as a conscious being. It is also possible, in principle, to transplant brains. Suppose your body is destroyed and neurologists transplant each half of your brain into a different body. Dr. Matthews transplants one-half of your brain into Maria Martin and the other half into the head of a seven-foot-tall basketball player. "You" wake up with two personalities. Do you survive the operation? There seem to be just three possible answers: (1) you do not survive; (2) you survive as one of the two; or (3) you survive as two people.

All these options seem unsatisfactory. It seems absurd to say (1) that you don't survive, for there is continuity of consciousness (in the Lockean sense), as though you had gone to sleep and awakened. If you had experienced the destruction of one-half of your brain, we would still say you survived with half a brain, so why not say so now when each half is autonomous? The logic of this thesis would seem to say that double life equals death.

But (2) seems arbitrary. Why say that you only survive as one of the two, and which one is it? And (3), that you survive as both, is not satisfactory either because it gives up the notion of identity. You cannot be numerically one with two centers of consciousness and two spatiotemporal bodies. Otherwise, we might say when we wreck our new Ford that the other one left in the automobile dealer's parking lot (the blue Ford that was exactly like ours) was indeed ours.

If this is an accurate analysis of the personal identity problem, what sense can we make of the concept? Not much, according to Parfit. We should speak of survival of the person, not the identity of the person. Persons, as psychological states, survive and gradually merge (like Theseus's rebuilt ship) into descendent persons. Your memories and personality gradually emerged from the 15-year-old who gradually developed from the 6-year-old and, before that, the 1-year-old who bore your name. These were your ancestor selves. But you too will merge with future or descendent selves as you have different experiences, take on new memories, and forget old ones. Suppose every year neurologists could transplant half of your brain into another body, in which a new half would duplicate the present state of the transferred half. In this way, a treelike operation would continue to spread successors of yourself as though by psychological parthenogenesis. You would survive in a sense, but it would make no sense to speak of personal identity, a concept that Parfit wants to eliminate. We could also imagine a neurological game of "musical hemispheres," as half of your brain was merged with half of someone else's brain in a third person's head. Suppose something like "The Branching Brain Game" catches on (see the figure below). The brains of John, Mary, Bill, Pat, and others are split every year or so and the hemispheres joined inside different heads. In year 1, half of Mary's brain is joined with half of John's, half of Bill's brain is joined with Mary's, and half of Pat's brain is joined with Bill's. The next year, they split again, and different halves are joined by the corpus callosum in a different head (Ross, *R*, and Arthur, *A*), and so on. Suppose you were one of these brain-branching people. You could continue the hemisphere-moving game every year so that you might even get remerged with your own other half at some future time—much like meeting your high school companion again after years of separation and interesting adventures. You'd have much to talk about through the medium of the corpus callosum!

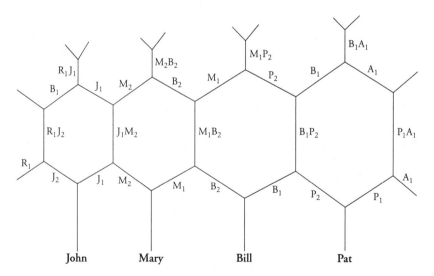

Of course, Parfit's point is that we are going through significant changes all the time, so that as we have new experiences, we take on new selfhood. Something in us survives but with a difference. If Parfit is right about the relativity of identity in survival, then we might be less interested in our distant future than our immediate future. After all, that person 10 years down the line is less like us than the person we'll be tomorrow. This might encourage a sort of general utilitarianism; because our distant interests really are not as closely related to us as the needs of our contemporaries, we could be free to work for the total greater good. On the other hand, it could have the deleterious effect of making us indifferent to the future of society. This notion of proximate identity also raises the question of whether we should be concerned about our distant death 50 years down the line, which one of our successor selves will have to face. Why should we fear death, when it won't touch us but only one of our successor selves in the distant future? Of course, one of our successor selves might be angry with us for not taking out an insurance policy or pension plan necessary for his or her well-being.

This notion of relative and proximate identity might also cause us to prohibit long-term prison sentences for criminal actions, for why punish a descendent for what one of his or her ancestors did? It could be used to argue against exorbitant awards in malpractice litigation. Often a jury is asked to award a sum of money (as high as $12 million) to a severely retarded child who had been damaged through medical malpractice. The justification for the large sum is the expectation that the child could have become a highly talented professional (physician or lawyer) and made an enormous sum of money in his or her lifetime. But if we were to take the notion of proximate identity seriously, we could only sue the physician for the damages done to the immediate person, not to the descendent selves.

What is the truth about personal identity? What constitutes the essential you? The issue is as perplexing as it is important. The challenge of solving this problem is before you. Who are you?

SUMMARY OF PART ONE

The problem of personal identity is a compound set of paradoxes and puzzles. It involves three difficult questions: What is a person? What is identity over time? What is it to be the same person through change and time? The first question relates to the body-mind problem in general and cannot be satisfactorily answered without a solution to that problem. The second question seems to be context dependent, that is, the answer will depend on subtleties of meaning that depend on various contexts. The third question, which depends, in part, on the first two, has been answered in two chief ways: the psychological state criterion and the body/brain criterion. Far-reaching implications flow from how we decide this issue.

❧ PART TWO: IS THERE LIFE AFTER DEATH?

LIFE AFTER DEATH?

Is there life after death? Few questions have troubled humans as deeply as this one. Is this finite, short existence of 70 or so years all that we have, or is there reason to hope for a blessed postmortem existence in which love, justice, and peace, which we now experience in fragmented forms, will unfold in all their fullness and enable human existence to find fulfillment? Are we merely mortal or blessedly immortal?

Anthropological studies reveal a widespread and ancient sense of immortality. Prehistoric societies buried their dead with food so that the deceased would not be hungry in the next life. Most cultures and religions have some version of a belief in another life, whether it be in the form of a resurrected body, a transmigrated soul, reincarnation, or an ancestral spirit present with the tribe.

Let us begin by understanding what we mean by "immortality." For our purposes, we will not mean living on through our works in the memories of our loved ones, but rather a conscious state in which the individual continues to exist. The definition given in *A Catholic Dictionary* is that attribute in virtue of which a being is free from death. A being is incorruptible if it does not contain within itself a principle of dissolution; it is indestructible if it can resist every external power tending to destroy or annihilate it. If the indestructible and incorruptible being is endowed with life it is called immortal. Annihilation is always possible to God by the mere withdrawal of his conserving act.[1]

Death for most humans is the ultimate tragedy. It is the paramount evil, for it deprives us of all that we know and love on earth. Although there may be fates worse than death for some of us (living a completely evil life, being a heavy burden on others), our fear of death is profound. We want to live as long as possible (given a certain quality of life). We have a general craving for continued existence. The more life, the better.

Unfortunately, there is precious little direct evidence for life after death. After the brain ceases to function, a person cannot be resuscitated. We don't know personally of anyone who has come back from the dead to tell us about the next life.

So. on the one hand, we have a passionate longing to live again and be with our loved ones; on the other hand, there is little or no direct evidence that we will live again. The grave seems the final environment for humankind. And yet we search for indirect evidence for immortality. We welcome any news from this possible distant clime as good news indeed and cannot help but regard the promise of eternal life as an incentive to meet whatever a credible guide states as the necessary conditions for entry.

In the Western tradition, three views have dominated the scene; one denies life after death, and two affirm it. The negative view, going back to the ancient Greek atomist philosophers Democritus (ca. 460–370 B.C.) and Leucippus (ca. 450 B.C.), holds that we are identical with our bodies (including our brains) so that when the body dies, so does our self. There is nothing more. We can call this view materialist monism because it does not allow for the possibility of a soul or spiritual self that can live without the body.

The positive views divide into dualist and monist theories of life after death. The dualist view separates the body from the soul or self of the agent and affirms that it is the soul or self that lives forever. This view was held by the pre-Socratic philosopher Pythagoras (ca. 580–496 B.C.) and developed by Plato (ca. 427–347 B.C.). In modern philosophy, it is represented by René Descartes (1596–1650). It is sometimes referred to as the Platonic-Cartesian view of immortality. These philosophers argue that we are essentially spiritual or mental beings and that our bodies are either unreal or not part of our essential selves, so that death is merely the separation of our souls from our bodies, a sort of spiritual liberation. Although Plato has many arguments for this thesis, one of the most famous is found in the *Phaedo,* in which he writes,

> When the soul employs the body in any inquiry, and makes use of sight, or hearing, or any other sense—for inquiry with the body must signify inquiry with the senses—she is dragged away by the body to the things which are impermanent, changing, and the soul wanders about blindly, and becomes confused and dizzy, like a drunken man, from dealing with things that are changing. . . . [But] when the soul investigates any question by herself, she goes away to the pure and eternal, and immortal and unchangeable, to which she is intrinsically related, and so she comes to be ever with it, as soon as she is by herself, and can be so; and then she rests from her wandering and dwells with it unchangingly, for she is related to what is unchanging. And is not this state of the soul called wisdom?[2]

The argument can be analyzed as follows:

1. If a person's soul while in the body is capable of any activity independently of the body, then it can perform that activity in separation from the body (i.e., after death, surviving death).
2. In pure or metaphysical thinking (i.e., in contemplating the eternal ideas and their interrelationships), a person's soul performs an

activity independently of the body. No observation is necessary for this investigation.

3. A person's soul can engage in pure or metaphysical thinking in separation from the body. That is, it can and must survive death.

This is a positive argument for the existence of the soul. It does seem that we can think about logic, mathematics, metaphysics, and other subjects without reference to bodies. Unfortunately, the second premise is dubious, for it could be the case that the mind's activity is epiphenomenal, that is, dependent on the brain. So, although Plato is right in saying that we need not make an empirical examination of the world in order to think analytically or metaphysically, he has not shown that analytic and metaphysical thinking can go on without a body or brain.

As far as I know, no one has offered a sound argument to prove that we have a soul that outlives our physical existence. However, this is not to say that there is no evidence for this point of view. We will note some below.

The second positive view on immortality is associated with the Christian tradition, namely, St. Paul's statement in 1 Corinthians 15. It is interesting to note that there is very little mention made in the Old Testament of life after death. It is at best a shadowy existence in Sheol, the place under Jerusalem where the dead lie dormant or vaguely aware, a place comparable to Hades in Greek mythology. The one exception, celebrated in Handel's *Messiah,* is the famous passage in the Book of Job (19:25–26).

> I know that my Redeemer liveth,
> And that He shall stand at the latter day upon the earth,
> And though after my skin worms destroy this body,
> Yet in my flesh shall I see God.

Note that it is *in the flesh,* not as a disembodied spirit, that Job expects to live again.

In the New Testament, although there are references to a spiritual existence, the soul (*psyche*) is not separated from the body (*soma*), but the person is a holistic, unified being with the soul or self being the form of the material body (in an almost Aristotelian sense). In death the soul is not liberated from the body as from a corpse, but rather a new, glorified *body* comes into being, which is somehow related to our present earthly body. The classic passage is from Paul's first letter to the Corinthians. It reads as follows:

> Now if Christ be preached that he rose from the dead, how say some among you that there is no resurrection of the dead? But if there be no resurrection of the dead, then is Christ not risen: And if Christ be not risen, then is our

preaching in vain, and your faith is also in vain. . . . Ye are still in your sins. Then they which are fallen asleep in Christ are perished. If in this life only we have hope in Christ, we are of all men most miserable.

But now is Christ risen from the dead, and become the first fruits of them that slept. For since by man came death by man came also the resurrection of the dead. . . . For Christ must reign until he hath put all enemies under his feet. The last enemy that shall be destroyed is death. But some man will say, How are the dead raised up? and with what body do they come? Thou fool, that which thou sowest is not quickened, except it die: and that which thou sowest, thou sowest not that body that shall be, but bare grain, it may chance of wheat, or of some other grain. But God giveth it a body as it hath pleased him, and to every seed his own body. All flesh is not the same flesh; but there is one kind of flesh of men, another flesh of beasts, another of fishes and another of birds. There are also celestial bodies, and bodies terrestrial: but the glory of the celestial is one, and the glory of the terrestrial is another. There is one glory of the sun, and another glory of the moon, and another glory of the stars: for one star differeth from another star in glory. So also is the resurrection of the dead. It is sown in corruption; it is raised in incorruption . . . it is sown in weakness; it is raised in power; It is sown a natural body; it is raised a spiritual body. . . . And so it is written, The first man Adam was made a living soul; the last Adam was made a quickening spirit. Howbeit that was not first which is spiritual, but that which is natural; and afterward that which is spiritual. The first man is of the earth, earthly: the second man is the Lord from heaven. As is the earthly, such are they also that are earthly: and as is the heavenly, such are they also that are heavenly. And as we have borne the image of the earthly, we shall also bear the image of the heavenly. Now this I say, brethren, that flesh and blood cannot inherit the kingdom of God; neither doth corruption inherit incorruption. Behold, I show you a mystery; We shall not all sleep, but we shall all be changed. In a moment, in a twinkling of an eye, at the last trump: for the trumpet shall sound, and the dead shall be raised incorruptible, and we shall be changed. For this corruptible must put on incorruption, and this mortal must put on immortality.[3]

When I approach the subject of immortality in an undergraduate philosophy class, I poll the students to ask them which is the Christian view of life after death: the view that in death the soul leaves the body and goes to heaven or the view that our bodies will be raised. Almost every student chooses the first view, which I then point out is basically Platonic, not Christian. This view is reflected in popular religion, not the least being the bedtime prayer taught to children. "Now I lay me down to sleep, / I pray the Lord my soul to keep. / If I should die before I wake, / I pray the Lord my soul to take." Of course, one could have a view that although there is eventually a new body, there is an intermediate state in which the soul dwells disembodied, waiting for the resurrection day, at which time it will receive its new form.

Are there good arguments for either of these versions of survival after death? Each raises the question of personal identity, discussed in Part One of this chapter. Given the fact that we all undergo physical and mental change, under what conditions can we be said to be the same person over time (i.e., what gives us the right to say that some person *P* is the same person at t_2 as *P* was at some time earlier, t_1)?

You will recall (from Part One) the two standard views on this matter: the psychological states criterion and the body (including the brain) criterion. The psychological states (or memory) criterion goes back to John Locke (1632–1704) and states that a person is the same person if and only if he or she is psychologically continuous in character, desires, and memories. There are, at least, three problems with this view:

1. There is no way to distinguish *apparent* memories from *genuine* remembering, so that it could be the case that someone came among us, detailing the events of Napoleon's life in such a way as to cause us to believe that he had somehow captured those memories. But we would probably be reluctant to say that this person was Napoleon, especially if we already knew him to be our uncle.
2. There is a problem with multiple rememberers. That is, it could be the case that our memories (and characters and desires for that matter) could be duplicated in other people, so that multiple subjects have the same "memories." We would not be able to tell which of the persons was the rememberer. As we noted in Part One, if Bill and Joyce both possess the same memories, they would be each other!
3. There is the problem of whether memory itself makes any sense apart from a body. What kind of existence would a purely mental existence be? Would it be in time and space? If it were in space, how does it, a nonsensory entity, perceive anything at all? It seems that memory and character predicates are tied to a physical existence. This leads us to consider the body criterion as the proper criterion for personal identity.

The body criterion states that a person is the same person over time if he or she is continuous with his or her body. The notion of resurrection (or reconstitution) states that I will continue to survive my death in a new glorified body. God will reconstitute me. This is eloquently stated on Benjamin Franklin's tombstone:

This body of B. Franklin in Christ Church cemetery,
Printer, Like the Cover of an old Book,
Its Contents torn out,

And stript of its Lettering and Gilding,
Lies here, Food for Worms.
But the work shall not be lost;
For it will, as he believed,
Appear once more in a new and more elegant Edition,
Corrected and Improved by its Author.

But the resurrection view supposes that God will create a new being like yourself. The problem with this view is that it does not seem all that comforting to learn that someday there will be someone just like you who will enjoy a blessed existence, for if there is no continuity between you and your future self, it is really not you but your successor (someone very similar, even exactly similar to you, a sort of twin) who will enjoy eternal life.

Taking this criterion literally, we would have to conclude that when a zygote divides into identical twins during the first weeks of its existence, the two resulting entities are identical to each other (rather than being exactly similar). Furthermore, we can imagine situations in which the personality of one person is transferred to another, such as in Locke's story of the prince and the pauper in which the body of the prince wakes up one day with all the memories, desires, and character of the pauper. We might be inclined to say that although the prince's body was before us, we were really speaking with the pauper. We could also imagine futuristic split body–brain operations in which our bodies and/or brains are divided and merged with prosthetic bodies or brains. The notions of continuity and uniqueness would conflict.

Suppose the ingenious neurologist Dr. Matthews were to design a brain just like yours in his laboratory and suppose he were to design a body like yours but virtually indestructible (well, a nuclear bomb could destroy it, but failing that it would be impervious to alteration). The brain is now dormant, but, at your death, Dr. Matthews will activate it and bring it to life within the prosthetic body. Now Matthews tells you that he needs to kill you in order to allow your alter ego to exist. You complain, but he assures you that one exactly similar to you will live again with all your memories (or copies of them, but Alter Ego won't know the difference). Would you be comforted by that news? Would you take comfort in the fact that "you" will live again?

Where does all of this leave us with regard to survival after death? If there is no continuity of consciousness, is it the same person who would be resurrected or reconstituted by God at some future time? Or is the reconstituted person like Matthews's replica? A different token of the same generic type? Could God make several tokens of your type—say, five of you—that could be reconstituted and go on to live a new and eternal life? Quintuple resurrection!

Is the survival of the disembodied memories of a person sufficient to satisfy you with regard to your survival after death? The question is perplexing. On the one hand, it seems that our identity is somehow tied to our psychological states (e.g., memories and personality traits), which don't seem to depend on a body. But then if this is so, would our survival occur if a computer stored much of the information about our personalities and memory states?

We seem to need both a body and brain to instantiate our consciousness and personalities. It is hard to imagine any learning or experiencing or communication with others without a recognizable body. And the brain seems to be the locus of conscious experience. But our bodies and brains die and are disintegrated. What happens to our consciousness and our personal identity? Is the gap between the present conscious life and the next simply like a long sleep during which God prepares a new and glorified body for our personality? Or does the fact that there will have to be a new creation rule out the possibility of personal survival altogether? Or can it be that there is an intrinsically spiritual character to ourselves that both survives the death of the body and purdures in a life beyond this one?

Of course, many Christians believe that although there must be a body for one's full existence, it could be the case that the personality is preserved in an interim state of disembodiment between the first corruptible bodily existence and the second incorruptible bodily existence. But this still has the problem of whether it makes sense to speak of a disembodied self.

REINCARNATION

Reincarnation is the view that after death human beings live again in other forms. The doctrine was held by Plato and is a tenet in Hinduism and Buddhism. In the Hindu scripture Bhagavad Gita (ca. 500 B.C.), Lord Krishna comforts the unenlightened Arjuna by telling him that there is no reason to grieve over the death of someone we love, for the "eternal in man cannot die." "We have all been for all time: I, and thou, and those kings of men. And we shall be for all time, we all for ever and ever."

A person's body is different in every incarnation, but the same mind inhabits each body. As the Bhagavad Gita states, "As a man leaves an old garment and puts on the one that is new, the Spirit leaves his mortal body and then puts on one that is new." The goal is to end the cycle of rebirths and be absorbed into God (or Nirvana). Reincarnation is typically linked with karma, the doctrine that whatsoever a person sows, whether in action or thought, he or she will eventually reap the fruits—if not in this life, then in the next. Thus a person who led an evil existence might be reborn as a lower animal (e.g., a reptile or an insect). Evidence cited for reincarnation includes déjà vu experiences, the sense that you've been in this place before, seen this person some other time—in another existence—as well as reports of children and other experiences that a person couldn't have had in this life.

Objections to reincarnation include the problem of uniform age. When a 90-year-old man dies, one would expect him to be reborn as an old man or at least with the maturity and the memories of an old man, but he is always born as a baby without wisdom, maturity, or apparent memories. Why is that? If memories are a criterion of personal identity, can the baby be said to be the same person as the 90-year-old man? Or is it simply a successor self—or does this problem indicate that reincarnation is a myth? Furthermore, what happens to the soul in the interregnum between incarnations? Where do these souls rest while they are awaiting rebirth?

Finally, if one holds the view that consciousness is dependent on the brain, then the very idea of a disembodied soul will seem implausible. The burden of proof will rest with the proponent of reincarnation to give us evidence as to why we should believe this doctrine.

However, there is indirect evidence for a soul or the disembodied survival of the self, evidence recorded by individuals who have had out-of-body experiences after being pronounced clinically dead. James Moody documents several cases of "clinically dead" persons who were revived and reported remarkably similar experiences. Moody sets down a composite of the reports in the following passage:

> A man is dying and, as he reaches the point of greatest physical distress, he hears himself pronounced dead by his doctor. He begins to hear an uncomfortable noise, a loud ringing or buzzing, and at the same time feels himself moving very rapidly through a long dark tunnel. After this, he suddenly finds himself outside of his own physical body, but still in the immediate physical environment, and he sees his own body from a distance, as though he is a spectator. He watches the resuscitation attempt from this unusual vantage point and is in a state of emotional upheaval.
>
> After a while, he collects himself and becomes more accustomed to his odd condition. He notices that he still has a "body," but one of a very different nature and with very different powers from the physical body he has left behind. Soon other things begin to happen. Others come to meet and to help him. He glimpses the spirits of relatives and friends who have already died, and a loving, warm spirit of a kind he has never encountered before—a being of light—appears before him. This being asks him a question, nonverbally, to make him evaluate his life and helps him along by showing him a panoramic, instantaneous playback of the major events of his life. At some

point he finds himself approaching some sort of barrier or border, apparently representing the limit between earthly life and the next life. Yet, he finds that he must go back to the earth, that the time for his death has not yet come. At this point he resists, for by now he is taken up with his experiences in the afterlife and does not want to return. He is overwhelmed by intense feelings of joy, love, and peace. Despite his attitude, though, he somehow reunites with his physical body and lives.[4]

This passage is not meant to represent any one person's report but is the model, or composite, of the common elements that are found in many stories. Moody himself makes no claims for the interpretation that the patients really experienced what they claim to have experienced. There could be neurological causes for the experiences, or they could be attributed to wish fulfillment. The point is, simply, that these experiences should be considered as part of the evidence to be examined carefully—perhaps being followed up with further research.

But even if these reports survive close scrutiny, in themselves they do not constitute a strong case for immortality. It could be the case that we do survive our death for one or two more existences but then perish. But for those who can find other arguments for life after death, the Moody reports may serve as a corroboration of this doctrine.

SUMMARY OF PART TWO

The question whether there is life after death has haunted human beings from time immemorial. Virtually every religion addresses it and attempts to answer it. Plato and many through the ages have held that our essential self is spiritual, so that it does not die with the body but endures, either in heaven or as reincarnated in another body. The Hebrew view, which is reflected in Paul's writings in the New Testament, holds that our personhood is a function of our bodies, so that you cannot separate body from soul in any absolute manner. Paul taught that after death the redeemed will inherit a new and glorified body. We noted problems with both views. James Moody has recorded evidence of out-of-body experiences, although these testimonies have been challenged.

Questions for Discussion

1. The noted anthropologist Sir James Frazier has written the following statement about immortality. Evaluate it.

Of all the many forms which natural religion has assumed none probably has exerted so deep and far-reaching an influence on human life as the belief in immortality and the worship of the dead; hence [a discussion] of this momentous creed and of the practical consequences which have been deduced from it can hardly fail to be at once instructive and impressive, whether we regard the record with complacency as a noble testimony to the aspiring genius of man, who claims to outlive the sun and the stars, or whether we view it with pity as a melancholy monument of fruitless labour and barren ingenuity expended in prying into that great mystery of which fools profess their knowledge and wise men confess their ignorance.[5]

2. Analyze the Platonic and Hebrew-Christian views on life after death. Which view is more plausible? Explain your answer.

3. What do you make of the evidence for out-of-body experiences described by James Moody? What are the arguments for and against using this evidence for the thesis that we survive our deaths?

4. How would you respond to the question raised by the brain operation? Do you survive the operation? Consider the three possible answers: (a) You do not survive; (b) you survive as one of the two; or (c) you survive as two people. Discuss the reasons for and against each answer.

5. How would you solve the puzzle about the identity of Theseus's ship? What happens to it at t_2? One of my students said, "It just disappears." Do you agree? Why, or why not?

6. Explain the difference between the psychological states criterion for personal identity and the body/brain criterion. Which has the best case in its favor? Why?

7. What do you make of the phenomenon of split personalities and multiple personalities, such as the case of Sybil, who allegedly expressed 16 different personalities with 16 different sets of memories? According to a psychological states account, would we have to say that one body contained 16 persons? Are there different persons inside each of us, expressed by different "sides" of our personalities?

8. In the last section of Part One, we discussed the implications flowing from relative and proximate identity. Discuss these consequences. Can you think of other implications?

For Further Reading

Ducasse, C. J. *Nature, Mind and Death.* La Salle, Ill.: Open Court, 1951. A defense of immortality.

Edwards, Paul, ed. *Immortality.* New York: Macmillan, 1992. The best collection of articles available. Edwards's own introductory article is valuable.

Flew, Anthony. "Immortality." In *Encyclopedia of Philosophy,* edited by Paul Edwards, Vol. 4, 139–150. New York: Macmillan, 1967.

Geach, Peter. *God and Soul.* London: Routledge & Kegan Paul, 1969. A defense of the Hebrew-Christian view of survival after death.

Johnson, Raynor. *The Imprisoned Splendor.* London: Hodder & Stoughton, 1953. A defense of reincarnation.

Moody, Raymond. *Life After Life.* New York: Bantam Books, 1976. A fascinating but controversial account of near-death experiences.

Parfit, Derek. *Reasons and Persons.* Oxford, England: Clarendon Press, 1984. Part 3 contains an excellent discussion.

Perry, John. *A Dialogue on Personal Identity and Immortality.* Indianapolis, Ind.: Hackett, 1978. A philosophically rich, entertaining discussion of the problem of personal identity.

Perry, John, ed. *Personal Identity.* Berkeley: University of California Press, 1975. Contains the essential classical readings.

Pojman, Louis, ed. *Philosophy: The Quest for Truth.* 2d ed. Belmont, Calif.: Wadsworth, 1992. Contains Parfit's discussion, as well as the first part of Perry's dialogue and other essays.

Rorty, Amelie, ed. *The Identities of Persons.* Berkeley: University of California Press, 1976. A good selection of essays on the nature of personhood.

Unger, Peter. *Identity, Consciousness, and Value.* New York: Oxford University Press, 1990. A highly imaginative, penetrating discussion of the issues discussed in this chapter.

Notes

1. *A Catholic Dictionary,* ed. D. Attwater (New York: Macmillan, 1941), 261.
2. Plato, *Phaedo,* 79c,d; my translation.
3. 1 Corinthians 15:12–53, King James Version, edited.
4. Raymond Moody, *Life After Life* (New York: Bantam Books, 1976), 21.
5. Sir James Frazier, *The Belief in Immortality,* vol. 1 (London: Macmillan, 1913), vii–viii.

9

FAITH AND REASON

The heart has reasons of its own which the mind knows nothing of.

—PASCAL

THE CLASSIC POSITIONS

Given the difficulty of establishing the truth of religion by reason alone, the question of faith becomes of supreme importance. In this chapter and the next I consider the question, What is the relationship of faith to reason? I discussed in Chapter 1 the idea that normally reason should be our final guide in life, both with regard to belief (Hume's declaration that the wise man "proportions the strength of his belief to the strength of the evidence") and action (justified beliefs give us the best chances of reaching our goals). But is religious belief rational? Or is faith essentially an irrational or, at least, an arational activity? If we cannot prove the claims of religious belief, is it nevertheless reasonable to believe these claims? For example, even if we do not have a deductive proof or strong inductive evidence for the existence of God, is it nevertheless reasonable to believe that God exists? In the debate over faith and reason, two opposing positions have dominated the field. The first position asserts that faith and reason are compatible—that is, that it is rational to believe in God. The second position denies this assertion. Those holding to the first position differ among themselves about the extent of the compatibility between faith and reason. Most adherents follow Thomas Aquinas (1224–1274) in relegating the compatibility to the "preambles of faith" (e.g., the existence of God and his nature) against the "articles of faith" (e.g., the doctrine of the Incarnation). Few have gone as far as Immanuel Kant (1724–1804), who maintained complete harmony between reason and faith—that is, a religious belief within the realm of reason alone.

The second position divides into two subpositions: (1) Faith is opposed to reason (a position held by such unlikely bedfellows as David Hume and Søren Kierkegaard), placing faith in the area of *irrationality;* and (2) faith, being *transrational,* is higher than reason. John Calvin (1509–1564) and Karl Barth (1886–1968) assert that a **natural theology** is inappropriate because it seeks to meet unbelief on its own ground (ordinary, finite reason). Revelation, however, is *self-authenticating,* "carrying with it its own evidence." We can call this position the transrational view of faith. Faith is not so much against reason as above and beyond it. Actually, Kierkegaard shows that the two subpositions are compatible, for he holds both that faith is above reason (superior to it) and against reason (because human reason has been corrupted by sin). The irrationalist and transrationalist positions are not always clearly separated in arguments about the incompatibility of faith and reason. At least, it seems that faith gets such a high value that reason comes off looking not simply inadequate but culpable. To use reason where faith claims the field is not only inappropriate but irreverent, faithless, and immoral.

In this chapter I examine three nonrationalist theories on faith and reason. First, I consider the claim of Pascal and William James that belief in God is pragmatically justified even where evidence is absent or weak. I next examine the claim that faith has its own value—so that it is higher than reason. Finally, we examine Alvin Plantinga's claim that we need not have evidence or arguments for our religious beliefs, because they may be properly basic for us.

PRAGMATIC JUSTIFICATION OF RELIGIOUS BELIEF

> Our passional nature not only lawfully may, but must, decide an option between propositions, whenever it is a genuine option that cannot by its nature be decided on intellectual grounds; for to say, under such circumstances, "Do not decide, but leave the question open," is itself a passional decision—just like deciding yes or no—and is attended with the same risk of losing the truth.[1]

Pascal's Wager

Sometimes religious philosophers concede that religion cannot be justified through rational argument. They maintain, however, that it can be justified by its practical results. Religious belief has a *practical* reasonableness.

That is, even if we cannot find good evidence for religious beliefs, it would perhaps be in our interest to convince ourselves to believe in these propositions anyway. Would such believing be morally permissible? In his classic work *Thoughts,* Blaise Pascal (1623–1662), a renowned French physicist and mathematician, sets forth the "wager" argument, contending that if we do a cost–benefit analysis of the matter, it turns out that it is eminently reasonable to get ourselves to believe that God exists regardless of whether we have good evidence for that belief. The heart of the argument is contained in the following passage:

> Either God exists or He does not. But to which side shall we incline? Reason can decide nothing here. A game is being played where heads or tails will turn up. What will you wager? According to reason, you can do neither the one thing nor the other; according to reason, you can defend neither proposition. But you must wager. It is not optional. You are embarked. Which will you choose then? Your reason is no more shocked in choosing one rather than the other, since you must of necessity choose. This is one point settled. But which course will affect your happiness? Let us weigh the gain and the loss in wagering that God is. Let us estimate these two chances. If you gain, you gain all; if you lose, you lose nothing. Wager, then, without hesitation that He is.
>
> "That is very fine," you say. "Yes, I must wager; but I may perhaps wager too much."
>
> Let us see. Since there is an equal risk of gain and of loss, if you had only to gain two lives, instead of one, you might still wager. But if there were three lives to gain, you would have to play, and you would be imprudent, when you are forced to play, not to chance your life to gain three at a game where there is an equal risk of loss and gain. But there is an eternity of life and happiness.
>
> You may object, "My hands are tied, my mouth is gagged. I am forced to wager, so I am not free. But, despite this, I am so made that I cannot believe. What then should I do?"
>
> I would have you understand your incapacity to believe. Labor to convince yourself, not by more "proofs" of God's existence, but by disciplining your passions and wayward emotions. You would arrive at faith, but know not the way. You would heal yourself of unbelief, yet know not the remedies. I answer you: Learn of those who have been bound as you are. These are they who know the way you would follow, who have been cured of a disease you would be cured of. Follow the way by which they began, by acting as if you believe, taking holy water, having masses said, and so forth. Even this will naturally make you believe.[2]

The argument follows something like this. Regarding the proposition "God exists," reason is neutral. It can neither prove nor disprove it. But we must make a choice on this matter, for not to choose for God is in effect to choose against him and to lose the possible benefits that belief would bring. Because these benefits promise to be infinite and the loss equally infinite, we might set forth the possibilities like this:

	God Exists	*God Does Not Exist*
I Believe in God	A. Infinite gain with minimal finite loss	B. Overall finite loss in terms of sacrifice of goods
I Do Not Believe in God	C. Infinite loss with finite gain	D. Overall finite gain

There are only these four possible outcomes. If I believe in God, two outcomes are possible, depending on whether God exists. If God exists, I win eternal happiness, an infinite gain. If God does not exist, I suffer minor inconvenience. Perhaps I could have better enjoyed using the money I gave to the church or synagogue, but the loss cannot be compared with the possibility of infinite gain. On the other hand, if I do not believe in God, two other outcomes are possible. If I do not believe and God does not exist, I may gain a little advantage in not having had to give my money to the church or sacrifice in other ways. But if I fail to believe and God does exist, I lose eternal bliss. I suffer infinite loss. No earthly gain can compensate me for missing God, "for what shall it profit a man if he gain the whole world but lose his own soul?" (Matthew 16:26)

Even if there is only a small chance that God exists (say 1 percent), it still pays to bet on God, for no matter how enormous the *finite* gain in C and D in the diagram, 1 percent probability multiplied by infinity equals infinity. So the only relevant considerations are A and C. Because A (believing in God) promises infinite happiness and C (not believing in God) infinite unhappiness, a rational cost–benefit analysis leaves no doubt about what we should do. We have a clear self-interested reason for believing in God.

You should go over this argument closely. Are there any serious weaknesses in it? Is Pascal consistent? At the beginning of his argument, he assumes that theoretical reason is neutral on the matter, but the logic of his wager advocates believing even when the evidence is against the God-hypothesis. Does this matter? Does his wager argument demonstrate that we all should do whatever necessary (e.g., take drugs, get brainwashed) to get ourselves to believe that God exists? Is such a belief necessary and sufficient for eternal happiness? Remember that the Epistle of James (2:19) states that even the devils, who are not saved, believe that God exists. There must be more to the wager than mere belief.

W. K. Clifford and the Ethics of Belief

In a famous rejoinder to such gambling with God, the British philosopher W. K. Clifford (1845–1879) argued that believing has moral ramifications, so that believing without sufficient evidence is immoral.[3] Pragmatic justifications are not justifications at all but counterfeits of genuine justifications, which must always be based on evidence.

Clifford illustrates his thesis with the example of a shipowner who sends an emigrant ship to sea. He knows that the ship is old and not well built, but he fails to have the ship inspected. Dismissing from his mind all doubts and suspicions of the unseaworthiness of the vessel, he trusts in Providence to care for his ship. He acquires a sincere and comfortable conviction in this way and collects his insurance money without a trace of guilt after the ship sinks, killing all the passengers.

Clifford comments that although the shipowner sincerely believed that all was well with the ship, his sincerity in no way exculpates him from blame because "he had no right to believe on such evidence as was before him." One has an obligation to get oneself in a position in which one will believe propositions only on sufficient evidence. Furthermore, it is not a valid objection to say that what the shipowner had an obligation to do was to *act* in a certain way (viz., inspect the ship), not to *believe* in a certain way. Although he does have an obligation to inspect the ship, the objection overlooks the function of believing as action guiding:

> No man holding a strong belief on one side of a question, or even wishing to hold a belief on one side, can investigate it with such fairness and completeness as if he were really in doubt and unbiased; so that the existence of a belief not founded on fair inquiry unfits a man for the performance of this necessary duty.

The general conclusion is that "it is wrong always and for anyone to believe anything on insufficient evidence." Clifford's argument is essentially rule-utilitarian. Generally, the best way to reach our goals is to engage in rational belief-forming processes. We need to know the facts or at least to have the best justified beliefs so that we reach our personal and social ends—to get our emigrant ship or our social ship safely to the port.

William James: The Will to Believe

The classic response to Clifford's ethics of belief is William James's "The Will to Believe" (1896),[4] in which James argues that life would be greatly impoverished if we confined our beliefs to such a Scrooge-like epistemology as Clifford proposes. In everyday life, when the evidence for important propositions is often unclear, we must live by faith or cease to act at all. Although we cannot make leaps of faith just anywhere, sometimes practical considerations force us to make a decision regarding propositions that do not have their truth value written on their faces.

In "The Sentiment of Rationality" (1879), James defines faith as "a belief in something concerning which doubt is still theoretically possible; and as the test of belief is willingness to act, one may say that faith is the readiness to act in a cause the prosperous issue of which is not certified to us in advance." In "The Will to Believe," he speaks of a live, momentous optional hypothesis on which we cannot avoid a decision, for not to choose is, in effect, to choose against the hypothesis. If we judge the hypothesis to be worth the venture, we should get ourselves to believe it. There is a good illustration of this notion of faith in "The Sentiment of Rationality." A mountain climber in the Alps finds himself in a position from which he can escape only by means of an enormous leap. If he tries to calculate the evidence, only believing on sufficient evidence, he will be paralyzed by emotions of fear and mistrust and hence be lost. Without evidence of being able to perform this feat successfully, the climber would be better off convincing himself to believe that he can and will make the leap: "In this case . . . the part of wisdom clearly is to believe what one desires; for the belief is one of the indispensable preliminary conditions of the realization of its object. *There are then cases where faith creates its own verification.*"

James claims that for many of us religion may be such a momentous optional hypothesis that the individual for whom it is so has the right to believe the better story rather than the worse. To do so, one must will to believe what the evidence alone is inadequate to support.

The reader should keep two questions in mind at this point; one is descriptive, and the other is normative. The first is whether it is possible to believe propositions at will. In what sense can we get ourselves to believe propositions that the evidence doesn't force on us? Normally, beliefs are not under our control. We do not choose to believe propositions; the belief comes naturally. By opening our eyes, we nonvoluntarily come to believe in what we perceive; seeing is believing. Surely we can't believe that the world is flat or that 2 plus 2 equals 5 simply by willing to do so, but which propositions (if any) are subject to volitional influences? Is it psychologically impossible to make the kinds of moves that Pascal and James advise? Does it involve self-deception? If we know that the only cause for our belief in a religious proposition is our desire to believe, can we, if we are rational, continue to believe that proposition? Is there something self-defeating about the whole enterprise of trying to get yourself to believe propositions just because they are comforting?

The second, normative, question deals with the ethics of belief, stressed by Clifford. Suppose that we can get ourselves to believe or disbelieve propositions—is this morally permissible? What are the arguments for and against integrity of belief? Clifford argued that volitional believing is socially corrupting and will likely lead to disutility in the long run. Others hold that we have a deontological duty to believe according to the evidence.

Note that Pascal's volitionalism is indirect, whereas James's might be interpreted as direct. In Pascal's case, one must will to believe the proposition *p*, discover the best means to get into that state (e.g., going to church, saying mass, taking holy water), and act in such a way as to make the acquisition of the belief likely. In direct volitionalism, one supposes that one can obtain some beliefs simply by fiat of the will.

Finally, note that there is a difference between getting oneself to believe propositions the truth of which one has no control over and getting oneself to believe propositions about which the truth has still not been decided but in which belief might help bring about the desired state of affairs. For example, the mountain climber may have good practical reasons for believing that convincing himself to believe he can leap over the gorge will help bring about that event, but my believing that $6,000,000 was miraculously deposited into my savings account yesterday won't help bring that state of affairs about. Should we have a different attitude about each of these types of cases?

FIDEISM: FAITH WITHOUT/AGAINST REASON

When subjectivity, inwardness, is truth, the truth becomes a paradox; and the fact that the truth is objectively a paradox shows in turn that subjectivity is truth.[5]

The position that holds that objective reason is simply inappropriate for religious belief is called **fideism.** Faith does not need reason for its justification, and the attempt to apply rational categories to religion is completely inappropriate. Faith creates its own justification, its own criteria of internal assessment. There are two versions of fideism. The first states that religion is bound to appear absurd when judged by the standards of theoretical reason. The second merely says that religion is an activity in which reason is properly inoperative. It is not so much against reason as above reason. The two positions are compatible. The third-century theologian Tertullian seemed to hold that religious faith was both against and beyond human reason (and perhaps St. Paul holds the same in 1 Corinthians 1), but many fideists (e.g., Calvin) would only subscribe to the latter position.

Søren Kierkegaard (1813–1855), the Danish philosopher and father of **existentialism,** seems to hold to both versions of fideism. For him faith, not reason, is the highest virtue a human can reach, a trait that is necessary for the deepest human fulfillment.[6] If Kant, the rationalist, adhered to a "religion within the limits of reason alone," Kierkegaard adhered to "reason within the limits of religion alone." He unashamedly proclaimed faith as being a virtue higher than reason in the development of essential humanness, that alone which promised eternal happiness. In a more everyday sense, Kierkegaard thought that we all lived by simple faith in plans, purposes, and people. It is rarely the case in ordinary life that reason is our basic guide. Paraphrasing Hume, he might have said that "reason is and ought to be a slave to faith," for we all have an essential faith in something, and reason comes in largely as an afterthought to rationalize our intuitions and commitments.

No philosopher writes more passionately about faith, nor values it more highly, than Kierkegaard. Whereas his predecessors had largely viewed faith as a necessary evil, a distant cousin to the princely knowledge, Kierkegaard reversed the order. Knowledge about **metaphysical** issues is really not a good thing, for it prevents the kind of human striving that is essential for our fullest development. Faith is the highest virtue precisely because it is objectively uncertain, for it is risk and uncertainty that are crucial for personal growth into selfhood. Spiritual self-realization needs to venture forth, to swim over 700,000 fathoms of ocean water. Faith is the lover's loyalty to the beloved when all the evidence is against her. Faith is the soul's deepest yearnings and hopes, which the rational part of us cannot fathom. Faith is risk, and the greater the risk, the greater the faith. "Whereas Hume asserted that 'probability is the guide of life,'" Kierkegaard wrote, "Probability is therefore far from sacred to the believer, but he fears it most of all, since he knows well that when [probability] is present, he has begun to lose faith."[7] Even if we had direct proof for theism or Christianity, we would not want it, for such objective certainty would take the venture out of the religious pilgrimage, reducing it to a set of dull mathematical certainties or statistical probabilities. Kierkegaard is arguing, following Pascal, that "the heart has reasons of its own which the mind knows nothing of." Religion is like a passionate love affair, not calculating but spontaneous, risky, and deeply fulfilling. He calls this passionate approach to belief *subjectivity* and argues that *subjectivity is truth,* "the highest truth there is for an existing human being."

Genuine theistic faith appears when reason reaches the end of its tether, when the individual sees that without God there is no purpose to life:

In this manner God becomes a postulate, but not in the otiose manner in which this word is commonly understood. It becomes clear rather that the only way in which an existing individual comes into relation with God, is when the dialectical contradiction brings his passion to the point of despair, and helps him to embrace God with the "category of despair" (faith). Then the postulate is so far from being arbitrary that it is precisely a life-necessity. It is then not so much that God is a postulate, as that the existing individual's postulation of God is necessary.[8]

One is not always sure how serious Kierkegaard is about this radical antirationalism, for he argues that his faith is not nonsense but a recognition of a deeper truth in the soul of a person. Often writing under pseudonyms such as Johannes Climacus (John the Climber—presumably, to heaven), he argues that there is something fundamentally misguided in trying to base one's religious faith on objective evidence or reason. It is both useless (it won't work) and a bad thing (it detracts one from the essential task of growing in faith). Then he goes on to develop a theory of subjectivity wherein faith finds an authentic home. One version of his argument is called the *approximation argument,* for it claims that reason and scholarship give us only approximate results, whereas faith demands infinite passion and subjective certainty. Here is a key passage:

If a naked dialectical analysis reveals that no approximation to faith is possible, that an attempt to construct a quantitative approach to faith is a misunderstanding, and that any appearance of success in this endeavor is an illusion; if it is seen to be a temptation for the believer to concern himself with such considerations, a temptation to be resisted with all his strength, lest he succeed in transforming faith into something else, into a certainty of an entirely different order, replacing its passionate conviction by those probabilities and guarantees which he rejected in the beginning when he made the leap of faith, the qualitative transition from non-belief to belief—if this be true, then everyone who so understands the problem, insofar as he is not wholly unfamiliar with scientific scholarship or bereft of willingness to learn, must feel the difficulty of his position, when his admiration for the scholars teaches him to think humbly of his own significance in comparison with their distinguished learning and acumen and well merited fame, so that he returns to them repeatedly, seeking the fault in himself, until he is finally compelled to acknowledge dejectedly that he is in the right.[9]

Kierkegaard is here examining the need for biblical scholarship to establish the credibility of the Bible and Christian claims of revelation, but in other places he discusses attempts to prove the existence of God through rational demonstrations, concluding that all they give us is probability or approximate objective results. For example, years ago most biblical scholars believed in the literal narrative of the Creation and Fall from

Grace of Adam and Eve (in Genesis 2 and 3). Today most biblical scholars do not believe in the literal interpretation of the Genesis account, so that the literal interpretation cannot serve as the basis for a believer's faith. But suppose tomorrow new evidence turns up against the authenticity of the New Testament Gospels. Or suppose a noted biblical scholar sets forth a plausible theory that explains how the disciples were deluded into believing that Jesus of Nazareth rose from the dead. Kierkegaard contends that if the believer's faith is hostage to the fortunes of scholarship, one week the faith may be strong, but the next week it may be very weak. Indeed, some weeks there may be no faith at all because the evidence is insufficient.

But this is just silly, argues Kierkegaard. Because Christianity has made eternal happiness dependent on faith, taking scholarship too seriously can cause us to lose eternity. Our eternal happiness can't rest on the luck of what scholars find or on intellectual hypotheses. Faith is not simply for scholars and intellectuals—perhaps it is least of all for them, for they are preoccupied with reason and miss the glory of faith. Faith is something even peasants and uneducated people can possess. It is certain, something absolute, that demands one's whole heart and soul. The leap of faith transcends all scholarly pretensions. It's more like falling in love than figuring out a crossword puzzle, to which the scholars would have us liken it.

What do you make of this argument? Is faith wholly cut off from reason? Or is it simply a fact of life that most of us, at least, have no rational basis for religious certainty?

A question may be asked: Why do we value reason so highly? In most areas of life, it seems to give us good results. In science, as well as in our daily lives, following reason is generally the best guarantee for success. Using reason, as we argued in Chapter 1, seems the best way to reach truth and provide the best evidence for guiding our action. Even the recognition of the limits of reason seems to be a function of reason at a higher reflective level, exactly what you might be doing right now—using reason to recognize the limits of reason.

But should we value faith over reason, as Kierkegaard argues? Is faith as a risk really a better guide to happiness or eternal happiness than reason? It is hard to believe it is. In fact by this logic of subjectivity (i.e., "the more risk, the greater the faith") we should believe in absurdities, for they demand the greatest epistemic risk possible. The rationalist has one big advantage over the fideist. He or she can bring evidence into the discussion so that we may all evaluate it and decide how credible it is, but the fideist has no such justification. In most other important areas of life, we trust the person with good reasons over the person with no reasons. Why should things be different with regard to religious belief?

REFORMED EPISTEMOLOGY: ALVIN PLANTINGA

One of the most innovative, brilliant, and controversial contributions to the debate on faith and reason is the theory set forth by Alvin Plantinga. It claims that the belief that God exists is rational even though it is not based on prior evidence. In a series of articles, Plantinga has juxtaposed what he calls "Reformed epistemology" (or Calvinist epistemology) with classical foundationalism (which he finds in Aquinas, Descartes, Locke, Hume, and many others) and has concluded that the theist is rationally justified in believing in God without further evidence.[10] Plantinga finds classical foundationalism wanting, but he himself seems to prefer a revised version of foundationalism as the best available epistemological theory. In this section I exposit Plantinga's arguments, using his classic article, "Reason and Belief in God," as the focal point of my analysis. After this, I discuss two criticisms of his position.

Classical foundationalism is the doctrine that all justified beliefs must either be properly basic by fulfilling certain criteria or be based on other beliefs, which eventually result in a treelike construction with properly basic beliefs resting at the bottom, or at the foundations. According to a typical classical foundationalism:

A proposition p is properly basic for a person S if and only if p is either self-evident to S or incorrigible for S or evident to the senses for S

Foundationalists may differ about the exact makeup of the definition (Descartes accepts only the first two disjuncts, but Aquinas and Locke accept all three), but they all agree that justified beliefs must be based on foundations having some of the above components. Self-evident propositions are those that a person just sees as true immediately, such as that $1 + 2 = 3$ or that nothing all green is all black, or that the law of noncontradiction is universally valid. Incorrigible propositions are those about one's states of consciousness in which one cannot mistakenly believe what is not true, such as "that I seem to see a red ball" or "I think, therefore I am" or "I am in pain." Aquinas and Locke add a third type of proposition, that which is evident to the senses, such as "that I see a tree" or "I see a red ball." The goal of the classical foundationalist is to protect our belief systems from error by allowing only solid or absolutely certain beliefs to make up the foundations of our belief systems. Actually, memory beliefs should be included in the class of properly basic beliefs, for it seems a fundamental belief that I remember going to bed last night and waking up this morning. I also remember (or seem to) seeing my son in his room at 10 P.M. last night, at the time a murder was committed across town. From the basic belief that I seem to remember my son in his room and other beliefs about the reliability of memory beliefs and the impossibility of being in two places at the same time, I can infer to the nonbasic belief that my son did not commit the murder across town, even if some evidence points in that direction. So the formula for foundationalism should be revised to read:

> A proposition p is properly basic for a person S if and only if p is either self-evident to S or incorrigible for S or evident to the senses for S or seems to be remembered by S.

Next, Plantinga develops the notion of a noetic structure. "A person's noetic structure is the set of propositions he believes together with certain epistemic relations that hold among him and these propositions" (p. 48). Plantinga analyzes the noetic structure from the point of view of foundationalism in general. There are three ways of classifying the contents of our noetic structure: (1) in terms of basicality, (2) in terms of degree of belief, and (3) in terms of the depth of ingress of a belief.

1. Basicality refers to the dependency relationship of all other beliefs on basic beliefs. The relationship is irreflexive (it can't be justified by itself), one-many (nonbasic beliefs may depend on more than one belief), and asymmetric (if belief A depends on belief B, belief B cannot legitimately depend on belief A).
2. We believe propositions in various degrees. Classical foundationalists such as Locke and Hume would define rationality in terms of believing propositions according to the strength of the evidence, but, whereas Plantinga agrees that we do believe in varying degrees, he rejects any attempt to work out an exact correlation of degrees of evidence and degrees of belief. He does so because the only candidate for such correlation is some sort of quantification test, which he rejects as unworkable.
3. Regarding the matter of depth of ingress, Plantinga says that beliefs play different roles within our noetic structure. Some of our beliefs are more central and some more peripheral to our **doxastic** system, so that losing some beliefs will have a greater effect on us than losing others. We are less worried about being wrong about the trivial proposition that there are X number of steps in the city of Dallas than about the proposition that the snake we are about to handle is nonpoisonous.

Applying this theory of classical foundationalism to religious claims, we see that, according to the theory, belief in God has no legitimacy. The thesis excludes the belief from the foundations of one's noetic structure, for belief in God is neither self-evident, incorrigible, nor evident to the senses. Furthermore, because it does not seem possible to get from the types of propositions allowed in our noetic structure by these conditions to the conclusion that God exists, the present-day foundationalists tend to reject the belief that God exists as unjustified or irrational.

But, Plantinga points out, classical foundationalism is not without problems. First of all, it seems that "relative to propositions that are self-evident and incorrigible, most of the beliefs that form the stock in trade of ordinary everyday life are not probable—at any rate there is no reason to think they are probable" (p. 59). Such propositions as that there are enduring physical objects and other minds and that the world has existed for more than five minutes "are not more probable than not with respect to what is self-evident or incorrigible for me." Nor are the propositions that there are other minds or that the world existed five minutes ago evident to the senses. Furthermore, many propositions that do not meet the criteria of classical foundationalism seem properly basic for me. "I believe, for example, that I had lunch this noon. I do not believe this proposition on the basis of other propositions; I take it as basic; it is in the foundations of my noetic structure. Furthermore, I am entirely rational in so taking it, even though this proposition is neither self-evident nor evident to the senses nor incorrigible for me" (p. 60).

The most devastating criticism of the formula of classical foundationalism, however, is that it is self-referentially incoherent. For the belief that we are rational only if the belief is either properly basic or derived from beliefs that are does not seem itself to be either properly basic or derived from other statements or beliefs that are properly basic. To be properly basic, the statement must be either self-evident, incorrigible, or evident to the senses. But the statement that prescribes such rules does not seem to be any of these. Nor does it seem to be derived from statements that are. Hence, it seems irrational to accept it by its own standards.

Plantinga's alternative to classical foundationalism is rooted in the Reformed theological tradition, which contains the core of a nonevidentialist epistemology. The Reformed thinkers have eschewed the attempt to demonstrate the existence of God. From the outset such theologians as John Calvin, Herman Bavinck, Benjamin Warfield, and, more recently, Karl Barth have seen dangers in trying to prove theism, have recognized that arguments are not the source of the believer's confidence, and have insisted that they are not needed for rational justification. As Scripture "proceeds from God as the starting point," so should the believer. In this sense, belief that God exists is like belief in other minds or that I had lunch this noon. It does not need argument before it can be properly basic.

There is within the human mind, and indeed by natural instinct, an awareness of divinity. This we take to be beyond controversy. To prevent anyone
from taking refuge in the pretense of ignorance, God himself has implanted
in all men a certain understanding of his divine majesty. Ever renewing its
memory, he repeatedly sheds fresh drops. Since, therefore, men, one and all,
perceive that there is a God and that he is their Maker, they are condemned
by their own testimony, because they have failed to honor him and to concen-
trate their lives to his will. There is no nation . . . so barbarous, no people so
savage, that they have not a deep-seated conviction that there is a God.[11]

Starting from that premise, the theist could then go on and adhere to
foundational rules: (1) In every rational noetic structure there is a set of
beliefs taken as basic—that is, not accepted on the basis of other beliefs;
and (2) in a rational noetic structure, nonbasic belief is proportional to
support from the foundations (p. 72).

Why is it, then, that both agnostics and atheists exist? The answer: Sin.
Disobedience and rebellion against God are the causes of unbelief. Following Calvin, Plantinga says, "Were it not for the existence of sin in the world,
human beings would believe in God to the same degree and with the same
natural spontaneity that we believe in the existence of other persons, an
external world, or the past." The atheist and agnostic, according to Reformed epistemology, are morally culpable for failing to believe that God
exists, for they are blocking their God-given tendency in that direction.

Plantinga does not offer criteria for proper basicality, but he does want
to protect Reformed epistemology from certain objections. Specifically, his
position should not be confused with the view that any belief may be part
of one's epistemic foundations, nor does he want to say that it is groundless. Some objectors have complained that Plantinga's views open the door
to all sorts of irrationality in the foundations of our noetic structure. Why
cannot belief in the Great Pumpkin be considered properly basic?

Plantinga's answer is that the Reformed epistemologist agrees with
Calvin that "God has implanted in us a natural tendency to see his hand in
the world around us; the same cannot be said for the Great Pumpkin, there
being no Great Pumpkin and no natural tendency to accept belief about
the Great Pumpkin" (p. 78).

We have noted that Plantinga does not give any criteria for distinguish-
ing unacceptable from acceptable candidates for proper basicality, but he
suggests that the manner of arriving at such will be broadly inductive.

We must assemble examples of beliefs and conditions such that the former
are obviously properly basic in the latter, and examples of beliefs and conditions such that the former are obviously not properly basic in the latter. We
must then frame hypotheses as to the necessary and sufficient conditions of

proper basicality and test these hypotheses by reference to those examples. (p. 76)

But there is a certain relativity in the process of searching for criteria for proper basicality. Each community will assemble a different set of examples of beliefs and accompanying conditions, so that there is no reason to assume that everyone will agree on the examples.

> The Christian will of course suppose that belief in God is entirely proper and rational; if he does not accept this belief on the basis of other propositions, he will conclude that it is basic for him and properly so. Followers of Bertrand Russell and Madelyn Murray O'Hare may disagree; but how is that relevant? Must my criteria, or those of the Christian community, conform to their examples? Surely not. The Christian community is responsible to its set of examples, not theirs. (p. 77)

It may well be the case that we shall never arrive at universal agreement regarding the conditions for proper basicality. This does not mean that there is no truth in this area, but simply that at least one set of criteria is wrong. It is important to point out that Plantinga is not stating that no argument could ever cause the theist to give up his belief in God but that the burden of proof is on the opponent to give good reasons why the believer should not accept belief in God into the foundations of her noetic structure. Until the opponent fulfills that task, there is no reason for the believer to be troubled. Plantinga distinguishes weak justification, by which one is in one's epistemic rights in accepting a proposition, from strong justification, by which one has what amounts to knowledge. He suggests that the believer may only have a weak justification for belief that God exists but indicates that, in the absence of a successful defeater, it is rational to believe in God. One is *prima facie*, but not *ultima facie*, justified in so doing (p. 84f.).

Regarding the objection that Reformed epistemology makes belief in God groundless, Plantinga answers that the belief is properly grounded in other beliefs, such as "God is speaking to me" and "God forgives me," which are properly basic. They are analogous to perceptual beliefs (e.g., "I see a tree"), memory beliefs ("I had breakfast this morning"), and beliefs ascribing mental states to other persons (e.g., "that person is in pain"). In the proper circumstances (e.g., when there is no reason to believe that my noetic structure is defective), my having an experience of a certain sort confers on me the right to hold the belief in question (p. 79). In like manner, having the experience that God is speaking to me or that God is forgiving me are properly basic in the right circumstances. In this sense, "it is not wholly accurate to say that it is belief in God that is properly basic."[12]

It is really these more experiential beliefs that are properly basic. They in turn entail that God exists. The proposition that God exists is a relatively high-level general proposition that is based on these other more basic propositions.

Finally, Plantinga's proposal is to be distinguished from fideism. Plantinga accepts the definition of fideism as "exclusive or basic reliance upon faith alone, accompanied by a consequent disparagement of reason and utilized especially in the pursuit of philosophical or religious truth" (p. 87). Extreme fideism disparages and denigrates reason, whereas moderate fideism simply prefers faith over reason in religious matters.

The Reformed epistemologist rightly rejects the extreme fideism of Kierkegaard (who, as noted in the previous section, makes faith in the absurdity of the eternal entering time a necessary condition for being a Christian) and Lev Shestov (who holds that one can attain religious truth only by rejecting the proposition that $2 + 2 = 4$ and accepting instead $2 + 2 = 5$). If we understand the deliverances of reason to include basic perceptual truths, incorrigible propositions, certain memory propositions, certain propositions about other minds, and certain moral or ethical propositions, then the Reformed epistemologist would say that belief in God fits into this scheme as properly rational, rather than being an instance in which faith overrides reason. There is a tendency, or nisus, to apprehend God's existence and to understand something of his nature and actions. "This natural knowledge can be and is suppressed by sin, but the fact remains that a capacity to apprehend God's existence is as much part of our natural noetic equipment as is the capacity to apprehend perceptual truths, truths about the past, and truths about other minds" (p. 90). Hence, belief that God exists is among the deliverances of reason as much as these other basic beliefs; hence, the theist need not be a fideist of any sort.

Plantinga is one of the growing number of philosophers of religion who are sensitive to the matter of **volitionalism** (the idea that we can choose our beliefs directly) and the ethics of belief (see Chapter 10). He rejects direct volitionalism as a plausible account of belief formation. We cannot make ourselves believe propositions simply by fiat. Beliefs are not normally, at least, within our control. But if they are not within our control, how can we be said to have duties to believe rationally or according to the evidence?

Plantinga begins his answer by appealing to almost universal beliefs about moral responsibility. Nearly all of us have a deep belief that we can be held morally responsible for our actions even when they are based on what we presently believe. Sincere, false belief does not excuse us from moral condemnation. The anti-Semite, who acts on the conclusion that

Jews are evil, and who believes that she is following the evidence to this abhorrent conclusion, is morally culpable. A person who believes that it is morally proper to arrive at beliefs carelessly or who is sincere in rejecting morality is still morally guilty. This is because we believe that there is an objective morality which each normal person could know if she cared to.

Although we cannot get ourselves to believe just anything at all by willing to believe it, we can affect our doxastic repertoires by paying attention to the evidence—in this case, to our inner moral prompting. The implication of this is that we may also be responsible for whether we believe in God. Perhaps the nonbeliever is one who has defiled his natural tendency to see God in nature.

CRITIQUE OF PLANTINGA'S REFORMED EPISTEMOLOGY

What should we say about this attempt to place belief in God in the foundations of one's noetic structure? Is Plantinga's rejection of traditional evidentialism justified? Is his attempt to place the burden on proof on the nonbeliever to dislodge theistic belief from the foundations well argued? Normally, we think that the proposer of a hypothesis, not the doubter, has the burden of proof. For example, if I say there are ghosts in this room, it would seem unfair to place the burden of proof on you to disprove this, for I could always discount your evidence ("You're not looking for ghosts in the right way or in the right place"). It is well known that existential statements are unfalsifiable and that universal statements (e.g., "All ravens are black") are unverifiable. A counterinstance could always turn up unexpectedly. It seems, then, that Plantinga is mistaken in shifting the burden of proof to the opponent.

Along this line, Gary Gutting is troubled by the ease with which Plantinga dismisses the views of those who differ from him, his epistemic peers who do not find the proposition "God exists" properly basic.[13] Let us take an instance of disagreement among epistemic peers.

> Suppose a mathematician has reflected long and hard on a given proposition (e.g., the axiom of choice) and, although he is not able to derive it as a theorem or even to put forward strong plausibility arguments for it, has come to an entirely firm conviction of its truth. He just 'sees' that it is true. However, when he proposes his proposition to his equally competent colleagues, he meets mixed reactions. Some share his intuitive acceptance of the proposition, others do not. In such a case, is he entitled to continue believing the proposition or should he withhold judgment on it? (p. 85)

It would seem that the mathematician ought to take account of his opponents' views. He should see whether they have any good arguments against his views and, if he concludes that they do not, "he must see if there is any reason to trust his opponents' judgment (intuition) rather than his own on this point." But even if there is no reason to prefer their judgment to his own, he should be moved from his certainty by the fact of their difference. To cling tenaciously to his intuition rather than weakening his hold on the proposition is to be guilty of "epistemological egoism," which is just as "arbitrary and unjustifiable as ethical egoism is generally regarded to be" (p. 86). That is, there is something like peer review of important propositions within any given field. Although such review may not always cause us to give up a belief that we cannot defend, it ought, at least, to cause us to loosen our grasp on the belief, to realize that we could be wrong.

A second criticism concerns Plantinga's dismissal of classical foundationalism, on which evidentialism is grounded. Although foundationalism may not be the complete account of justification and knowledge, it does seem to have strong *prima facie* force. Generally, we do trace our beliefs back to self-evident and empirical beliefs in order to justify them. Perhaps there are some beliefs that are justified abductively or through a comprehensive coherent system—for example, that the world has a past and that other minds exist—but even these seem to have an empirical or self-evident core. I seem to remember past events, and it's simply self-evident that there are other minds. Generally, we think that our beliefs have to be backed up by evidence and withstand evidential scrutiny. My small daughter once was convinced about the existence of Santa Claus. She was quite exasperated by those who doubted her testimony about this, for she thought she saw "him" climb through our window to place presents under our Christmas tree. One Christmas morning she saw "him" climbing through the window (from the fire escape) and came up to address him. She suddenly noticed he was wearing a wedding ring similar to her father's. She yanked at his beard, dislodging it from his face, and cried in discovery, "You're not Santa Claus. You're my Daddy!" The falsification of her hypothesis completely undermined her faith in Santa. She no longer believed in Santa. But suppose that her younger brother Paul objected that discovering one impersonator doesn't prove that Santa doesn't exist somewhere else. But doesn't the burden of proof now pass on to Paul to give reasons or evidence for the existence of Santa Claus? Existential propositions can't be absolutely disproved (if the ghost isn't in this room, it could be in a million other places—all of which we cannot check at once).

A third criticism, which has been made by Robert Audi[14] and others, is that Plantinga has not shown us why almost anything cannot be allowed into the foundations of one's noetic structure. In letting belief in God in as properly basic, he seems to be permitting belief in the Great Pumpkin and much more—and this in spite of his asseverations that there are limits on what is acceptable. His response that "God has implanted in us a natural tendency to see his hand in the world around us; the same cannot be said for the Great Pumpkin, there being no Great Pumpkin and no natural tendency to accept belief about the Great Pumpkin" (p. 78) seems circular, for the Pumpkin theologian could claim the same argument as the reason that there are not more followers of the Pumpkin, viz., that unbelievers are disobeying their true nature or not being sufficiently reflective. Is Plantinga making a natural tendency to believe something a criterion for proper basicality? If so, belief that God exists does not seem to have that property. At least it does not have it to the extent that belief in other minds or in *modus ponens* has it. If there is a strong person-relative aspect to rationality, why can it not be the case that someone comes to believe some strange things about the Great Pumpkin? Plantinga's point seems to be that there is no reason to worry about fictions (or bizarre beliefs) such as the Great Pumpkin that are not serious candidates for proper basicality, but he has not shown what is wrong with such a belief. Likewise, someone could well believe that God is evil or that Krishna is the unique manifestation of God or that Satan is the creator of heaven and earth and claim this belief as properly basic. I've met people who believe this and that God is a sadist who is out to harm them. As Plantinga himself points out, it may turn out that we will not find clear criteria to separate the theist's beliefs from the atheist's or Satanist's beliefs. It may be that the different sets of criteria that characterize what is properly basic for different groups and persons will never be entirely harmonized, but it may also be true that rationality directs us to be deeply respectful of our epistemic peers and moderate our judgment in matters in which we have great differences and cannot give good reasons for preferring our positions. Belief that God exists or that he is speaking to me is not, after all, subject to the almost universal confirmability of the statement "I see a tree."

These criticisms need further attention and debate, which I must leave to you. But this much must be added. In the end, it seems that Plantinga is, his protestations notwithstanding, not a foundationalist at all but a coherentist, who thinks that Christian theism is the most cogent explanatory theory available. Coherentists do not worry much about basic beliefs but seek to justify each belief by its relationship with all other beliefs in the system. Note, in this regard, his rejection of the Great Pumpkin theory, which fails because it does not satisfy the theist's criteria, and his critique of atheism. According to Reformed epistemology, the atheist doesn't believe in God because he is sinful. But if sin is defined as disobedience to God, as it usually is, then Plantinga's rejection of the atheist's position is circular. Plantinga presupposes the existence of God to argue against those who disagree with him over the very issue in question: the existence of God.

Not only does Plantinga seem to be a coherentist, but his theory suffers from the same problems as coherentism, a lack of grounding in empirical data. He doesn't tell us how to test his theory. Good coherent theories supplement themselves by appealing to an empirical core. Evolutionary theory predicts that we will discover genetic processes that result in mutations, which sometimes enable members of a species to adapt more successfully to an environment. Einstein's coherent relativity theory predicted that the perihelion of the planet Mercury would occur in a different location than Newtonian physics predicted. Capitalist economic theory predicts that free market processes will result in greater material wealth and well-being than those of any other economic system. If another system outperforms capitalism, the theory has been falsified. But what crucial experiment does Plantinga propose to test Christianity or theism? Until he makes this task clear, we have reason to doubt that his proposal is sound.

Finally, we should note one further issue: Plantinga's claim that accepting belief in God into the foundations is similar to our basic belief in other minds, the external world, and the past. Perhaps he is correct about these latter beliefs being basic. Suppose he is. Still we can justify them indirectly—or at least give a coherent explanation for why we have them. From an evolutionary perspective, we have been selected to have these beliefs, without which we probably would not have survived in the development of species. Granted, evolutionary theory may be considered (as it is by Plantinga) as a rival explanatory theory to theism, but, as argued in the previous paragraph, it can be corroborated by fossil evidence, the symmetrical structure of animals, vestigial organs, and other phenomena. It also fits in with our knowledge about genetics. Furthermore, to some degree, these other basic beliefs can be tested. For instance, take the idea of the past. I seem to recall leaving my keys on the dining room table. I can check this out by walking into the dining room and looking on the table. The best explanation of their being there is that in the near past I placed them there. Similarly with the existence of other minds. Although no deductive argument for other minds is successful, the best explanation for the behavior of others is that their behavior is intentional, which presupposes a mind. Again, our beliefs about intentions and minds takes place within a wider explanatory context. But we make predictions about these hypotheses and test them. What predictions does Plantinga's Reformed epistemology make? What crucial experiment does he propose to confirm or disconfirm the God hypothesis?

The refusal to enter into the reasoning process seems to remove Plantinga's theory from the domain of philosophy altogether, because philosophy is just that process, as we argued in Chapter 1, of supporting our beliefs and hypotheses with evidence and arguments. Perhaps he offers an alternative to classical philosophy, but, if so, he needs to do a lot more arguing to convince us.

Summary

There are three main positions regarding the relationship of faith to reason:

1. Faith and reason are compatible; they work in harmony.
2. Faith transcends reason, so that there are limits to reason. But faith never contradicts reason rightly used.
3. Faith is against reason. Human reason is fallible and should not be given much weight in religious affairs.

The weakness of positions 2 and 3 is that, if we give up reason, how do we distinguish nonsense that claims to be transcendent from the veridical message of God?

Pascal's wager offers a pragmatic justification for believing in God without sufficient evidence. We examined Clifford's critique and other problems with Pascal's position, as well as James's defense.

At this point, at the beginning of the twenty-first century, the debate in Philosophy of Religion is largely between the evidentialists, both theists and nontheists, on the one side and fideists or neofideists such as Plantinga on the other side. The foremost evidentialist, Swinburne, has made a cumulative case for the existence of God. Taking all the evidence into consideration, the cosmological and teleological arguments and the argument from religious experience, the case for theism has a slight edge. Swinburne's controversy with the agnostics and atheists looks like a family quarrel compared with Plantinga's work on religious foundationalism, which rejects the notion of needing arguments for one's belief in God. God is the beginning point for the religious person, not something we arrived at by argument. The role of Philosophy of Religion becomes very limited, at best a negative enterprise of marshalling attacks that will be met by a polite rebuttal by the theist who will not let anything come in the way of his faith in God. Plantinga's work is, at present, a central focus of debate. I argued that this defensive procedure was fraught with serious problems.

In the next chapter I continue the discussion of faith and reason, arguing that one way to reconcile the tensions between these categories is to substitute the concept of hope for belief.

Questions for Discussion

1. Examine the three major positions regarding faith and reason. What are the strengths and weaknesses of each one? Which seems the most plausible to you and why?

2. Examine Pascal's Wager. What are its strengths and weaknesses?

3. Do you think that you can make yourself believe propositions (e.g., that God exists or that Hinduism is the true religion) just by willing to do so? Or do beliefs force themselves on people depending on how the evidence or testimony of others affects them? Discuss your answer.

4. Is it immoral to believe a proposition against the evidence? Why, or why not?

5. In arguing for the strongest fideism, in which we claim that reason is contrary to faith, don't we use rational arguments to show it is reasonable to abandon reason? Does this prove that the fideist is still a rationalist?

6. Consider a woman who has faith in the faithfulness of her husband who has been accused of committing adultery. Suppose the evidence is strong but not conclusive. Is she morally virtuous in persisting in believing in his fidelity, or is she simply foolish? What if the case against him is conclusive? Does reason ever tell us that it is rational to believe despite the evidence?

7. Examine Plantinga's rejection of evidentialism and classical foundationalism. Are his arguments cogent, or can we defend evidentialism? Is the Santa Claus analogy a good analogy to belief in God?

8. Review and evaluate Plantinga's Reformed epistemology. Is it a sound theory? Are criticisms of it sound?

9. Do you agree with Calvin and Plantinga that all humans have a natural tendency to believe in God but that it has been suppressed because of sin? Is there evidence for this view?

10. Is the problem of faith and reason the same for all religions? Those who come from non–Judeo-Christian traditions might throw light on this issue from within your own tradition.

For Further Reading

Kenny, Anthony, *Faith and Reason.* New York: Columbia University Press, 1983.
Mackie, J. L. *The Miracle of Theism.* Oxford, England: Oxford University Press, 1982. An atheist's defense of rationality against religious belief.
Penelhum, Terrence, ed. *Faith.* New York: Macmillan, 1989. A good collection of classical and contemporary articles on the nature of faith.

Plantinga, Alvin, and Nicholas Wolterstorff, eds. *Faith and Rationality*. Notre Dame, Ind.: University of Notre Dame Press, 1983. Contains a set of articles defending the rationality of theism from the perspective of Reformed epistemology.

Pojman, Louis. *Kierkegaard's Philosophy of Religion*. Bethesda, Md.: International Scholars Publications, 1999. An analysis of Kierkegaard's philosophy of religion.

Pojman, Louis. *Religious Belief and the Will*. London: Routledge & Kegan Paul, 1986. An examination of the relationship between faith and reason, arguing for a compatibilist position.

Pojman, Louis, ed. *Philosophy of Religion: An Anthology*, 3d ed. Belmont, Calif.: Wadsworth, 1998. Contains many of the readings discussed in this chapter.

Swinburne, Richard. *Faith and Reason*. Oxford, England: Clarendon Press, 1981. A strong defense of the rationality of religious belief.

Notes

The quotations in the first three sections of this chapter are from selections found in Part VII.B of Louis Pojman, *Philosophy of Religion: An Anthology*, 3d ed. (Belmont, Calif.: Wadsworth, 1998).

1. William James, "The Will to Believe," in Pojman, op. cit.
2. Blaise Pascal, *Thoughts*, trans. W. F. Trotter (New York: Collier, 1910).
3. W. K. Clifford, "The Ethics of Belief," in Pojman, op. cit.
4. William James, "The Will to Believe," in Pojman, op. cit.
5. Søren Kierkegaard, *Concluding Unscientific Postscript* (1846), my translation.
6. Ibid.
7. Ibid., italics added.
8. Ibid.
9. Ibid.
10. Alvin Plantinga, "Is Belief in God Rational?" in *Rationality and Religious Belief*, ed. C. F. Delaney (Notre Dame, Ind.: University of Notre Dame Press, 1979) and "Reason and Belief in God," in *Faith and Rationality*, eds. A. Plantinga and N. Wolterstorff (Notre Dame, Ind.: University of Notre Dame Press, 1983). All references to Plantinga refer to this work.
11. Ibid.
12. Ibid.
13. Gary Gutting, *Religious Belief and Religious Skepticism* (Notre Dame, Ind.: University of Notre Dame Press, 1982). See Chapter 3.
14. Robert Audi, "Direct Justification and Theistic Belief" in *Religious Belief and Moral Commitment*, ed. R. Audi and W. Wainwright (Ithaca, N.Y.: Cornell University Press, 1986). In this regard we might mention Anthony Kenny's attempt to answer Plantinga's critique of standard foundationalism, found in Anthony Kenny's lectures at Columbia University, published as *Faith and*

Reason (New York: Columbia University Press, 1983). Kenny has been influenced by Plantinga and agrees that classical foundationalism is dead. However, he thinks that Plantinga's version of allowing belief in God into the foundations of one's noetic structure opens the door for letting in any proposition whatever, including the proposition that there is no God. Kenny's alternative version of foundationalism, which escapes both the self-referential incoherence of classical foundationalism and the liberality of Plantinga, states that a belief is properly basic if and only if it is "self-evident or fundamental, evident to the senses or to memory, defensible by argument, inquiry or performance" (p. 27).

By "fundamental" Kenny means such universal beliefs as that there are other minds, that cats do not grow on trees, that the earth has existed for many years, and the like. By being defensible by inquiry, Kenny merely means that sometimes we ourselves do not have the requisite evidence at our fingertips but are ready to take steps to get it. By being defensible by performance, he means such situations as those in which the person always gets the right answers even though he or she may not know how it was done—for example, the water diviner who knows but can't tell how he knows that there is water in certain places. Kenny believes that this reconstructed evidentialist version of foundationalism escapes the liabilities of classical foundationalism, as well as the attacks by the antievidentialists. Whether it does or not will doubtless be the subject of forthcoming work in the area of faith and reason.

15. Plantinga has responded to my critique, indicating that his new book, *Warranted Christian Belief* (Oxford University Press, 2000) deals with these items.

10

FAITH, HOPE, AND DOUBT

He that doubteth is damned. . . . Whoever is not of faith is sin.
—ROMANS 14:23

Whoever desires to be saved must above all things hold the Catholic faith.
Unless a man keeps it in its entirety inviolate, he will assuredly perish
eternally. Now this is the Catholic faith, that we worship one God in Trinity
and Trinity in unity without either confusing the persons or dividing the
substance. . . . So he who desires to be saved should think thus of the Trinity.

It is necessary, however, to eternal salvation that he should also faithfully
believe in the Incarnation of our Lord Jesus Christ. Now the right faith is
that we should believe and confess that our Lord Jesus Christ, the Son of
God, is equally both God and man.

This is the Catholic faith. Unless a man believes it faithfully and
steadfastly, he will not be able to be saved.
—ATHANASIAN CREED, FIFTH CENTURY

WE HAVE BEEN EXAMINING arguments for and against such metaphysical propositions as "God exists" and "we will survive our death,"
endeavoring to determine whether belief in these propositions is justified.
Traditionally, in Judaism, Christianity, and Islam, right belief (*orthodoxy*) is
necessary for salvation or pleasing God.

Traditionally, orthodox Christianity has claimed (1) that faith in God
and Christ entails belief that God exists and that Christ is God incarnate,
and (2) that without faith we are damned to eternal hell. Similarly, in
Islam, belief that Allah alone is God is necessary for salvation. So doubt is
an unacceptable propositional attitude. In this chapter I argue that this
thesis is misguided. One may doubt, that is, lack propositional belief, and
yet have faith in God (and Christ).

135

Let me relate the incident that originally provoked my thinking on this subject. When I was about 15 years old, having studied naturalistic evolution in a biology class, I began to doubt the religion in which I had been raised, especially the account of Creation in Genesis 1 through 3, leading me to doubt the inerrancy of the Bible and even whether there was a God. Finally, I went to a minister and confessed my doubts about God and Christianity. He listened carefully, and, to my consternation, offered no sympathy, let alone arguments against the evidence that provoked my doubts, but reprimanded me for my unfaithfulness to God. He said the situation was grave, indeed. My eternal soul was at stake. So I must will myself to believe the message of Christianity. He quoted Romans 14:23, "He that doubteth is damned . . . for whatsoever is not of faith is sin." I was thrown into paroxysms of despair, for the attempt to get myself to believe that God exists or that Christ is perfect God and perfect man failed. Yet I wanted to believe with all my heart (after all, I believed that my salvation depended on it), and some days I would find myself believing—only to wake up the next day with doubts. Hence, this preoccupation with faith and doubt. Hence, this chapter.

IS BELIEF A NECESSARY CONDITION FOR SAVING FAITH?

According to traditional Christianity, belief is a necessary condition for salvation. Paul says in Romans 10:10, "If you confess with your lips that Jesus is Lord and believe in your heart that God raised him from the dead, you will be saved." In Hebrews 11 we are told that he who would please God must believe that He exists and is a rewarder of them that seek Him. The Athanasian Creed, an official doctrine of orthodox Christianity (quoted above), states that salvation requires that one believe not only that God exists but also that God is triune and that Christ is perfect God and perfect man. Most theologians and philosophers, from Athanasius to Pascal to Plantinga, hold, at least, that Christian faith requires propositional belief.[1] You can be judged and condemned according to your beliefs. As in Romans 14:23, "He that doubted is damned." The basic argument goes like this:

1. Faith in God through Christ is a necessary and sufficient condition for eternal salvation.
2. Belief that God exists is a necessary condition for faith.
3. Therefore, belief is a necessary condition for salvation.

4. Therefore, doubt, the absence of belief, is an unacceptable attitude for salvation. No doubter will be saved.

Let us begin with some definitions:

1. **Belief** = df* an involuntary assenting of the mind to a proposition (a "yessing" to a proposition), a feeling of conviction about p. As such, obtaining a belief is a *nonvolitional event.*

   Consider this Belief Line, defined in terms of subjective probability, the degree to which I think the proposition is probable. Let "S" stand for the believer or *subject,* "B" for *believe,* and "p" for the proposition in question. Then we can roughly locate our beliefs on the Belief Line. Above 0.5 equals various degrees of positive belief in p. Below 0.5 equals various degrees of unbelief (or belief that the complement, "not-p" is true). 0.5 equals agnosticism or suspension of judgment.

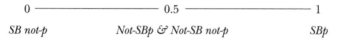

2. **Acceptance** = df deciding to include p in the set of propositions that you are willing to act on in certain contexts, a *volitional act.* For example, in a legal context, say a jury, when evidence is insufficient to convict an accused criminal, I may believe the subject is guilty but accept the proposition that he is not because the high standards of criminal justice have not been met. In a scientific context, say in testing the hypothesis that a formula will lead to the development of cold fusion, I may not believe the hypothesis I am testing is true but accept it for purposes of the experiment. Acceptance is different from belief in that we do have some direct control over our acceptances, whereas we don't over our beliefs. We may or may not believe our acceptances and we may or may not accept our beliefs.

3. **Faith** = df a commitment to something X (e.g., a person, hypothesis, religion, or worldview). Faith is a deep kind of acceptance. An acceptance can be tentative. For example, when I make the marriage vow that I will to be faithful until death to my beloved, I make it whether or not I believe that I will succeed. Normally, given background considerations, the performative "I [N] take you [N] to be

---

*"df" stands for "definition."

my wedded wife," entails commitment. If my marriage vow was
merely an acceptance, I suppose, it would be "I promise to be faithful to you for at least three years or until I lose interest in you."
Faith involves commitment to its object. Under normal circumstances, it involves trusting and obeying the object of faith or doing
what has the best chance of bringing its goals to fulfillment. It is a
volitional act.

We may note at this point that the New Testament word *pistis* can be
translated as either belief or faith. The distinction is discernible primarily
by the context of its use.

THE PHENOMENOLOGY OF BELIEF

To begin with, we must understand what is involved in direct volitionalism
or **voliting** (the act of acquiring a belief directly by willing to have it). The
following features seem necessary and jointly sufficient conditions for an
interesting thesis of volitionalism:

1. The acquisition is a basic act. That is, some of our beliefs are
   obtained by acts of will directly on being willed. Believing itself
   need not be an action. It may be dispositional. The volitionalist
   need not assert that all belief acquisitions occur via the fiat of the
   will, only that some of them do.
2. The acquisition must be done in full consciousness of what one is
   doing. The paradigm cases of acts of will are those in which the
   agent deliberates over two courses of action and decides on one of
   them. However, acts of will may take place with greater or lesser
   awareness. Here our notion of will is ambiguous, having two mean-
   ings: "desiring" and "deciding." Sometimes we mean by "act of will"
   simply a desire which manifests itself in action, such as my being
   hungry and finding myself going to the refrigerator or being tired
   and finding myself heading for bed. We are not always aware of our
   desires or intentions. There is a difference between this type of willing and the sort in which we are fully aware of a decision to perform an act. If we obtain beliefs via the will in the weaker sense of
   desiring, of which we are only dimly aware, how can we ever be sure
   that it was really an act of will that caused the belief directly rather
   than the will simply being an accompaniment of the belief? That is,
   there is a difference between willing to believe and believing will-
   ingly. The latter case is not an instance of acquiring a belief by fiat

of the will; only the former is. In order for the volitionalist to make his case, he must assert that the acts of will that produce beliefs are decisions of which he is fully aware.

3. The belief must be acquired independently of evidential considerations. That is, the evidence is not what is decisive in forming the belief. Perhaps the belief may be influenced by evidence (testimony, memory, inductive experience, and the like), so that the leap of faith cannot occur just any time over any proposition but only over propositions that have some evidence in their favor, though still inadequately supported by that evidence. They have an initial subjective probability of, or just under, 0.5. According to Descartes, we ought to withhold belief in such situations in which the evidence is exactly equal, whereas for Kierkegaard religious and existential considerations may justify leaps of believing even when the evidence is weighted against the proposition in question. William James prescribes such leaps only when the option is "forced, living and momentous." It may not be possible to volit in the way Kierkegaard prescribes without a miracle of grace, as he himself suggests; but the volitionalist would have to assert that volitional belief goes beyond all evidence at one's disposal, and hence the believer must acquire the belief through an act of choice that goes beyond evidential considerations. It is as though we place our volitional finger on the mental scales of evidence assessment, tipping the scale one way or the other.

In sum, then, a *volit* must be an act of will whereby I acquire a belief directly on willing to have the belief, and it is an act made in full consciousness and independently of evidential considerations. The act of acquiring a belief may itself not be a belief but a way of moving from mere entertainment of a proposition to the disposition of having the belief. There is much to be said in favor of volitionalism. It seems to extend the scope of human freedom to an important domain, and it seems to fit our experience of believing when we are conscious of having made a choice. The teacher who sees that the evidence against a pupil's honesty is great and yet decides to trust him, believing that somehow he is innocent in spite of the evidence, and the theist who believes in God in spite of insufficient evidence seem to be everyday examples confirming our inclination toward a volitional account of belief formation. We suspect, at times, that many of our beliefs, although not formed through fully conscious volits, have been formed through half-aware or subconscious desires, for on introspection we note that past beliefs have been acquired in ways that could not have taken the evidence seriously into consideration. Volitionalism seems a good explanatory theory to account for a great deal of our cognitive experience.

Nonetheless, there are considerations which may make us question whether on reflection volitionalism is the correct account of our situation. I will argue that it is not the natural way in which we acquire beliefs, and that, although it may not be logically impossible that some people volit, it seems psychologically odd and even conceptually incoherent.

Beliefs Are Not Chosen

Beliefs are not chosen but occur involuntarily, as responses to states of affairs in the world. Beliefs are, to use the late British philosopher Frank Ramsey's famous metaphor, mappings in the mind by which we steer our lives. As such, the states of affairs that beliefs represent exist independently of the mind; they exist independently of whether we want them to exist. Insofar as beliefs presume to represent the way the world is, and hence serve as effective guides to action, they are not actions. The will seems superfluous. Believing seems more like seeing than looking, falling than jumping, catching a cold than catching a ball, getting drunk than taking a drink, blushing than smiling, getting a headache than giving one to someone else. Indeed, this involuntary, passive aspect seems true on introspection of most propositional attitudes: anger, envy, fearing, suspecting, doubting, though not necessarily of imagining or entertaining a proposition, where an active element may often be present.

In acquiring a belief, the world forces itself on one. Consider perceptual beliefs. If I am in a normal physiological condition and open my eyes, I cannot help but see certain things, for example, this piece of white paper in front of me. It seems intuitively obvious that I don't have to choose to believe that I see this piece of white paper before I believe I see it. Here "seeing is believing." This is not to deny a certain active element in perception. I can explore my environment, focus in on certain features, turn from others. I can direct my perceptual mechanism, but once I do this the perceptions I obtain come of themselves whether or not I will to have them. I may even have an aversion to white paper and not want to have such a perception. Likewise, if I am in a normal physiological state and someone nearby turns on loud music, I hear it. I cannot help believing that I hear it. Belief is forced on me.[2]

We may speak of the difference in the direction of fit between beliefs and actions. In an action, the direction of fit is from subject to world: The subject desires to change the world in conformity to his desire or will $(S \rightarrow W)$, whereas in believing, the direction of fit is from world to subject.

The perception of states of affairs in the world effects a change in the subject, so that, if successful, the belief corresponds to the world (S ← W). To make believing itself an act is to confuse this direction of fit, as though my wishing it to be the case made it so.

Logic of Belief Argument Against Volitionalism

The notion of volitional believing involves a conceptual confusion; that is, it is broadly a logical mistake. It argues that there is something incoherent in stating that one can obtain or sustain a belief in full consciousness simply by a basic act of the will, that is, purposefully disregarding the evidence connection. This strategy does not altogether rule out the possibility of obtaining beliefs by voliting in less than full consciousness (not truly voliting) but asserts that, when full consciousness enters, the "belief" will wither from one's noetic structure. One cannot believe in full consciousness "that p and I believe that p for other than truth considerations."[3] If you understand that to believe that p is to believe that p is true and that wishing never makes it so, then there is simply no epistemic reason for believing p.

If I said that I somehow find myself believing that I have $1,000,000 but don't know why, we might suppose that there was a memory trace of having deposited $1,000,000 into my account or evidence to that effect in the guise of an intuition that caused my belief. But if I denied that and said, "No, I don't have any memory trace regarding placing $1,000,000 into my account. In fact, I'm sure that I never placed $1,000,000 into the account. I just find it good to believe that it's there; it makes me happy to believe this, so I have chosen to believe it," you would be stumped. And if I started acting on this belief, by writing checks for merchandise purchased, serious problems would arise.

The point is that because beliefs are about the way the world is and are made true (or false) depending on the way the world is, it is a confusion to believe that any given belief is true simply on the basis of being willed. As soon as the believer, assuming that he understands these basic concepts, discovers the basis of his belief—as being caused by the will alone—he must drop the belief. In this regard, saying "I believe that p, but I believe it only because I want to believe it," has the same incoherence attached to it as the British philosopher G. E. Moore's paradoxical, "I believe p but it is false that p." Structurally, neither is a strictly logical contradiction, but both show an incoherence that might be called broadly contradictory.[4]

If this reasoning is sound, then, since beliefs are not actions, we cannot be judged for our beliefs. That is, if ought implies can, and we cannot acquire beliefs directly by choosing them, we cannot be judged according to what beliefs we have. Of course, we can be judged by our actions, by how well we have investigated the evidence and paid attention to the arguments on the various sides of the issue. That leads to the matter of the ethics of belief.

THE ETHICS OF BELIEF

Of course, we can sometimes indirectly obtain beliefs by willing to have them. I can desire to believe that I am innocent of an unjust act against my neighbor, say, directing my drain pipes to drain onto his property; I can bring to mind all the nasty things my neighbor may have done, use auto-suggestion to convince myself I was justified in redirecting the drain pipes toward his property, and thus bring the desired belief about. This manipulation of the mind is immoral. At least, there is a strong case against indirect volitionalism.

W. K. Clifford, as we noted in Chapter 9, has given a classic absolutist injunction against voliting: "It is wrong always, everywhere and for anyone to believe anything on insufficient evidence." This may have the sound of too "robustious pathos in the voice" as William James notes, but it may sound hyperbolic only because we have not taken truth seriously enough. Nevertheless, I defend the principle of an ethic of belief only as a *prima facie* moral principle, one which can be overridden by other moral principles but which has strong presumptive force.[5]

Why do we want true justified beliefs, beliefs based on the best evidence available? Because beliefs make up our road map of life and guide our desires. If I believe that I can fly and jump out of the top of the Empire State Building in order to take a short cut to Columbia University, I'm likely to be disappointed. If I want to live a long life and believe that living on alcohol and poison ivy will enable me to do that, I will not attain my desire. Referring to our earlier example, if, without good evidence, I somehow find myself believing that I have $1,000,000 in my bank account and start writing checks on the supposed deposit, reality will soon correct me—at some inconvenience.

The importance of having well-justified beliefs is connected with truth seeking in general. We believe that these two concepts are closely related, so that the best way to assure ourselves of having true beliefs is to seek to develop one's belief-forming mechanisms in such ways as to become good judges of various types of evidence, attaining the best justification of our beliefs that is possible. The value of having the best justified beliefs possible can be defended on both deontological grounds with regard to the individual and teleological or utilitarian grounds regarding the society as a whole. The deontological argument is connected with our notion of autonomy. To be an autonomous person is to have a high degree of warranted beliefs at one's disposal on which to base one's actions. There is a tendency to lower one's freedom of choice as one lowers the repertoire of well-justified beliefs regarding a plan of action, and because it is a generally accepted moral principle that it is wrong to lessen one's autonomy or personhood, it is wrong to lessen the degree of justification of one's beliefs on important matters. Hence, there is a general presumption against attaining beliefs by willing to have them. Cognitive voliting is a type of lying or cheating in that it enjoins believing against what has the best guarantee of being the truth. When a friend or doctor lies to a terminally ill patient about her condition, the patient is deprived of the best evidence available for making decisions about her limited future. She is being treated less than fully autonomously. Although a form of paternalism may sometimes be justified, there is always a presumption against it and in favor of truth telling. We even say that the patient has a right to know what the evidence points to. Cognitive voliting is a sort of lying to oneself, which, as such, decreases one's own freedom and personhood. It is a type of doxastic suicide which may only be justified in extreme circumstances. If there is something intrinsically wrong abut lying (making it *prima facie* wrong), there is something intrinsically wrong with cognitive voliting, either directly or indirectly. Whether it be Blaise Pascal, William James, John Henry Newman, or Søren Kierkegaard, all prescriptive volitionalists (consciously or not) seem to undervalue the principle of truthfulness and its relationship to personal autonomy.

The utilitarian, or teleological, argument against cognitive voliting is fairly straightforward. General truthfulness is a desideratum—an essential desire—without which society cannot function. Without it language itself would not be possible, because language depends on faithful use of words and sentences to stand for appropriately similar objects and states of affairs. Communication depends on a general adherence to accurate reporting. More specifically, it is very important that a society have true beliefs with regard to important issues, so that actions that are based on beliefs have a firm basis.

The doctor who cheated her way through medical school and who, as a consequence, lacks appropriate beliefs about certain symptoms may endanger a patient's health. If we all volited such beliefs that we had millions of dollars in our bank accounts, our financial institutions and use of the check system would collapse. A politician who fails to take into consideration the amount of pollutants being discharged into the air or water by large corporations that support his candidacy may endanger the lives and health of his constituents. Even the passerby who gives wrong information to a stranger who asks directions may seriously inconvenience the stranger. Here Clifford's point about believing against the evidence is well taken, despite its all-too-robustious tone: The shipowner who failed to make necessary repairs on his vessel and "chose" to believe that it was seaworthy is guilty of the deaths of the passengers. "He had no right to believe on such evidence as was before him." It is because beliefs are action guiding, maps by which we steer, and, as such, tend to cause actions, that society has a keen interest in our having the best justified beliefs possible regarding important matters.

Some people object to my model of the **verific** person, the truth seeker, as being neutral on the matter of religion. They point out that the issue is too important to permit neutrality as an appropriate attitude. Let me clear this up by making a distinction between *neutrality* and *impartiality*. The verific person is not neutral but impartial. For the proper model of the verific person, one seeking to proportion his or her beliefs to the strength of the evidence, consider the referee in an Army–Notre Dame football game. The veterans of foreign wars and Army alumni will tend to be biased toward Army, considering close calls against their team by the referee as clear instances of poor officiating, even of injustice. Roman Catholics throughout the nation, unless they are Army alumni, will tend to be biased toward Notre Dame, seeing close calls against their team by the referee as clear instances of poor officiating, even of injustice. The neutral person is the atheist pacifist in the crowd, who couldn't care less who wins.[6] But the impartial person is the referee, who, knowing that his wife has just bet their family fortune on the underdog, Notre Dame, still manages to call a fair game. He is able to separate his concerns about his financial security from his ability to discern the right calls in appropriate situations. The verific person is one who can be trusted to reach sound judgments when others are riven by bias, prejudice, and self-interest.

If we have a moral duty not to volit, but to seek the Truth impartially and passionately, then we ought not obtain religious beliefs by willing to have them but should follow the best evidence available.

HOPE AS THE PROPER RELIGIOUS PROPOSITIONAL ATTITUDE FOR DOUBTERS

For those who find it impossible to believe directly that God exists and who follow an ethic of belief acquisition, hope may be a sufficient substitute for belief. I can hope that God exists without believing that He does. Let us first analyze the concept of hope in order to determine whether this is a viable option. Consider some examples of hope:

1. Ryan hopes that he will get an A in his philosophy course.
2. Mary hopes that Tom will marry her.
3. Susan hopes that Happy Dancer will win the Kentucky Derby next week.
4. Steve hopes that the Braves won their game yesterday.
5. Although Bill desires a cigarette, he hopes he will not give in to his desire.
6. Christy hopes her saying "No" to Ron's proposal of marriage is the right decision.
7. William hopes that the Serbs lose the war, because he believes they are the aggressors.

If we look closely at these examples of hoping, we can pick out salient features of the concept. First of all, **hope** involves *belief in the possibility* of a state of affairs obtaining. We may wish for, but cannot hope for, what we believe to be impossible. If Ryan hopes to get an A in philosophy, he must believe that it is possible to do so, though he need not believe it will happen; and if Mary hopes that Tom will marry her, she must deem it, at least, possible, though not highly probable. The *Oxford English Dictionary* defines *hope* as an "expectation of something desired," but this seems too strong. Expectation implies belief that something will occur, whereas we may hope even when we do not expect the object to obtain, as when Mary hopes that Tom will marry her or Steve hopes the languishing Braves won their game against the awesome Yankees. Susan may hope that Happy Dancer wins the race, even though she doesn't expect that to happen. So belief that the object of desire will obtain does not seem necessary for hope. It is enough that the hoper believe that the proposition in question is possible, though not necessarily probable (it has a subjective probability of greater than 0 but not necessarily more than 0.5).

Second, hope precludes certainty. Mary cannot be certain that Tom will marry her, and Susan is uncertain whether Happy Dancer will win the race. There must be an apparent possibility of the state of affairs not obtaining. We would think it odd to say, "Steve knows that the Braves won the game yesterday, for he was there, but he still hopes that the Braves won the game." As Paul wrote in Romans 8:24, "For hope that is seen is not hope: for what a man sees, why does he yet hope for?" Hope entails uncertainty, a subjective probability index of greater than 0 but less than 1.

Third, hope entails desire (or a pro-attitude) for the state of affairs in question to obtain or the proposition to be true. In all of the above examples, a propositional content can be seen as the object of desire. The state of affairs envisaged evokes a pro-attitude. The subject wants some proposition p to be true. It matters not whether the state of affairs is past (case 4) or present (cases 5 and 6) or future (cases 1 through 3), though it generally turns out, because of the role hope plays in goal orientation, that the state of affairs will be a future situation.

Fourth, the desire involved in hoping must be motivational, greater than mere wishing. I may wish to live forever, but if I don't think it is sufficiently probable or possible, it will not serve as a spring for action. I can wish, but not hope, for what I believe to be impossible—as when I wish I were 20 years old again. If I hope for some state of affairs to occur, under appropriate circumstances I will do what I can to bring it about, as Ryan will study hard to earn his A in philosophy. Bill's hope that he will not give in to his first-order (or unreflective) desire for a cigarette will lead him to strive to reject the weed now being offered him.

In this regard, hoping involves a willingness to run some risk because of the positive valuation of the object in question. Consider case 3 (Susan hopes Happy Dancer will win the Kentucky Derby). For this to be the case, Susan must be disposed to act in some way as to manifest trust in Happy Dancer. She may bet on the horse without believing he will win the race, and the degree to which she hopes Happy Dancer will win the race may be reflected in how much she is willing to bet.

Fifth, hoping, unlike believing, is typically under our direct control.[7] I may decide to hope that the Braves will win, but it doesn't make sense to decide to believe that they will win. I hear that my enemy is suffering and find myself hoping that he will suffer great harm. Then I reflect that this schadenfreude* is a loathsome attitude and decide to change it (to hoping he will suffer only as he deserves!). I may or may not be able to give up a hope, but, unlike beliefs, normally I am able to alter the degree to which I hope for something. I find that I am hoping too strongly that I will get an A, notice that it is preoccupying me to the point of distraction, and decide to invest less hope in that goal. It seems that the degree of hope has something to do with cost–benefit analysis about the payoff involved in obtaining a goal.[8] The greater the combination of the (perceived) probability of p obtaining and the value of its obtaining to me (or someone whose fate I care about), the more I am likely to hope for p. So reflection on the costs and benefits of p will affect hope. Still, I can exercise some voluntary con-

---

Schadenfreude refers to feeling pleasure at someone's suffering or misery.

trol over my hopes in a way I can't over beliefs. I say, hope is *typically* under one's control. Admittedly, it is not always so. In Example 7, "William hopes that the Serbs lose the war, because he believes they are the aggressors," if William discovers that the Serbs are really the innocent victims, he will probably involuntarily hope for their victory, not their defeat.

Sixth, hoping, like wanting, is evaluative in a way that believing is not. We may have morally unacceptable hopes, but not morally unacceptable beliefs. Consider the difference between:

> "I believe that we are heading toward World War III in which nuclear weapons will destroy the world."

and

> "I hope that we are heading toward World War III in which nuclear weapons will destroy the world."

Beliefs may be formed through a culpable lack of attention and thus have a moral dimension, but the belief itself cannot be judged moral or immoral. This is applicable to beliefs about racial or gender differences. Sometimes being a "racist" or "sexist" is defined by holding that people of different races or genders have on average different native cognitive (or personality) abilities. The inference is then made that because racism and sexism are immoral, anyone holding these beliefs is immoral. But this is a confusion. Racism and sexism involve unjust discrimination, treating individuals not as individuals but simply as members of a class or race, and this is wrong because it fails to judge the individual by his or her own merit. But beliefs about average race or gender differences are not moral or immoral but true or false. The way to deal with false beliefs is to argue with the believer, presenting the best evidence available, not to condemn the believer, as happened during the Inquisition when Galileo was forced to recant the unorthodox belief that the sun, not the Earth, was the center of the solar system and when Giordano Bruno paid for this true belief by being burned at the stake.[9]

Finally, we must make a distinction between ordinary hope and a deep hope. Consider Susan's situation as she hopes in Happy Dancer. She may only believe that horse has a 1 in 10 chance to win the Kentucky Derby, but she may judge this to be significantly better than the official odds of 100 to 1 against him. Suppose that she has only $10 but wants desperately to enter a professional program which costs $1,000. She has no hope of getting the money elsewhere but sees that if she wins on Happy Dancer, she will get the required amount. Because she believes that the real odds are better than the official odds and that winning will enable her to get into the professional program, she bets her $10 on the horse. She commits her-self to Happy Dancer, though she never believes that he will win. We might call these cases in which one is disposed to risk something significant on the possibility of the proposition's being true *deep* or *profound* hope. When the risk involves something of enormous value, we might call it *desperate* hope.

We conclude, then, that hoping is distinguished from believing in that it may involve a strong volitional or affective aspect in a way that believing does not and that, as such, it is subject to moral assessment in a way that believing is not. Hoping is desiderative but is more inclined to action than mere wishing. Hope may be ordinary or profound.

Let us apply this to religious faith. Can hope serve as a *type of faith* in religions such as Judaism, Christianity, or Islam, without belief that the object of faith exists? Let me tell a story in order to focus our discussion. Suppose when Moses decides to launch a preemptive strike against the Canaanites in obedience to the command of Yahweh (in the book of Exo-dus in the Hebrew Bible), his brother Aaron doubts whether such a pre-emptive strike is morally right, let alone the command of God. He is inclined to make a treaty with the neighboring tribe. He doubts whether Yahweh has revealed such a command to Moses, doubts whether God appeared to Moses in the burning bush, and wonders whether Moses is hal-lucinating. When Moses points out that God annihilated the Egyptian pharaoh's army by causing the waters of the Red Sea to rush over them, Aaron is inclined to view that as an occurrence of getting caught in a flash flood. When Moses offers the fact that a pillar of cloud leads them by day and fire by night, Aaron entertains the supposition that the clouds are nat-ural phenomena and the appearance of "fire" is simply the effect of the rays of the setting sun on the distant sands. Aaron is agnostic about both the existence of Yahweh and the "revelation" to Moses. Although he can-not bring himself to overcome his doubt, he plumbs for the better story. He decides to accept the proposition that Yahweh exists and has revealed himself to Moses, and so lives according to this hypothesis as an experi-mental faith. He assists Moses in every way in carrying out the campaign against the Canaanites. He proclaims the need for his people to fight against the enemy, helps hold up Moses' arms during the battle, and urges the warriors on to victory in the name of God.

True, Aaron may not act out of spontaneous abandon as Moses does. On the other hand, his scrupulous doubt may help him to notice problems and evidence which might otherwise be neglected, to which the true believer may be impervious. This awareness may signal danger that may be avoided, thus saving the tribe from disaster. Doubt may have as many virtues as belief, though they may be different virtues.

Moses is the true believer, whereas Aaron, the doubter, lives in hope, profound hope. He believes that it would be a good thing if Moses' convictions are true and that it is possible that they are true, and so he decides to throw in his lot with his brother, living as if God exists and has revealed his plan to Moses.

The point may be put more simply. Suppose you are fleeing a murderous gang of desperados, say the Mafia, who are bent on your annihilation. You come to the edge of a cliff that overlooks a yawning gorge. However, there is a rope spanning the gorge, tied to a tree on the cliff on the opposite side of the gorge. A man announces that he is a tightrope walker who can carry you on the rope over the gorge. He doesn't look like he can do it, so you wonder whether he is insane or simply overconfident. He takes a few steps on the rope to assure you that he can balance himself. You agree that it's possible that he can navigate the rope across the gorge, but you have doubts whether he can carry you. But your options are limited. Soon your pursuers will be on you. You must decide. Although you still don't believe that the tightrope walker can save you, you decide to trust him. You place your faith in his ability, climb on his back, close your eyes and do your best to relax and obey his commands in adjusting your body as he steps onto the rope. You have a profound, even desperate, hope that he will be successful.[10]

This is how I see religious hope functioning in the midst of doubt. The verific person recognizes the tragedy of existence, that unless there is a God and life after death, our lives lack a grand purpose and have no deep value, but if there is a God and life after death, that meaning is glorious. There is just enough evidence to whet his or her appetite, to inspire hope, a decision to live according to theism or Christianity as an experimental hypothesis, but not enough evidence to cause belief. So keeping one's mind open, the hoper plumbs for the better story, gets on the back of what may be the Divine Tightrope Walker, and commits him- or herself to the pilgrimage.[11] Perhaps the analogy is imperfect, for it may be possible to get off the Tightrope Walker's back in actual existence and to get back to the cliff. Perhaps the Mafia make a wrong turn or take their time searching for you. Still, the alternative to the Tightrope Walker is not exactly welcoming: death and the extinction of all life in a solar system that will one day be extinguished. We may still learn to enjoy the fruits of finite love and resign ourselves to a final, cold fate. As Bertrand Russell wrote:

> Brief and powerless is man's life; on him and all his race the slow, sure doom falls pitiless and dark. Blind to good and evil, reckless of destruction, omnipotent matter rolls on its relentless way; for man, condemned today to lose his dearest, tomorrow, himself to pass through the gate of darkness, it remains

only to cherish, ere yet the blow fall, the lofty thoughts that ennoble his little day; disdaining the coward terrors of the slave of Fate, to worship at the shrine that his own hands have built; undismayed by the empire of chance, to preserve a mind free from the wanton tyranny that rules his outward life; proudly defiant of the irresistible forces that tolerate, for a moment, his knowledge and his condemnation, to sustain alone, a weary but unyielding Atlas, the world that his own ideals have fashioned despite the trampling march of unconscious power.[12]

But if there is some evidence for something better, something eternal, someone benevolent who rules the universe and will redeem the world from evil and despair, isn't it worth betting on this worldview? Shouldn't we, at least, consider getting on the back of the Tightrope Walker and letting him guide us across the gorge?

Summary

What's so great about belief? Note that the Epistle of James tells us that belief is insufficient for salvation, for "the devils believe and also tremble" (James 2:19). Note, too, that the verse quoted by the minister to me as a 15-year-old (Romans 14:23) was taken out of context. The passage reads: "For meat destroy not the work of God. All things are pure; but it is evil for that man who eateth with offense. It is good neither to eat flesh, nor to drink wine, nor any thing whereby thy brother stumbleth, or is offended, or is made weak. Hast thou faith? Have it to thyself before God. Happy is he that condemneth not himself in that thing which he alloweth. And he that doubteth is damned if he eats, because he eateth not of faith, for whatsoever is not of faith is sin." The passage is not about one's eternal salvation but about eating meat previously offered to idols. Paul is saying, "Let your conscience be your guide here. If your conscience condemns you—if you have doubts about this act—refrain!" True, beliefs are action guiding, but only true beliefs are reliable guides in the long run, and the best way to have true beliefs is by rational justification, believing in accordance with the evidence.

Can we be judged (condemned) for our beliefs? No, not for our beliefs as such, for they're not things we choose, so we're not (directly) responsible for them; we can only be judged according to what we have responsibly done (*ought* implies *can*).

1. We can only be judged for what we have control over.
2. We have control only over our actions.

3. Beliefs are not actions.
4. Therefore, we cannot be judged for our beliefs, but only for our actions.

Although we have some indirect control over acquiring beliefs, we ought not violate the Ethics of Belief and get ourselves to believe more than the evidence warrants.

We can be judged by how faithful we have been to the light we have, to how well we have lived, including how well we have impartially sought the Truth. We may adopt theism, or a particular brand of theism, such as Judaism, Islam, Hinduism, or Christianity, as an experimental faith, living by hope in God, yet keeping our minds open to new evidence which may confirm or disconfirm our decision.

If this argument is sound, the people who truly have faith in God are those who live with moral integrity within their lights. Some unbelievers will be in heaven and some religious, true believers, who never doubted, will be absent. However, my supposition is that the uncritical believers will be in purgatory. What is purgatory? It is a large philosophy department where people who compromised the truth and the good will be taught to think critically and morally, according to the ethics of belief. The faculty, God's servants in truth seeking, will be Giordano Bruno,[13] David Hume, J. S. Mill, Voltaire, Immanuel Kant, and Bertrand Russell.[14]

Questions for Discussion

1. Do you agree with the arguments in the chapter against volitionalism? Explain your answer. What is the direction of fit theory and how does it affect the main thesis of this chapter?

2. Analyze the arguments for religious faith without belief. Are they plausible, or do you find problems with the idea that we can have faith in God without believing he exists? According to the arguments in this chapter, could an atheist have faith in God? Could he or she be a Christian?

3. Is there an Ethics of Belief? If so, how does it work? Can we be held directly responsible for what we believe?

4. Examine the concept of hope as discussed in this chapter. Is it an adequate substitute for belief in one's religious life?

5. Have ever found yourself doubting something others thought you ought to believe (these need not be religious beliefs—they may be political, moral, anthropological, or cultural)? Discuss your experience and evaluate it.

For Further Reading

See "For Further Reading" at the end of Chapter 9.

Notes

1. Most theologians and Christian philosophers hold that belief is a necessary condition for faith. For example, Alvin Plantinga writes, "The mature theist does not typically accept belief in God tentatively or hypothetically or until something better comes along. Nor, I think, does he accept it as a conclusion from other things he believes; he accepts it as basic, as a part of the foundations of his noetic structure. The mature theist commits himself to belief in God: this means that he accepts belief in God as basic" ("Is Belief in God Rational" in *Rationality and Religious Belief,* ed. C. F. Delaney (Notre Dame, Ind.: University of Notre Dame Press, 1979), 27.

2. Much more needs to be said than can be said here. I have developed the fuller argument against direct volitionalism in my book *Religious Belief and the Will* (London: Routledge & Kegan Paul, 1986).

3. Of course, I might will to forget the evidence against p and so succeed indirectly in obtaining or sustaining my belief that p.

4. Imagining is within our control, and perhaps people with unusually active imaginations can imagine things so vividly that they come to believe them. This still would not be a case of direct, but only indirect, volitionalism.

5. Many philosophers have criticized Clifford's advice as being self-referentially incoherent. It doesn't have sufficient evidence for itself. But, suitably modified, I think this problem can be overcome. We can give reasons why we ought generally to try to believe according to the evidence, and, if these reasons are sound, then we do have sufficient evidence for accepting the principle. See W. K. Clifford "The Ethics of Belief" in L. Pojman, ed. *Philosophy of Religion: An Anthology,* 3d ed. (Belmont, Calif.: Wadsworth, 1998).

6. People confuse *neutrality* with *impartiality,* but they are very different concepts. Neutrality entails not taking sides, whereas impartiality entails taking a stand, not whimsically but on the basis of an objective criterion. I am not advocating neutrality toward religion but impartiality, according to the standard of available evidence.

7. At times it seems that hope is not under our control, as in the statement, "I cannot help but hope that the Serbs lose the war." But we can alter such hopes by focusing on their moral bases. Suppose I discover that the Serbs are actually the innocent ones in the conflict. Won't that tend to affect my hoping?

8. I owe this example to an anonymous reviewer. This reviewer also questions my thesis that faith need not entail belief. He offers the following counterexample: "Suppose that I have a child who has gone cross-country skiing in an area with major avalanches. She has been missing three days. I personally know the first-rate rescue team that has been out looking for her. I have faith

in them that if she can be rescued alive, they will do it. But it has now been three days with no sign; the temperatures are below zero. I can still hope, deeply hope, that she will be found alive and rescued. I may commit all of my resources to the search. But due to the length of time and temperature, I don't have *faith that the team will find her alive precisely because I now believe that she will not be found alive.*" So faith does entail belief.

My response to this is that the reviewer simply defines *faith* as entailing *belief.* He admits one can be hopeful and committed to the rescue but denies that one can have faith that the daughter will be found alive. But recall that my definition of faith was "a commitment to something," a "deep kind of acceptance," so the reviewer is simply begging the question against me, asserting that my characterization of faith is improper because it leaves out belief. But if the reviewer and reader thinks that faith requires belief, then substitute *commitment* for all the places I use *faith* and my thesis will stand. There is no need to haggle about words.

9. In the 1980s the television sports announcer "Jimmy the Greek" was fired from CBS for suggesting that blacks had on average superior athletic ability, and in 1994 Charles Murray's fellowship with the American Enterprise Institute was terminated for his unorthodox belief, set forth in his and Richard Herrnstein's *The Bell Curve,* that there were average differences in intelligence between racial groups. My point is that we can hold people responsible for their behavior, including how they investigate the evidence for hypotheses, but beliefs themselves are not good or bad, but either rational or irrational. For the classic defense of this point, see J. S. Mill, *On Liberty* (1861).

10. Compare my theory about faith as hope with that of Thomas Aquinas. St. Thomas makes an important distinction between *unformed* and *formed* faith: *Unformed faith* is mere belief, whereas *formed faith* is deeper and mature, involving both hope and love. I differ from St. Thomas in that I hold that *formed* faith need not include *belief* at all. You can have a commitment to some policy even though you are agnostic (or even believe the contrary). Because faith is an act, all that is necessary is that one hold that it is worthwhile. I suppose this is a practical belief, so, in a sense, we have not gotten rid of belief—only changed it from an attitude about the state of affairs in the world to a cost–benefit analysis about action.

11. The analogue of the tightrope walker is not God, but the system, such as a religious way of life that provides the best chance to obtain eternal salvation.

12. Bertrand Russell, "A Free Man's Worship" in L. Pojman, ed., *Classics of Philosophy* (New York: OUP, 1998), 1138.

13. Girodano Bruno (1548–1600) was burned at the stake by the Inquisition for believing that the Earth revolved around the sun.

14. Earlier versions of this chapter were read as a paper to philosophy departments at the University of Utah, Brigham Young University, Utah Valley State College, and the Irish National University in Maynooth. I am grateful to the participants for their comments. Jonathan Harrison, Richard Gale, and two anonymous reviewers made incisive comments on the penultimate version of this chapter, for which I am deeply grateful.

11

RELIGION AND ETHICS

Does God love goodness because it is good, or is it good because God loves it?

—PARAPHRASE OF SOCRATES' QUESTION
IN PLATO'S *EUTHYPHRO*

The attempts to found a morality apart from religion are like the attempts of children who, wishing to transplant a flower that pleases them, pluck it from the roots that seem to them unpleasing and superfluous, and stick it rootless into the ground. Without religion there can be no real, sincere morality, just as without roots there can be no real flower.

—LEO TOLSTOY, "RELIGION AND MORALITY,"
FROM HIS *SELECTED ESSAYS*

A DAM AND EVE DISOBEYING GOD in the Garden of Eden and bringing suffering and death on themselves and all people for all time; Moses receiving the Ten Commandments from the hand of God and delivering them to the people of Israel as laws to be obeyed on pain of death; the prophets Amos, Hosea, Isaiah, and Jeremiah warning the people that to disobey God's laws is to ensure doom and destruction; Jesus' Sermon on the Mount, Golden Rule, and Parable of the Good Samaritan, his teaching that we should not only love God with all our hearts and our neighbor as ourselves, but also our enemy; visions in the Apocalypse of the Last Judgment, wherein God shall reward every man and woman according to his or her deeds on Earth; the hope of heaven and the fear of hell—all these items have profoundly influenced conscious life and moral behavior for two millennia. For the majority of humanity throughout the ages, morality has been identified with adherence to religion, immorality with sin, and the moral law with the command of God. Even Plato, Locke, and Rousseau advocated banishing professed atheists from the state, because they would

lack sufficient incentive for being moral, especially under strong temptation. The moral life in most cultures in human history has been viewed as
a personal relationship between the individual or the community and a
heavenly parent. David, after committing adultery with Bathsheba and
arranging for the death of her husband, Uriah, can say to God without
being misunderstood, "Against Thee only have I sinned" (Psalm 51).

Whether it be the poor Calcutta harijan (untouchable) accepting his
degradation as his karma, the Shiite Muslim fighting a jihad in the name of
Allah, the Jew circumspectly striving to keep kosher, or the Christian giving
to charity in the name of Christ, religion has so dominated the moral land-
scape as to be virtually indistinguishable from it. There have been excep-
tions to be sure: Confucianism in China is essentially a secular system;
there are nontheist versions of Buddhism; and the philosophers of Greece
contemplated morality independent of religion. But, throughout most of
our history, most people have identified morality with religion, with the
commands of God.

The question remains whether the equation is a valid one. Is morality
so essentially tied to religion that the term *secular ethic* is an oxymoron, a
contradiction in terms? Can morality survive without religion? Is it the
case, as Tolstoy declares in the chapter-opening quotation, that to separate
morality from religion is like cutting a flower from its roots and trans-
planting it rootless into the ground? Is Dostoevsky's character Ivan Karamazov correct when he proclaims that "If God doesn't exist, everything is
permissible"?

Essentially, our inquiry comes down to addressing two questions:
(1) Does morality depend on religion? (2) Is religious ethics essentially
different from secular ethics?

DOES MORALITY DEPEND ON RELIGION?

The first question is whether moral standards themselves depend on God
for their validity, or whether there is an autonomy of ethics, so that even
God is subject to the moral order. This question first arises in Plato's dialogue *Euthyphro,* in which Socrates asks the pious Euthyphro, "Do the gods
love holiness because it is holy, or is it holy because the gods love it?"[1]
Changing the terms but still preserving the meaning, we want to know
whether God commands what is good because it is good, or whether the
good is good because God commands it. According to one theory, called
the **Divine Command Theory** (DCT), ethical principles are simply the
commands of God. They derive their validity from God's commanding
them, and they *mean* "commanded by God." Without God, there would be

no universally valid morality. Here is how theologian Carl F. H. Henry states this view:

> Biblical ethics discredits an autonomous morality. It gives theonomous ethics its classic form—the identification of the moral law with the Divine will. In Hebrew-Christian revelation, distinctions in ethics reduce to what is good or what is pleasing, and to what is wicked or displeasing to the Creator-God alone. The biblical view maintains always a dynamic statement of values, refusing to sever the elements of morality from the will of God. . . . The good is what the Creator-Lord does and commands. He is the creator of the moral law, and defines its very nature.[2]

We can analyze the DCT into three separate theses:

1. Morality (i.e., rightness and wrongness) originates with God.
2. *Moral rightness* simply means "willed by God," and *moral wrongness* means "being against the will of God."
3. Because morality essentially is based on divine will, not on independently existing reasons for action, no further reasons for action are necessary.

There are modified versions of the Divine Command Theory that drop or qualify one or more of these three theses, but the strongest form includes all three theses. We may characterize that position thusly:

> Necessarily, for any person S and for all acts A, if A is forbidden (required) of S, then God commands that not-A (A) for S. Likewise, if A is permitted for S, then God has commanded neither A nor not-A for S.

Bringing out the implications of this, we may list four propositions:

1. Act A is wrong if and only if it is contrary to the command of God.
2. Act A is right (required) if and only if it is commanded by God.
3. Act A is morally permissible if and only if it is permitted by the command of God.
4. If there is no God, then nothing is ethically wrong, required, or permitted.

We may summarize the Divine Command Theory this way: Not only does morality originate with God, but *moral rightness* simply means "willed by God," and *moral wrongness* means "being against the will of God." That is, an act is right *in virtue of* being permitted by the will of God, and an act is wrong *in virtue of* being against the will of God. Because morality essentially is based on divine will, not on independently existing reasons for action, no further reasons for action are necessary. As Ivan Karamazov asserts, "If God doesn't exist, everything is permissible." Nothing is forbidden or required. Without God we have moral nihilism. If there is no God, then nothing is ethically wrong, required, or permitted.

The opposing viewpoint—call it the **autonomy thesis** (standing for the independence of ethics)—denies the theses of the Divine Command Theory, asserting, to the contrary, the following:

1. Morality does not originate with God (though the way God created us may affect the specific nature of morality).
2. Rightness and wrongness are not based simply on God's will.
3. Essentially, there are reasons for acting one way or the other, which may be known independent of God's will.

In sum, ethics is autonomous, and even God must obey the moral law, which exists independent of himself—as the laws of mathematics and logic do. Just as even God cannot make a three-sided square or make it the case that he never existed, so even God cannot make what is intrinsically evil good or make what is good evil.

Theists who espouse the autonomy thesis may well admit some epistemological advantage to God: God knows what is right—better than we do. And because he is good, we can always learn from consulting him. But in principle we act morally for the same reasons that God does: We follow moral reasons that are independent of God. We are against torturing the innocent because it is cruel and unjust, just as God himself is against torturing the innocent because it is cruel and unjust. By this account, if there is no God, then nothing is changed; morality is left intact, and both theists and nontheists have the very same moral duties.

The attractiveness of the Divine Command Theory lies in its seeming to do justice to the omnipotence or sovereignty of God. God somehow is thought to be less sovereign or necessary to our lives if he is not the source of morality. It seems inconceivable to many believers that anything having to do with goodness or duty could be "higher" than or independent of God, for he is the supreme Lord of the believer's life, and what the believer means by *morally right* is that "the Lord commands it—even if I don't fully understand it." When the believer asks what the will of God is, it is a direct appeal to a personal will, not to an independently existing rule.

There are two problems with the Divine Command Theory that need to be faced by those who hold it. One problem is that the Divine Command

Theory would seem to make the attribution of "goodness" to God redundant. When we say "God is good," we think we are ascribing a property to God; but if *good* simply means "what God commands or wills," then we are not attributing any property to God. Our statement "God is good" merely means "God does whatever he wills to do" or "God practices what he preaches," and the statement "God commands us to do what is good," merely is the tautology "God commands us to do what God commands us to do."

A second problem with the Divine Command Theory is that it seems to make morality into something arbitrary. If God's fiat is the sole arbiter of right and wrong, it would seem to be logically possible for such heinous acts as rape, killing of the innocent for the fun of it, and gratuitous cruelty to become morally good actions—if God suddenly decided to command us to do these things. The radicality of the DCT is set forth by a classic statement of William of Occam:

> The hatred of God, theft, adultery, and actions similar to these actions according to common law, may have an evil quality annexed, in so far as they are done by a divine command to perform the opposite act. But as far as the sheer being in the actions is concerned, they can be performed by God without any evil condition annexed; and they can even be performed meritoriously by an earthly pilgrim if they should come under divine precepts, just as now the opposite of these in fact fall under the divine command.[3]

The implications of this sort of reasoning seem far-reaching. If there are no constraints on what God can command, no independent measure or reason for moral action, then anything can become a moral duty, and our moral duties can change from moment to moment. Could there be any moral stability? The proponent of the Divine Command Theory may object that God has revealed what is his will in his word, the sacred scriptures. But the fitting response is: How do you know that God isn't lying? For if there is no independent criterion of right and wrong except what God happens to will, how do we know God isn't willing to make lying into a duty (in which case believers have no reason to believe the Bible)?

When I was a teenager I read in the newspaper of a missionary in Africa who put a knife through the hearts of his wife and five children. On his arrest for murder, he claimed God commanded him to kill his family and he was only obeying God.

The missionary might reply, "Didn't God command Abraham to kill his son Isaac in Genesis 22?" How do we know that God didn't command him to do this horrible deed? He would only be sending his family to heaven a bit sooner than normal. Insane asylums are filled with people who have heard the voice of God commanding them to do what we normally regard as immoral: rape, steal, embezzle, and kill. If the Divine Command Theory is correct, we could be treating these people as insane simply for obeying God.

If God could make what seems morally heinous morally good simply by willing it, wouldn't morality be reduced to the right of the powerful—Nietzsche's "might makes right"? Indeed, what would be the difference between the devil and God if morality were simply an arbitrary command? Suppose we had two sets of commands, one from the devil and one from God. How would we know which set was which? Could they be identical? What would make them different? If there is no independent criterion by which to judge right and wrong, then it's difficult to see how we could know which was which; the only basis for comparison would be who won. God is simply the biggest bully on the block (granted it is a pretty big block—covering the entire universe).

Furthermore, the Scriptures speak of God being love. "Beloved, let us love one another, for love is of God, and he who loves is born of God and knows God. He who does not love does not know God; for God is love" (I John 4:7, 8). Could you truly love people and at the same time rape, kill, or torture them? Could a loving God command you to torture them? If so, then I suppose that Auschwitz could be considered God's loving act to the Jews.

The opponent of the Divine Command Theory (i.e., the proponent of the autonomy thesis) denies that God's omnipotence includes his being able to make evil actions good. Even as God's power does not include being able to override the laws of logic (e.g., He cannot make a contradiction true or $2 + 2 = 5$), so likewise God cannot make rape, injustice, cruelty, and the torturing or killing of innocents good deeds. The objective moral law, which may be internal to God's nature, is a law that even God must follow, if He is to be a good God.

Some philosophers and theologians acknowledge that God cannot change the moral law any more than He can change the laws of logic, but claim that He is, nevertheless, the source of the moral law. I recently heard the Christian philosopher William Lane Craig set forth the following argument:[4]

1. If there is no God, no moral absolute values exist.
2. Evil exists (which is a negative absolute value and implies that the Good exists as an positive absolute value).
3. Therefore, God exists.

Craig assumes that unless God is the ultimate source and authority of morality, it cannot have absolute or objective status. But if the autonomy thesis is correct, objective moral principles exist whether or not God exists. They are the principles that enable human beings to flourish, to make life more nearly a heaven than a hell. Rational beings can discover these principles independently of God or revelation—using reason and experience alone.[5]

ARE RELIGIOUS ETHICS ESSENTIALLY DIFFERENT FROM SECULAR ETHICS?

The second problem related to the matter of religion and morality has to do with the relationship between religion and secular morality. Are they essentially compatible or incompatible? We can divide this question into two subquestions: (1) Does religion actually do moral harm and detract from deep morality? (2) Does religion provide, and do secular systems fail to provide, ethics with the necessary motivation to be deeply moral?

Immanuel Kant (1724–1804), who held to the autonomy thesis, thought that there could be no difference between valid religious ethics and valid philosophical ethics. God and humanity both have to obey the same rational principles, and reason is sufficient to guide us to these principles:

> [Christianity] has enriched philosophy with far more definite and purer concepts than it had been able to furnish before; but which, once they are there, are freely assented to by Reason and are assumed as concepts to which it could well have come of itself and which it could and should have introduced. . . . Even the Holy One of the Gospels must first be compared with our ideal of moral perfection, before we can recognize him as such.[6]

Kant's system exalts ethics to an intrinsic good; indeed, doing one's duty for no other reason but that it is one's duty is the highest good there is. As such it is related to religion; it is our duty to God. God loves the virtuous and finally will reward them with happiness in proportion to their virtue. In fact, God and immortality are necessary postulates of ethics. Immortality is necessary in this way: According to Kant, we are commanded by the moral law to be morally perfect. Because *ought* implies *can,* we must be *able* to reach moral perfection. But we cannot attain perfection in this life, for the task is an infinite one. So there must be an afterlife in which we continue to make progress toward this ideal.

God is a necessary postulate in that there must be someone to enforce the moral law. That is, in order for the moral law to be completely justified there must finally be a just recompense of happiness in accordance with virtue. The good must be rewarded by happiness in proportion to their virtue, and the evil punished in proportion to their vice. This harmonious correlation of virtue and happiness does not happen in this life, so it must happen in the next life. Thus there must be a God, acting as judge and enforcer of the moral law, without which the moral law would be unjustified.

Kant is not saying that we can *prove* that God exists or that we ought to be moral in order to be happy. Rather, the idea of God serves as a completion of our ordinary ideas of ethics. Is Kant right about this?

IS RELIGION IRRELEVANT OR EVEN INIMICAL TO MORALITY?

Many secularists, such as Bertrand Russell and Kai Nielsen, have argued against both the stronger claim of the Divine Command Theory (that religion is the basis of ethics) and the weaker, Kantian claim (that religion completes ethics). They contend that morality has no need of God: One can be moral and, within the limits of thoughtful stoic resignation, even happy. The world may well be a product of blind evolutionary striving, ultimately absurd, but this doesn't remove our duty to fill our lives with meaning and goodness. As Russell put it:

> Nature, omnipotent but blind, in the revolutions of her secular hurryings through the abysses of space, has brought forth at last a child, subject still to her power, but gifted with sight, with knowledge of good and evil, with the capacity of judging all the works of his unthinking Mother.[7]

It is this conscious power of moral evaluation that makes the child superior to his omnipotent Mother. He is free to think, to evaluate, to create, and to live committed to ideals. So in spite of suffering, despair, and death, humans are free. Life has the meaning that we give it, and morality will be part of any meaningful life.

But theists may counter that secularists such as Russell are "whistling in the dark." Christian philosopher George Mavrodes has criticized Russell's secular view as puzzling.[8] If there is no God, then doesn't secular ethics suffer from a certain inadequacy? Mavrodes argues that the Russellian world of secular morality can't satisfactorily answer the question, Why should I be moral?, for, on its account, the common goods, at which morality in general aims, are often just those that we sacrifice in carrying out our moral obligations. Why should we sacrifice our welfare or self-interest for our moral duty?

The second oddity about secular ethics, according to Mavrodes, is that it is superficial and not deeply rooted. It seems to lack the necessary metaphysical basis afforded by a Platonic worldview (i.e., the view that reality and value essentially exist in a transcendent realm) or a Judeo-Christian worldview:

> Values and obligations cannot be deep in such a [secular] world. What is deep in a Russellian world must be such things as matter and energy, or perhaps natural law, chance, or chaos. If it really were a fact that one had obligations in a Russellian world, then something would be laid upon man that might cost a man everything but that went no further than man. And that difference from a Platonic world seems to make all the difference.[9]

Of course, the secularist will continue the debate. If what morality seeks is the good, as I have argued, then secular morality based on a notion of the good life is inspiring in itself, for it promotes human flourishing and can be shown to be in all of our interests, whether or not a God exists. A religious or Platonic metaphysical orientation may not be necessary for a rational, secular, commonsense morality. To be sure, there will be differences in the exact nature of the ethical codes—religious ethics will be more likely to advocate strong altruism, whereas secular codes will emphasize reciprocal altruism—but the core morality will be the same.

Some secularists—call them antireligious secularists—go even further than Russell or Nielsen, claiming that not only are religious and secular morality dissimilar but religious morality is an inferior brand of morality that actually prevents deep moral development. Both P. H. Nowell-Smith and James Rachels have argued that religion is (or gives rise to) an inferior morality.[10] Both base their contention on the notion of autonomy. Nowell-Smith's argument is based on child psychologist Jean Piaget's research in child development: Very small children have to be taught to value rules. When they do, they tend to hold tenaciously to those rules, even when games or activities would seem to call for a suspension of the rules. For example, suppose 10 children are to play baseball on a rectangular lot that lacks a right field. Some children might object to playing with only five on a side and no right field because that violates the official rules. Religious morality, in being deontologically rule governed, is analogous to the children who have not understood the wider purposes of the rules of games; it is an infantile morality.

Rachels's argument alleges that believers relinquish their autonomy in worship and so are immoral. Using Kant's dictum that "kneeling down or groveling on the ground, even to express your reverence for heavenly things, is contrary to human dignity," he argues that since we have inherent dignity, no one deserves our worship. But since the notion of God implies "being worthy of worship," God cannot exist. Rachels writes:

1. If any being is God, he must be a fitting object of worship.
2. No being could possibly be a fitting object of worship, since worship requires the abandonment of one's role as an autonomous moral agent.
3. Therefore, there cannot be any being who is God.[11]

Are Nowell-Smith's and Rachels's arguments sound? They seem to have problems. Take Nowell-Smith's contention that religious morality is infantile: Perhaps some religious people, and some secularists as well, are rigidly and unreasonably rule bound, but not all religious people are. Indeed, Jesus himself broke the rule regarding not working on the Sabbath day to heal and do good, admonishing his critics, the Pharisees, saying, "The Sabbath was made for man, not man for the Sabbath." Does not the strong love motif in New Testament religious morality indicate that the rules are seen as serving a purpose—the human good?

With regard to Rachels's argument, premise 2 seems false. In worshipping God, you need not give up your reason, your essential autonomy. Doesn't a rational believer need to use reason to distinguish the good from the bad, the holy from what is not holy? A mature believer does not (or need not) sacrifice his or her reason or autonomy in worship; rather, these traits are part and parcel of what worship entails. The command to love God is for one to love him with one's whole *mind*, as well as one's heart and strength. If there is a God, he must surely want us to be intelligent and discriminating and sensitive in all of our deliberations. Being a religious worshipper in no way entails or condones intellectual suicide.

Of course, a believer may submit his or her judgment to God's, when there is good evidence that God has given a judgment. If this is sacrificing one's autonomy, then it only shows that autonomy is not an absolute value but rather a significant *prima facie* value. If I am working in the physics laboratory with Albert Einstein, whom I have learned to trust as a competent authority, and he advises me to do something different from what my amateur calculations dictate, I am likely to defer to his authority. But I don't thereby give up my autonomy. I freely and rationally judge that in this particular matter I ought to defer to Einstein's judgment on the grounds that it is more likely to be correct. Functioning autonomously is not to be equated with deciding each case from scratch; nor does it require self-sufficiency in decision making. Autonomy is higher-order reflective control over one's life; a considered judgment that in certain kinds of cases someone else's opinion is more likely to be correct than one's own is an exercise of autonomy rather than an abdication of it.[12] Similarly, the believer may submit to God whenever he or she judges God's authority to override his or her own finite judgment. It seems eminently rational to give up that kind of autonomy. To do otherwise would be to make autonomy a foolhardy fetish.

DOES RELIGION ENHANCE THE MORAL LIFE?

Contrary to the views of philosophers such as Nowell-Smith and Rachels (and even Russell and Nielsen), there may be some morally relevant advantages to theism. Theists argue that there are at least five ways in which morality may be enriched by religion.

1. *If there is a God, good will win out over evil.* We're not fighting alone— God is on our side in the battle. Neither are we fighting in vain— we'll win eventually. As William James (1842–1910) said,

   > If religion be true and the evidence for it be still insufficient, I do not wish, by putting your extinguisher upon my nature, to forfeit my sole chance in life of getting upon the winning side—that chance depending, of course, on my willingness to run the risk of acting as if my passional need of taking the world religiously might be prophetic and right.[13]

   This thought of the ultimate Victory of Goodness gives us confidence to go on in the fight against injustice and cruelty when others calculate that the odds against righteousness are too great to oppose. Whereas the secularist may embrace a noble stoicism, resigned to fate, as Russell asserts, the believer lives in faith, confident of the final triumph of the kingdom of God on earth.

2. *If God exists, then cosmic justice reigns in the universe.* The scales are perfectly balanced so that everyone will eventually get what he or she deserves, according to their moral merit. It is true that in most religious traditions God forgives the repentant sinner his or her sins—in which case divine grace goes beyond what is strictly deserved. It's as though a merciful God will never give us *less* reward than we deserve, but if we have a good will, will give us more than we deserve. Nonetheless, the idea that "whatsoever a man sows, that will he also reap" (Galations 6:7) is emphasized in Judaism, Islam, Christianity, and most other world religions. In Hinduism it is carried out with a rigorous logic of karma (that is, what you are

now is a direct result of what you did in a previous life, and what you do with your life now will determine what kind of life you inherit in the next life).

The question that haunts secular ethics—Why should I be moral, when I can get away with being immoral? (for often, it seems we can profit by being immoral)—has a ready answer: I will not get away with immorality. God is the perfect judge who will bring my works to judgment, so that my good works will be rewarded and my bad works punished.

3. *If theism is true, moral reasons always override nonmoral reasons.* Let me illustrate this controversy: I once had an argument with my teacher Philippa Foot of Oxford University over the Gauguin case. Paul Gauguin abandoned his family and moved to Paris and then to Tahiti in order to fulfill his artistic dream. I argued that Gauguin did wrong, all things considered, to abandon his family. Foot, however, to my utter amazement, argued that although Gauguin did what was morally wrong, he did what was right, all things considered, for sometimes nonmoral reasons override moral ones. From a secular perspective, Foot's argument seems plausible: Why should moral reasons always override nonmoral ones? It is true that philosophers such as R. M. Hare build overridingness into the definition of a moral principle but then stipulate that we are *free to choose* our principles. Here is the dilemma for secular ethics: *either* overridingness *or* objectivity but not both. If you believe in moral realism, the idea that moral principles are universally valid whether or not anyone recognizes them, then the secularist is faced with the question, Why should I adhere to a given moral principle when I can get away with violating it? If you hold to overridingness, that is, if you believe that moral reasons are always the highest motivating reasons, the best reasons all things considered, then it seems likely that we will adopt some sort of agent relativity with regard to morals. From a religious perspective, however, the world is so ordered that the question, Why be moral? can hardly be taken seriously: To be moral is to function properly, the way God intended us to live, and he will see that the good are ultimately rewarded and the wicked punished. God ensures the supremacy of morality.[14] Moral reasons always override other reasons. We preserve both overridingness and objectivity.

4. *If theism is true, then there is a God who loves and cares for us—his love inspires us.* A sense of gratitude pervades the life of the believer so that he or she is ready to make greater sacrifices for the good of

others. That is, the believer has an *added reason* to be moral, beyond the ones a secular person already has, beyond even rewards and punishments: He or she wants to please a perfect God.

5. *If there is a God who created us in his image, all persons are of equal worth.* Theism claims that God values us all equally. If we are all his children, then we are all brothers and sisters; we are family and ought to treat each other benevolently, as we would family members of equal worth. Indeed, modern secular moral and political systems often assume the equal worth of the individual without justifying it. But without the parenthood of God, it makes no sense to say that all persons are innately of positive equal value. What gives us animals, the products of a process of the survival of the fittest, any value at all, let alone equal value? From a perspective of intelligence and utility, Aristotle and Nietzsche seem to be right; there are enormous inequalities, and why shouldn't the superior persons use the baser types to their advantage? In this regard, secularism, in rejecting inegalitarianism, seems to be living off the interest of a religious capital that it has relinquished.

In sum, if theism is false, then it may be doubtful whether all humans have equal worth, or any worth at all, and it may be more difficult to provide an unequivocal response to the question, Why be moral even when it is not in my best interest? If there is no sense of harmony and objective purpose in the universe, many of us will conclude that we are sadder and poorer because of it.

Add to this the fact that theism doesn't deprive us of any of the autonomy that we have in nontheistic systems. If we are equally free to choose the good or the evil whether or not God exists (assuming that the notions of good and evil make sense in a nontheistic universe), then it seems plausible to assert that in some ways the world of the theist is better and more satisfying than one in which God does not exist. It could also be the case that via revelation the theist has access to deeper moral truths that are not available to the secularist.

Of course, two important points may be made on the other side: First, a lot of evil has been done by religious people in the name of religion. We have only to look at our sordid history of heresy hunts, religious bigotry, and religious wars, some of which are still being fought. Religion may be used as a powerful weapon with which to harm others. Second, we don't know for sure whether a benevolent God exists. The arguments for the existence of God are not obviously compelling. Furthermore, even if a divine being exists, we don't have the kind of compelling evidence needed to prove that our interpretation of God's will and ways is the right one. Religion is based largely on faith rather than on hard evidence, so that it behooves believers to be modest about their policies. It would seem that most of us are more certain about the core of our morality than about the central doctrines of theology. So it is ill advised to require society to give up a morality based on reason for some injunctions based on revelation. Sometimes a religious authority claims to put forth a command that conflicts with our best rational judgments, giving rise to the kind of confrontation that can rip society apart.

The medieval Crusades and Inquisition, the religious wars of the Reformation period; the present religious conflict in Northern Ireland between Roman Catholics and Protestants; the current devastation of the former Yugoslavia, where Christians and Muslims are killing each other; the Hindu–Muslim massacres in India; and the Ayatollah Khomeini's order to kill author Salman Rushdie for writing his allegedly blasphemous book *The Satanic Verses* rightly cause apprehension in many fair-minded people. Religion can be a force for good or for evil, but dogmatic and intolerant religion deeply and rightly worries the secularist, who sees religion as a threat to society.

Our hope in solving such problems rests in working out an adequate morality on which theists and nontheists alike can agree. If there is, as I have argued elsewhere, an ethics of belief, then we can apply rational scrutiny to our religious beliefs, as well as to all our other beliefs, and work toward a better understanding of the status of our belief systems.[15] It is a challenge that should inspire the best minds, for it may turn out that it is not science or technology but rather deep, comprehensive ethical theory and moral living that will not only save our world but also solve its perennial problems and produce a state of flourishing.[16]

Summary

I began by asking whether Morality depends on religion. I examined whether moral standards themselves depend on God for their validity or whether there is an autonomy of ethics so that even God is subject to the moral order. Does God command what is good because it is good, or is the Good good because God commands it? We saw that the autonomy thesis was correct. God, if he exists, loves the Good because of its intrinsic value. Morality has independent value, so that moral truth exists whether or not God does. We argued that although religious ethics are not essentially different from secular ethics, religion can enhance the moral life by providing motivating reasons to be moral. If there is a God, Good will win out over evil and universal justice will prevail.

Questions for Discussion

1. Evaluate Leo Tolstoy's statement quoted at the beginning of this chapter:

> The attempts to found a morality apart from religion are like the attempts of children who, wishing to transplant a flower that pleases them, pluck it from the roots that seem to them unpleasing and superfluous, and stick it rootless into the ground. Without religion there can be no real, sincere morality, just as without roots there can be no real flower.[17]

2. In your judgment, how important is religion for a meaningful moral life? How would a secularist respond to the five claims made in favor of religion's ability to give added meaning to morality? Do you think that religion really does enhance the moral life?

3. Karl Marx said that religion was the opium of the people (today, the metaphor might better be changed to "cocaine" or "crack"): It deludes them into thinking that all will be well with the world, leading to passive acceptance of evil and injustice. Is there some truth in Marx's dictum? How would a theist respond to this?

4. Imagine that a superior being appears to you and says, "I am God and I am good; therefore, obey me when I tell you to torture your mother." (In case you don't think that a religious tradition would set forth such a message, read Genesis 22, in which God commands Abraham to kill his son Isaac, offering him as a sacrifice to God.) How would a proponent of the Divine Command Theory deal with this problem?

5. Discuss the problems connected with religious revelation and rational morality. Suppose that one's religion prohibits certain types of speech and requires the death penalty for those who disobey, such as was the case when the Ayatollah Khomeini condemned author Salman Rushdie to death for blasphemous words in the novel *The Satanic Verses*. Some religious people believe that abortion or homosexual behavior is morally wrong based on religious authority. How should a secular ethicist who believes that these practices are not morally wrong argue with the believer? Can there be a rational dialogue?

For Further Reading

Adams, Robert M. "A Modified Divine Command Theory of Ethical Wrongness." In *The Virtue and Faith*. New York: Oxford University Press, 1987.

Hare, John. *The Moral Gap*. Oxford University Press, 1996.

Helm, Paul, ed. *The Divine Command Theory of Ethics*. Oxford University Press, 1979. Contains valuable articles by Frankena, Rachels, Quinn, Adams, and Young.

Kant, Immanuel. *Religion Within the Bounds of Reason Alone,* translated by T. M. Greene and H. H. Hudson. Harper & Row, 1960.

Kierkegaard, Søren. *Fear and Trembling,* translated by Howard and Edna Hong. Princeton, N.J.: Princeton University Press, 1983.

Mitchell, Basil. *Morality: Religious and Secular.* Oxford, England: Oxford University Press, 1980.

Mouw, Richard. *The God Who Commands.* Notre Dame, Ind.: University of Notre Dame Press, 1990.

Nielsen, Kai. *Ethics Without God.* Pemberton Books, 1973. A very accessible defense of secular morality.

Outka, Gene, and J. P. Reeder, eds. *Religion and Morality: A Collection of Essays.* Anchor Books, 1973. Contains Robert M. Adams's "A Modified Divine Command Theory of Ethical Wrongness."

Pojman, Louis. "Ethics: Religious and Secular," *The Modern Schoolman* 70 (November 1992), 1–30.

Pojman, Louis, ed. *Ethical Theory: Classical and Contemporary Readings.* Belmont, Calif.: Wadsworth, 1998. Part XI contains important essays by Kant, Bertrand Russell, George Mavrodes, and Kai Nielsen.

Quinn, Philip. *Divine Commands and Moral Requirements.* Clarendon Press, 1978.

Robinson, Richard. *An Atheist's Values.* Clarendon Press, 1964.

Ward, Keith. *Ethics and Christianity.* Allen & Unwin, 1970.

Notes

1. Plato, *Euthyphro,* trans. William Jowett (Charles Scribner's Sons, 1889).
2. Carl F. Henry, *Christian Personal Ethics* (Eerdmans, 1957), 210.
3. William of Occam, quoted in *Divine Command Morality,* ed. J. M. Idziak (Mellon, 1979).
4. William Lane Craig set forth this argument in a debate with Paul Draper at the United States Military Academy, September 30, 1997.
5. More sophisticated versions of the Divine Command Theory exist. See Robert Adams, "A Modified Divine Command Theory of Ethical Wrongness," in his *Virtue and Faith* (New York: Oxford University Press, 1987). See also Louis Pojman, "Analysis of the Modified Divine Command Theory," in *Ethics: Discovering Right and Wrong* (Belmont, Calif.: Wadsworth, 1999).
6. Immanuel Kant, *Critique of Judgment,* trans. J. Bernard (Haefner, 1951), 410. See also *Fundamental Principles of the Metaphysics of Ethics,* trans. T. K. Abbott (Longmans, Green, 1898).
7. Bertrand Russell, "A Free Man's Worship," in *Ethical Theory: Classical and Contemporary Readings,* 3d ed., ed. Louis Pojman (Belmont, Calif.: Wadsworth, 1998). Note also the comment of my former student Laura Burrell (University of Mississippi):

> God is like a cosmic gardener—he tends and protects individual morality, he nourishes it and helps it bloom. Some people, like a hothouse orchid

or a fancy rose, do seem to need religion for their morality to have a purpose or justification. Others are like the Queen Anne's Lace (QAL)—able to withstand almost anything on their own. And many are borderline QAL, who need just that extra bit of fertilizer to break into bloom—and God provides it. But mankind could do as well. The relationship between God and morality is as simple as that—God is a parent, gardener, etc. He strengthens and cushions individual morality, he gives motivation (in the form of the outcomes: heaven or hell) and justice and order in a sometimes extremely chaotic world. But morality exists apart from God, and as hard as it is for some to accept it, could survive and even flourish in a world without God.

8. George Mavrodes, "Religion and the Queerness of Morality," in *Philosophy of Religion,* 3d ed., ed. Louis Pojman. (Wadsworth, 1998).
9. Mavrodes, "Religion and the Queerness of Morality," 539.
10. Patrick H. Nowell-Smith, "Morality: Religious and Secular," in *Philosophy of Religion,* 3d ed., ed. Louis Pojman. (Wadsworth, 1998).
11. James Rachels, "God and Human Attitudes," in *Religious Studies* 7 (1971); reprinted, with a reply by Philip Quinn, in *Divine Commands and Morality,* ed. Paul Helm (Oxford University Press, 1979).
12. For a fuller defense of this thesis, see Arthur Kuflik, "The Inalienability of Autonomy," *Philosophy and Public Affairs* (Fall 1984). My ideas have been influenced by Kuflik's work here.
13. William James, *The Will to Believe* (Longmans, Green, 1897).
14. For a fuller account of the differences between religious and secular morality, see Louis Pojman, "Ethics: Religious and Secular," in *The Modern Schoolman* 70 (November 1992), 1–30.
15. See Louis P. Pojman, "Believing, Willing and the Ethics of Belief," in *The Theory of Knowledge,* 2d ed. (Belmont, Calif.: Wadsworth, 1999), 525–543. Samuel Scheffler in *Human Morality* (Oxford University Press, 1992), like Foot, rejects the overridability thesis.
16. I am indebted to Michael Beaty and Arthur Kuflik for criticisms of an earlier draft of this chapter.
17. Leo Tolstoy, "Religion and Morality," in *Leo Tolstoy: Selected Essays,* trans. Aylmer Mande (New York: Random House, 1964), 31f.

CONCLUSION

THROUGHOUT THIS BOOK we have sought to let reason (in the form of argument) have the decisive word, to guide us in our delibera-tions—even if only to show us where reason has limits.

We have examined several arguments for and against the existence of God, survival after death, the relationship between faith and reason, and the relationship between ethics and religion. We have seen that the argu-ments regarding God's existence are inconclusive, that the idea of survival after death, while not impossible, is accompanied by serious difficulties, and that although religion is not necessary for morality, it can significantly enhance it, providing people with additional motivation and insight. We saw that the central issue is the existence of a omnipotent, omnibenevolent God. If we can establish the existence of God, we can probably use that datum to provide evidence for life after death and the probability of mira-cles. But can we come to any conclusions with regard to the existence of God? If we grant that the arguments examined do not individually make a good case for the existence of God, they might together constitute a cumu-lative case. Although one wooden leg may be too weak to support a chair, four of them may be sufficient. Or, with regard to a murder, if the testi-mony of witness A fails to establish the guilt of M, the testimony of witness B does not of itself provide strong evidence for the guilt of M, and similarly with witnesses C and D, still the cumulative testimony of A, B, C, and D might establish the guilt of M beyond reasonable doubt. Could the argu-ments examined together establish the existence or nonexistence of God? That is, if we brought together the cosmological argument, the teleological argument, and the argument from religious experience and put these alongside the argument from evil against the existence of God, what would our conclusion be? An ideal way to decide this matter would be to quantify the strength of each argument, adding the individual sums in order to see whether it was more likely that God exists than not. But this is not possible. The best we can do is look at the arguments carefully and allow their force to affect our noetic structure. Ideally, humans will eventually reach a rational consensus regarding the truth of religion. There are objective features to reasoning, for example, deductive and inductive processes, testing procedures, principles of predictability, coherence, and simplicity, and how we use these in coming to a conclusion may vary according to the issue and context. Rationality in these global situations is *person relative:* What is good evidence for you might not be good evidence for me. Two competent detectives, looking at the same evidence, may come to opposite conclusions. Mature scientists, examining the same data, may see it radically differently. Ultimately, because evidence is person relative, everyone will have to let the evidence lead him or her to an individual conclusion. Such weighty decisions are personal matters.[1] All we can do is inculcate epistemic virtues, like an expert referee or judge who is skilled at evaluating evidence and who loves the truth and seeks to attain it.[2] That is, we must each become what I have called a *verific person,* someone who lets reason form his or her beliefs. Let me illustrate the person relativity of evidence with the following.

Consider the situation of three German wives who are each suddenly confronted with evidence that their husbands have been unfaithful. Their surnames are Uberglaubig, Misstrauish, and Wahrnehmen. Each is disturbed by the evidence and determined to make further inquiries. Mrs. Uberglaubig is soon finished with her investigation, satisfying herself that her husband is innocent of the charges. Others, even relatives of Mr. Uberglaubig, are surprised by her credulity, for the evidence against her spouse is the sort that would lead others to conclude that he is unfaithful indeed. No matter how much evidence is adduced, Mrs. Uberglaubig is unflinching in her judgment. She seems to have a *blik* (an unfalsifiable conviction). Mrs. Misstrauish seems to be afflicted with an opposite malady. If Mrs. Uberglaubig overbelieves, Mrs. Misstrauish underbelieves. She suspects the worst, even though others who know Mr. Misstrauish deem the case against him weak (especially in comparison to the evidence against Uberglaubig). No evidence seems sufficient to reassure her of her husband's fidelity. Mrs. Wahrnehmen also considers the evidence against her spouse, which is considerable, and comes to a tentative judgment. Suppose she finds herself believing that her husband is faithful. Others may differ in their assessment of the situation, but Mrs. Wahrnehmen is willing and able to discuss the matter, give her grounds, and respond to the objections of others to her position. Perhaps we can say that she is more self-aware, more self-secure, and a better weigher of evidence than the others. She, unlike the other two women, seems to have a capacity for separating her hopes and desires from her ability to assess the evidence impartially.

Mrs. Wahrnehmen exemplifies the verific person. She may not always have the truth in the matter at hand, but her beliefs are well justified and tend toward truth. Although the rational person aims at truth, rationality does not guarantee the truth; it does, however, typically provide the best chance of reaching that desideratum. Mrs. Wahrnehmen and Mrs. Misstrauish both care about the truth in a way that Mrs. Uberglaubig does not. But rationality also entails a skill or behavioral capacity, utilizing but not confined to formal logical processes, involving an ability to judge impartially. It is as though Mrs. Wahrnehmen alone were able to see clearly through the fog of emotion and self-interest, focusing on some ideal standard of evidence—proportioning the strength of her belief to the strength of the evidence. Of course, there is no simple algorithm by which one can do this, any more than there exists such for the art critic in making a judgment on a controversial work of art or for the wise judge who adjudicates a difficult legal case. Still, the metaphor of the ideal standard is useful, for it draws attention to the objective features in rational judgment and at the same time shows how these features are internalized in the noetic structure of the verific person. Like learning to discriminate between works of art or with regard to criminal evidence, rationality is a learned trait that calls for a long apprenticeship (a lifetime?) under the cooperative tutelage of other rational persons. Some people with little formal education seem able to learn how to do this better than some "well educated" people, but in spite of this uncomfortable observation, I would like to think that it is the job of education to inculcate in people the virtue of impartial assessment of the evidence according to rational criteria over a broad range of human experience.

Let us continue our story. Suppose now Mrs. Wahrnehmen receives some new information to the effect that her husband has been unfaithful. Suppose it becomes known to others who were previously convinced by her arguments acquitting her husband, and suppose that the new evidence weakens many of those arguments, so that the third parties become convinced that Mr. Wahrnehmen is an adulterer. What should Mrs. Wahrnehmen do? Give up her belief that her spouse is innocent? Not necessarily. At least, it may not be a good thing to give it up at this point. If she has worked out a theory to account for a great many of her husband's actions, she might better cling to her theory and work out possible explanations of some of his actions. This activity of clinging to one's theory in the face of recalcitrant evidence is what Charles Peirce debunkingly, and Imre Lakatos approvingly, call the *principle of tenacity*.[3] It receives special treatment in Lakatos's treatment of progressive research programs. In science, theoretical change often comes as a result of persevering with a rather vaguely formulated hypothesis (the core hypothesis) which the researcher will hold onto in spite of a good many setbacks. The scientist must be ready to persevere (at least for a time) even in the face of his opponents' objections. If maximum fruitfulness of the experiment is to be attained, it must endure through many modifications as new evidence comes in. As Basil Mitchell has pointed out, the researcher's thesis is like a growing infant, which "could be killed by premature antisepsis."[4] The biographies of eminent scientists and scholars are replete with instances of going it alone in the face of massive intellectual opposition and finally overturning a general verdict. Hence the researcher cushions the core hypothesis against the blows and shocks that might otherwise force him to give it up. He invents ad hoc explanations in hopes of saving the core hypothesis. He surrounds the core hypothesis with a battery of such hypotheses, and as they fall, he invents new ones. Mitchell compares this process to a criminal network in which the mastermind (the core hypothesis) always manages to escape detection and punishment "by sacrificing some of his less essential underlings, unless or until the final day of reckoning comes, and the entire empire collapses." Admittedly, each ad hoc hypothesis weakens the theory, but the core hypothesis may nevertheless turn out to approximate the truth—or to be the best theory overall. But the more ad hoc hypotheses it is necessary to invent, the less plausibility the theory retains. Eventually, the theory stands in danger of becoming what Lakatos calls "a degenerative research project," one that has no promise of yielding new information.

Applying this to the religious believer, once he or she finds him- or herself with deep conviction, the believer has a precedent in science for clinging to it tenaciously. The religious person, as I argued in Chapter 10, need not actually believe the hypothesis; one may hope in it, but one must commit oneself to it sufficiently to give it a fair run for its money, drawing out its full implications and exploring its deeper explanatory scope. Nevertheless, if the analogy with science holds, the believer must recognize that the time may come when he or she is forced to abandon the theory because of the mountain of evidence against it. The rational person probably cannot say exactly at what point this should happen and does not expect it to happen, but he or she acknowledges the possibility and rather fears it. Still, he or she continues to live in hope, always recognizing a moral duty to seek to evaluate the evidence impartially. On the other hand, the unbeliever has a duty to examine the evidence for religion as impartially as possible.

Whether this assessment of the relation between the believer (or unbeliever) and the evidence is plausible, you must decide. The journey is worth the trouble.

Notes

1. Applying this discussion to Chapter 9, I think this is what William James and Alvin Plantinga are really saying. We can only do our epistemic best and trust that our best will lead us close to the truth.
2. Some people object to my model of the verific person, the truth seeker, as being neutral on the matter of religion. They point out that the issue is too important to permit neutrality as an appropriate attitude. Let me clear this up by making a distinction between *neutrality* and *impartiality*. The verific person is not neutral but impartial. For the proper model of the verific person, one seeking to proportion his or her beliefs to the strength of the evidence, consider the discussion of the referee in an Army–Notre Dame football game in Chapter 10.
3. For a good discussion of this issue, see Imre Lakatos, "Falsification and Methodology of Scientific Research Programs," in *Criticism and the Growth of Science*, eds. I. Lakatos and A. Musgrave (Cambridge, England: Cambridge University Press, 1970), 91–196.
4. Basil Mitchell, "Faith and Reason," an unpublished manuscript. I am indebted to my teacher Basil Mitchell for many of the ideas in this conclusion.

GLOSSARY

abduction A form of nondeductive reasoning. Sometimes referred to as *inference* to the best explanation in which the proponent argues that this explanation beats all its rivals as a plausible account of the events in question. A cumulative case argument is a form of abduction. (See Chapter 1 and Conclusion.)

acceptance: Deciding to include p in the set of propositions that you are willing to act on in certain contexts; a *volitional act*. (See Chapter 10.)

ad hoc A *proposition* added to a theory in order to save it from being considered logically impossible or implausible. As ad hoc, the proposition itself may have little or no support but simply serve to stave off rejection of the original theory. (See Chapter 1.)

agnosticism The view that we do not know whether God exists. It is contrasted with *theism,* the belief in God, and *atheism,* the belief that there is no such being. Although the term is used loosely, a popular way of describing agnostics versus believers and atheists is to say that the believer in God holds that the probability of God's existence is greater than 50 percent, the atheist holds that it is less than 50 percent, and

the agnostic holds that it is right at 50 percent. T. H. Huxley coined the phrase to point to a less dogmatic attitude than either theism or atheism. (See Chapter 1.)

anthropomorphism From the Greek, meaning "form of humanity." The tendency to see the divine as having human properties. David Hume argued that when theists view God as a superhuman being, rather than as something infinitely beyond humanity, they sacrifice the essence of God's transcendence. (See Chapter 3.)

anti-induction A process in which the normal regular or uniform causal processes of the past do not hold for the future. For example, dropped objects fly upward instead of falling to Earth. (See Chapter 1.)

a posteriori From the Latin, meaning "the later." Knowledge that is obtained only from experience, such as sense perceptions or pain sensations. (See Chapter 2.)

a priori From the Latin, meaning "preceding." Knowledge that is not based on sense experience but is innate or known simply by the meaning of words or definitions. David Hume limited the term to "relations of ideas," referring to analytic truths and mathematics. (See Chapter 2.)

argument   A process of reasoning from a set of statements, or premises, to a conclusion. Arguments are either valid or invalid. They are valid if they have proper logical form and invalid if they do not. (See Chapter 1; see also *deductive argument* and *inductive argument*.)

assumption   A principle or *proposition* that is taken for granted in an argument.

atheism   The view that there is no such being as God. (See Chapter 1; see also *agnosticism* and *theism*.)

autonomy thesis   The view that ethics is self-sufficient, so that even God must obey the moral law. The opposite of the *Divine Command Theory*. (See Chapter 11.).

belief   An involuntary assenting of the mind to a *proposition* (a "yessing" to a proposition), a feeling of conviction about p. (See Chapter 10.)

contingent   A *proposition* is contingent if its denial is logically possible and is not contradictory. A being is contingent if it is not logically necessary. (See Chapters 2 and 4.)

contradiction   When one statement denies another, both of which cannot be true. For example, "God exists" and "God does not exist." (See Chapter 4.)

deductive argument   An *argument* is a sound deductive argument if it follows a valid form and has true premises. In that case, the truth of its conclusion is guaranteed. A deductive argument is valid (but not necessarily sound) if it follows an approved form that would guarantee the truth of the conclusion if the premises were true. (See Chapter 1.)

deism   The view that God exists but takes no interest in human affairs. He

wound up the world like a clock and then left it to run itself down. (See Chapter 1.)

demiurge   Plato's name for the semidivine finite creator of the world. (See Chapter 5.)

Divine Command Theory   The view that right and wrong are defined by what God commands and forbids. (See Chapter 11.)

doxastic   From the Greek word *doxa*, having to do with beliefs or opinions. (See Chapter 9.)

existentialism   The name of the philosophical movement which began with the Christian Existentialist, Søren Kierkegaard (1813–1855) and reached its climax in the work of Jean-Paul Sartre (1905–1980). It emphasizes human freedom and the absurdity of existence over against the classical emphasis on reason and science. (See Chapter 9.)

faith   a commitment to something X (e.g., a person, hypothesis, religion, or worldview). Faith is a deep kind of acceptance. (See Chapter 10.)

fideism   The theory that reason is not necessary for religious faith. One should believe in religion without evidence. (See Chapter 9.)

hope   a deep acceptance of a hypothesis, involving desire for and belief in the possibility of a state of affairs obtaining. (See Chapter 10.)

inductive argument   An *argument* in which the premises support the truth of the conclusion but do not guarantee it (as a *valid deductive argument* would). (See Chapter 1.)

innate ideas   The theory that we first read of in Plato's *Meno* and later in René Descartes that states all humans are born with certain knowledge. Some philosophers and theologians hold that their idea of God is such an idea (see Chapter 9.)

isotropic The feature in biological being wherein physical properties are replicated on both sides of the body, such as eyes, ears, limbs, and lungs. This common feature is often cited as evidence for our common evolutionary origin. (See Chapter 1.)

metaphysics "Beyond physics." The study of ultimate reality, that which is not readily accessible through ordinary empirical experience. Metaphysics includes within its domain such topics as free will, causality, the nature of matter, immortality, and the existence of God. (See Chapter 9.)

naturalism The theory that ethical terms are defined through factual terms in that ethical terms refer to natural properties. Ethical hedonism is one version of ethical naturalism, for it states that the good that is at the basis of all ethical judgment refers to the experience of pleasure. Some naturalists such as Geoffrey Warnock speak of the content of morality in terms of promoting human flourishing or ameliorating the human predicament. The term also has a broader metaphysical meaning: as opposed to supernaturalism, explanations that appeal only to the natural, physical order of things. (See Chapter 1.)

natural theology The view that knowledge of God can be obtained through the use of reason. Strong versions hold that we can prove the existence of God. It is contrasted with revealed theology, which holds that all knowledge of God must come from a revelation of God. (See Chapter 9.)

noetic Having to do with the content of the mind, one's beliefs, desires, and values. (See Chapter 5.)

panentheism The view that God is in everything. A notable group called "process theologians" holds that God is limited, finite, and in all of nature. (See Chapters 1 and 6.)

pantheism The view that God is everything and everything is God. (See Chapter 1.)

proposition A sentence or statement that must either be true or false. Every statement that "states" how the world is is a proposition. Questions and imperatives are not propositions. "Would you open the door?" and "Please, open the door" are not propositions, but "The door is open" is because it claims to describe a situation. (See Chapter 1.)

rationality The process of using reliable patterns of argument to form conclusions. (See Chapter 1.)

theism The belief that a personal God exists and is providentially involved in human affairs. It is to be contrasted with *atheism,* which believes that no such being exists, and *deism,* which holds that God exists but that he is not providentially concerned with human affairs. (See Chapter 1.)

theodicy The view that evil can be explained in the light of an overall plan of God and that, rightly understood, this world is the best of all possible worlds. John Hick holds to a version of this doctrine in Chapter 6.

verific A verific person is a truth seeker, who judges impartially, though not neutrally, on disputes. (See Chapter 10.)

voliting The act of acquiring a belief directly by willing to have it. (See Chapter 10.)

volitionalism The thesis that we can (or ought to) obtain beliefs by willing to have them. (See Chapter 9.)

INDEX